Kemp, Sparrow and Greenwood Families

— of —

Norfolk, Virginia

Their Ancestors and Descendants

Kemp

Sparrow

Greenwood

Rev. C. Bernard Ruffin, III

HERITAGE BOOKS
2015

HERITAGE BOOKS

AN IMPRINT OF HERITAGE BOOKS, INC.

Books, CDs, and more—Worldwide

For our listing of thousands of titles see our website
at
www.HeritageBooks.com

Published 2015 by
HERITAGE BOOKS, INC.
Publishing Division
5810 Ruatan Street
Berwyn Heights, Md. 20740

International Standard Book Numbers
Paperbound: 978-0-7884-1466-4
Clothbound: 978-0-7884-6264-1

Table of Contents

Preface

Kemp, Sparrow, and Greenwood Families of Norfolk, Virginia traces the history of an "African-American" family that arose, after the Civil War, through the marriage of Benjamin Franklin Kemp and Mary Louisa (Dodie) Sparrow, from several very different strains: African slaves and Scots aristocrats through the Kemps; free people of color and native American Indians on the side of the Sparrows (the ancestors of Dodie's mother); and German burghers in the Greenwood inheritance (from Dodie's father). This history seeks to trace these three families to their earliest known origins, as well as present a narrative history of the nineteenth and twentieth century representatives down to the present time. Of immediate interest to those of the Kemp, Sparrow, Taylor, Vagner, Curdts, McGehee, Williams, Vanderbilt, Marlborough, and other related families (the name Greenwood died out of the family in 1944) as well as possible members of the lost lines of the Kemp and Sparrow families, it portrays a mixed race, or "mulatto" African-American family in such a way as to provide clues to others of similar background as to how their own roots can be unearthed, despite scanty information at the beginning of the search and the reluctance of older family members to discuss and acknowledge "skeletons in the closet." It also presents vignettes of local history and life and customs in Tidewater Virginia and north central North Carolina in the mid-nineteenth century and in the District of Columbia in the early twentieth, and depicts such important periods as the Civil War, Reconstruction, the World Wars, and the Depression as they related to particular people in particular places, contributing, hopefully, to the overall understanding of the larger picture. It includes six genealogical appendices that might prove to be of use to Kemp, Sparrows, Greenwoods, and others who are seeking their roots.

Some important sources are:

> The records of the Norfolk City Corporation Court
>
> The records of the Norfolk County Corporation Court
>
> Marriage and Death Records, New York City (Municipal Archives)
>
> The Personal Tax Records of Norfolk City (in the Virginia State Library, Richmond)
>
> The parish registers of Altheim, Germany (on microfilm through

the Church of Jesus Christ of Latter-Day Saints)

The parish registers of Babenhausen, Germany (LDS)

The parish registers of Frankfurt, Germany (LDS)

Vertical files, genealogical room, Kirn Library, Norfolk, VA

The U.S. Census, 1840, 1850, 1860, 1870, 1880, 1900, 1910, 1920

City Directories, Norfolk, VA

I would like to acknowledge the assistance of dozens of kind people, including the following:

Helen Ogle Atkins
The late Marian Elliott Bess
Tommy L. Bogger
Dorothy Goude Bryant
The late Kathryn Payne Carr
The late Mary Jones Nightengale Carter
The late Helen Quetrell Dancy
Grace Ridgeley Drew
The late Joseph L. Drew
The late George Elliott, Sr.
The late Louise Jackson Elliott
The late Mildred Curdts Fitzpatrick
The late Marie Madden Williams Ford
Louise Yoder Games
Wilhelmina Allen Garner
The late Ernst C. Helmreich
Elaine Gates Magruder
The late Margaret Saunders Manning
Ethel Browne O'Mealley
Maxine Baker Reynolds
The late C. Bernard Ruffin, Jr.
Benjamin L. Spaulding
Jayne Kemp Taylor
The late Pierre McKinley Taylor
The late Sara Davis Taylor
The late Dudley Tucker
Audrey Elliott Vagner
The late Helena Volp
The late Elinor Robinson Waller
The late Dorothy Douglas Williams
The late Mary Taylor Williams
Friedrich Wollmershauser
The late Sterling N. Yoder, Sr.

Chapter One

"Genealogy? You have no genealogy! Negroes have no genealogy! Negroes have no heritage!" These words, spoken more than once by my father, in response to my persistent questionings, also reflected of my mother and most of my other relatives when, as a boy of twelve or thirteen, I began the odyssey that has resulted in this narrative.

History, for me, was always a passion. When our household (which consisted of my parents, my mother's widowed sister, and me) assembled at dinner promptly at six, as it did for most of my childhood, my usual question, "Daddy, tell me what it was like when you were a little boy," prompted nightly stories that transported me into a different world, the world of Washington, D.C. in the 'teens and twenties.

It was a world of games of "King of the Hill" at Daddy's boyhood home on Euclid Street; of sledding on some vanished promontory known as "Snake Hill"; of rainy afternoons spent in the parlor listening to the singing of Daddy's eldest sister "Vie", who had come to some early, tragic, mysterious, and unmentionable death. It was a world of baseball at nearby Griffith Stadium; of Walter Johnson, whose pitches traveled at such speed that they could not be seen in the late afternoon when the pitcher's mound was in the sun and the batter's box was in the shadows; of Babe Ruth, who once, when the Yankees were visiting, hit a pop fly so high and hard that when Washington center fielder Tris Speaker caught it and tossed it into the crowd, the ball was flat as a pancake; Babe Ruth, whose favorite target was a towering elm tree above the right field wall, into whose boughs he drove innumerable home runs; Babe Ruth, who once hit a ball beyond the elm tree into Florida Avenue, perhaps a thousand feet from home plate in those days before anyone bothered to measure home runs with the tape measure.

Daddy spoke of the Knickerbocker Theatre, which collapsed, with much loss of life, in a snowstorm when he was about seven years old. Granddaddy wrapped newspapers around the boy's legs so that the two of them could trudge through more than two feet of snow to view the ruined theatre, which was several blocks away (and looked normal, because the lobby was not affected by the caving in of the roof of the auditorium).

Then there were the paddle-wheeled and stern-wheeled steamers which Daddy and his mother and sisters took each summer on their annual journey to Norfolk, Virginia. He mentioned three boats that made the trip down the Potomac and into the Chesapeake Bay: the *Northland*, the *Southland*, and the *Midland*. The *Northland* was the newest and nicest, the *Midland* the smallest and most dilapidated. The paddle-wheels made the sound, "Ka-tosh-ka-tee! Ka-tosh-ka-tee!" One day the *Midland* caught fire at its dock at "The Wharves" and blazed so furiously that the flames could be seen five miles away from the window of the house on the hill where Daddy and his family lived.

Such were the stories with which I was entertained. These recollections included reminiscences about people: about Granny and Granddaddy when they were young; about Aunt Elinor, the tomboy who physically defended her little brother; about the lost sister Viola, so smart, so talented, and so good. I was intrigued by the fact that Daddy himself had a grandmother, an unlovely old lady who lived with his family for some time until her death, so demented with age that everyone called her "Dodie." Daddy, in fact, remembered his *great*-grandmother, "Grandma Lydie", a dark, aged former slave who made "ladyfingers".

My mother, although sweet and loving, seldom if ever discussed her girlhood, except by way of example or illustration. For example, she might say, "When I was a girl, children were seen and not heard," or "Don't complain because you're not allowed to play with the children in the next block. When I was a child we weren't allowed out of the yard!" My father, to humor my interest in dinosaurs, concocted stories about my maternal grandfather "Farmer Jones" (who was not a farmer at all!) hunting dinosaur in the wilderness of Chambersburg, Pennsylvania. As for my mother's family, it remained for her sisters to supply details of their childhood and family circle--and there were *many* mysteries there.

In all these stories and anecdotes, from both sides of the family, there was little about "race." Daddy did mention a race riot in which "barricades" were erected not far from his home, but it was all a very hazy business that occurred when he was five. He ridiculed his mother for an unseemly deference to "whites" that led her to disparage all "colored" people and institutions, and for her habit of referring to "Mr. Campbell's Soup", "Mr. Gulden's Mustard", and "Mr. Muller's Spaghetti", because of a bizarre compulsion never to mention a white person without the handle "Mr." or "Mrs." He spoke of how his father dropped him and his sister Elinor at various theatres for whites only, so that the children could "pass" and see the feature, while Granddaddy dared not enter, lest decorum force him to remove his hat, revealing hair "so bad it carried pistols" and thus the negritude of all three. (This story, incidentally, was later furiously denied by Aunt Elinor, who insisted that her stepfather had never taken her anywhere or ever showed affection or concern). Daddy spoke of a time, when, as a teenager, he sat at a downtown lunch counter, only to have a waitress snarl, "We don't serve colored here!" in response to which he slammed his fist on the table, glaring at her in histrionic indignation, declaring haughtily, "Well, I don't blame you!" and was served! But such racial recollections were infrequent.

The family circle of my childhood was a close one, in which I was the only juvenile. Until I was three, my parents and I lived on the second floor of an apartment building at 2201 2nd Street, N.W. in the LeDroit Park section of Washington, near Howard University, which, in many ways, was and remained the center of my parents' lives. On the very same floor, just two doors from us, lived my mother's sister Amy and her husband Allan. Around the corner, in the same apartment complex, was the home of two other maternal aunts: Mary, a divorcee, and Louise, a widow. Six blocks to the south, on 124 Randolph Place, Granny Ruffin lived with her daughter Elinor, son-in-law "Big Art" Waller, and their son "Little Art", who was eleven years my senior. I never quite knew where Granddaddy Ruffin lived. He stayed in rented rooms and every time we visited him he seemed to be in a different place. It never occurred to me as a child that there was something strange about the fact that my grandparents Ruffin did not live together.

On a spring day in 1951 that I well recall, my parents and I followed a moving van to our new house on Taylor Street, about two miles from the old apartment. That same day we were joined by my mother's sister Louise, who was to make her home with us. I now understand that my mother had searched for a house large enough to accommodate Mary, Amy, and Allan as well. Even though such a dwelling was not available, these childless relatives, who joined us every Friday night to watch "I Remember Mama" (which reminded them of their own childhood) and shared nearly every family holiday and vacation, continued to comprise an integral part of my immediate family. Sometimes it seemed that the family decisions were made by the Council of Jones Sisters, frequently augmented by "The General", my mother's oldest sister Blondine, who came to Washington several times a year from her home in Orange, New Jersey.

I do not know into which stratum of "Negro Society", to use the terminology current at the time, my family fit. It was certainly not the very highest, which was comprised mainly of doctors and lawyers, many of whom boasted descent from presidents, congressmen, supreme court justices, and the First Families of Virginia. Various relatives, over the years, would recount cruel snubs suffered at the hands of the "old Washingtonians", "the Old Light People", "the Hinkties", the "Hoidie-Toidies", the "Swells." My parents and their siblings were nearly all educated at Howard and moved in a circle of teachers, social workers, postal employees, and government clerks. My father, who majored in Art at Howard, taught certain nights at the Letcher School of Art at Logan Circle, but made his living (somewhat unhappily, I think) as a police officer. He was put in charge of Division Two of the Metropolitan Police Boys' Clubs—which served Negro youth. He was also the police department's "first colored corporal." When I was a small boy, the people along U Street, where Daddy had his office in the Knights of Pythias Building, across from the Lincoln Theatre, treated their "first colored corporal" like royalty. Once, during an unhappy summer at the Police Boys Club Summer Camp, which my father supervised in Southern Maryland, near Point Lookout, one of his assistants, finding me in a tantrum of tears, remonstrated, "Here you're the son of *the first colored corporal* and you're crying the St. Louie Blues!"

My mother, a Howard graduate, was trained as a teacher, but never taught, spending most of her working life as a secretary "on the hill", as she and my family and their circle referred, not to Capitol Hill, but to Howard University. Eventually she became the assistant director of the personnel office. All my Washington aunts were teachers. Daddy's sisters both taught elementary school and Elinor went on to become a principal. Mummy's sisters Mary and Louise taught at the prestigious Dunbar High School, reputed to be one of the finest institutions of secondary education in America during the days of widespread segregation and the paucity of opportunities for educators who, under more favorable circumstances, might have taught in "white" universities. Amy was a professor at Morgan State College in Baltimore, whither she commuted every Sunday evening and from whence she returned on Friday afternoons. The biweekly trip to Union Station was one of the highlights of my week when I was a little boy. I looked forward to the ride to the station with my mother and aunts in Uncle Allan's Packard. We would park in a subterranean area, dark and excitingly mysterious (and later ruined when a train crashed into the main concourse and fell through the floor!) and ascend an escalator through the baggage room into the immense space of the concourse. Usually we went across the street to the vast ornate post office, where, looking up at the great gilded chandeliers and playing around the figures of lions and eagles and griffins that graced the bases of the massive Greek columns and the feet of the tremendous stone tables in the hall, I was, as it were, drawn into another world.

Race was seldom spoken of, at least in my presence, during these years. Washington was still partially segregated when I was a small boy, but, since the center of my world was my family, this meant little to me, since I went where I was taken. The social life of my parents in those years revolved around the businesses and theatres and restaurants of U Street. I was certainly aware that there were theatres elsewhere, but when I asked why we did not go there, I was always told something like, "Oh, sometime we will." I was attracted to the Little Tavern hamburger shops with their Elizabethan leaden-glass windows with diamond-shaped panels. I could never understand why my parents always refused my request to be taken inside.

"Why can't we go there?"

"Well, you wouldn't like it. Those people are very rough."

"I still want to go there."

"No! They're very, very rough, you see. They'd throw you out on your ear."

"I still want to go."

"Well, the food isn't very good. It's no good."

Then, one day, when I was about seven, my father asked, "Would you like to eat at the Little Tavern?" We went and we ate and I never stopped going to that chain as long as it was in operation. Only later, under what circumstances I can no longer remember, did one or both parents explain the reason why, at first, they would not take me to the Little Tavern.

Gradually, when I was eight or nine, I became aware that in Maryland and Virginia and in "The South" there were separate hotels, motels, washrooms, theatres, and, in some cases, even drinking fountains for "white" and "colored." When our family visited Jamestown Memorial Park in 1957 my father took a slide of the "Colored Men" sign that marked the lavatory we used. But, not knowing well any "white" people and having no understanding that the "white" facilities were often superior to the "colored", this seldom troubled me. The only thing that *did* bother me was Glen Echo Amusement Park in Maryland, which was constantly advertised on the children's television programs. That the hosts of the cartoon programs were urging me to visit a park they "knew darned well" was off-limits to a goodly percentage of their viewers infuriated me. One host urged young viewers to get hamburgers at a drive-in chain, which was prevalent in Maryland and Virginia. My mother informed me that this business was segregated. I must have written a half dozen letters to the host of the cartoon show, saying, " I am a colored boy. Can *I* go to ---- Drive In?" There was never a reply.

All of this is in the way of furnishing background for the story that I am about to tell, a story that begins in the summer of 1957 and works itself back into the Middle Ages. My aunt Louise, who was normally my summer child sitter, was in Mexico, and since my parents both worked, I spent my days divided between Amy and Mary, who, being teachers, had the summer off. Now I had to remember to spend precisely the same amount of time with each. Otherwise a horrid scene might ensue! One day Amy exploded when I spent more time with Mary than with her! That summer Mary taught me how to type. (It was also that summer that her elderly, irritable, neurotic cocker spaniel Oscar attempted to bite off my nose!) When I went to visit Amy, I sat with her in her living room, asking her questions about the family. As in the case of my father's family, there were siblings whom I never knew, including Uncle Paul, who died ten years before I was born. Amy recounted how their mother accidentally spilled scalding coffee on him when he was a little boy, disfiguring him in a frightful way. When Amy described graphically the hideous scars that she said covered every part of his body except his face, I froze with horror. I fantasized that perhaps Uncle Paul *was not really dead* and that one day I would come home from school and find this nightmare figure there in the house! For years, even when I had begun to ask other questions and inquire about other people, I dread to ask anyone about Paul Winston Jones. (Later I learned from my mother and other family members that Paul, who had in fact been burned as a small child, was a handsome man and that the story of gross disfigurement was, in my mother's words, "a product of Amy's imagination.")

In the fall of 1958 my paternal grandmother ("Granny") died. Several relatives I had never seen or even heard of appeared at the funeral. Among them was Granny's sister, Aunt Nonie. On the way to the cemetery I listened to different relatives mentioned that "of all those girls" Nonie was the oldest and now "she's the only one left." I listened to them recount stories about her four husbands. I listened as they recalled that Aunt Nonie was "the most beautiful girl in Norfolk" whose image at one time appeared on "baseball cards."

Not long afterwards I came upon a Bible in my parents' study in which Daddy had made some entries in fancy calligraphy. In it were inscribed the names of Granny's parents: Franklin Kemp and Mary Louisa Sparrow. Mary Louisa was clearly the "Dodie" my father had talked about. In the same chart Granny's siblings were listed: Elnora (Nonie), but three additional sisters, Carrie, Mattie, and Emma, and a brother, Franklin, Jr. Who were they? Why were they unknown to me? When and how had they died? I asked Daddy. He said that Mattie and Emma had died in the 1920s, when they were in their forties, and Carrie had died before he was born. How had they died? "They *just died!*" said my father with some irritation. Uncle Frank had gone to New York where he "passed for white", working as a cab driver. I pumped my father with more questions about our ancestry, questions that elicited the response that Negroes, except for the "elite", have no ancestry, no heritage. It was my task to *make my own genealogy*, to become a success and have a family for whose descendants *I* would be the ancestor. As to ancestors beyond my great-grandparents, I should not even be curious!

It troubled me, however, that there were certain "Negroes" or "colored people" who *could* trace their ancestry when we could not. Colored "Society" was made up of people who (with disputed degrees of accuracy) claimed descent from George Washington, Thomas Jefferson, the Harrisons, the Lees, and other founding fathers. A friend of my father claimed to be the grandson of Ulysses S. Grant. Another claimed to be the granddaughter of Judah P. Benjamin, the Confederate statesman. There was a man in my church, a physician, who was said to be a *direct* descendant of George Washington. It was explained that most of the so-called "descendants of George Washington" were the descendants of a son of Martha, who had been married before. But this doctor was different. He was the *direct* descendant to the First President. Moreover, he *looked exactly* like the Father of the Country, and it was said to be an awesome sight when this tall, elegant old man, strode down the aisle to his seat at church "the very spitting image of George Washington." It *seemed* as if one were excluded from the highest social circles unless one could sport such a pedigree. I felt vaguely different in a nebulously negative way from people with such illustrious antecedents.

Now, my father pretended to have nothing but contempt for those who boasted of glorious ancestry. More than once he told of a schoolmate who never tired of telling everyone that he was a direct descendant of George Washington, until a "U Street hustler" told him, "You may be a descendant of George Washington, but I bet I have more pictures of your great granddaddy in my pocket than you do." Yet, as I grew older, I detected in my father and in some of my mother's relatives an unspoken by nonetheless evident sense of inferiority that they were not of the "elite", but were, in the words of Aunt Blondine "just little people passing through." I often asked, "Who were *our* ancestors?" The answer, from my mother, from my father, from my aunts, was always, "We don't know. Don't worry about that. Make your own successes."

A painful moment occurred when I was looking through a book given me at Christmas, about the ways in which the holiday was celebrated in other lands. The last page described was the author claimed was a traditional American Christmas celebration. American children, at Christmas, were said to dress up in the national costume of their ancestors as they assembled in church to sing Christmas carols.

"Why can't *I* do that?" I asked an aunt. "What country do *our* ancestors come from?"

"You can't do that," it was explained, "because that is only for white people. Their ancestors came from different countries: England, Ireland, Germany, Italy, France, for example."

"But what country did *our* ancestors come from?"

"We *don't know.*"

"What about Africa? Could I dress up like an African?"

"Certainly not!"

"Didn't our ancestors come from Africa?"

"Well, some of them did. But from what part of Africa, we don't know. Africa is a big place, with many nations, many peoples, many cultures."

I was on a Sunday ride, uncharacteristically with only my parents, when I asked, probably from the hundredth time, "Where do our ancestors come from?" My mother, hesitantly, answered, "Well, I think you should know that we have some white blood. But *never speak of that!* That's not something we want to talk about."

Actually, my mother was proud of her Indian ancestry. To this she attributed the fact that her father and brothers did not have to shave regularly as well as the less attractive family proclivity towards what she always referred to as "firewater." She said that both of her parents were part Indian. In fact, her father's mother was a real Indian. But she never knew the tribe. "I should *like to think* that they were of the proud Iroquois," she once said tentatively. My father dismissed outright the notion of any Indian blood on his side, although, apparently his mother, Granny, always thought of herself as an Indian. When I tried to learn the name of the tribe involved, playing on the name of a Virginia tribe, the Pamunkeys, he laughed, " My people were po' monkeys."

It was January, 1961, when I was thirteen, that my interest in genealogy was further piqued when I just happened to be standing by while my mother was cleaning out one of her closets, and several photocopied pages fluttered down from a top shelf. They were copies of the family register of a Bible that had belonged to her own parents. Picking up the photocopies, I saw not only the dates of birth of my mother and her siblings, but also the dates of birth and death of the siblings of my grandmother Jones.

The discovery provoked a stream of questions directed to my mother and aunts. Mummy, characteristically, provided very little information and tried to divert my mind to "the present." Louise and Mary were a bit more helpful, but it was Amy who invited me to see the Bible from which the copies were made, which she kept in her apartment. She went down the list of names and recounted what she knew of each family member, showing me stains on the page recording the family deaths, stains she insisted came from her mother's tears. She horrified me when she recounted how her uncle Sylvestus Cato died when "he fell under a subway." I dared asked no more. For weeks my mental reconstruction of this gruesome incident revolved in my tortured mind until I asked my mother what she knew about the death of Uncle Sylvestus. "All I know is that he fell on a subway. See what you learn when you ask too many questions! Now, forget it!" That summer, when I asked her about her grandmother, Fannie Cato, she responded with annoyance, "You *know very well* that she was found in the creek! Now, don't ask any more questions!"

My interest, the next two years, was confined to questions put to my mother and aunts, which revealed a number of fascinating anecdotes about events contemporary to them, but little about previous generations, about which they made clear they knew nothing. I was fifteen when I seized the initiative and began my own research. From reading the preface to the then current *Baseball Encyclopedia*, I learned that the editors obtained vital information on athletes of the past thought their death certificates. Going through my parents' papers, I had found the death certificates of my paternal grandparents did indeed provide their dates of birth and their parents' names. I decided to send to Pennsylvania for the death certificates of the two maternal great-grandparents whose dates of death appeared in the family Bible. Great-grandfather James Cato had died before the state had begun issuing death certificates, but the death record of Fannie Cato gave an approximate age, the state of her birth, and the names of her parents--and the fact that her death was the result of "suicide by drowning." This was the beginning.

I began to write various localities for death certificates and other vital records, and this is how I began to prize open the door of the history of my ancestors. Not every line proved equally traceable. My mother's mother, Sarah Louisa Cato, was born in Chambersburg, PennsIvania. Marriage records were not kept in Pennyslvania before 1885, and birth and death records were not kept until the 1890s. Not only this, but the fact that my maternal grandmother was apparently rather close-mouthed and also because she did not live to old age resulted in a dearth of clear family traditions. My maternal grandfather was a native of Jefferson County, West Virginia, which, being originally a part of Virginia, kept records that went back to the 1850s. Some of his white ancestors were extensively chronicled by others[1]. I have so far been able to trace the lineage of my paternal grandfather back only to about 1800. It so happened that the ancestors of of my father's mother, Blanche Kemp Ruffin, proved easiest to trace, and which will be the subject of the following pages.

Chapter Two

There were, I think, two deep reasons for the reluctance on the part of my parents to discuss what little they knew of their ancestry. First, there was the matter of unsavory or embarrassing people and incidents. Second, there was the matter of the white ancestors. Both of these factors comprised what one aunt called "skeletons in the closet." She told me, "If you're too insistent, you'll come across the skeletons in the closet. And then, when they come tumbling out, *you'll be sorry!*"

Subsequent research, for example, revealed many such "skeletons". It brought to light characters who seem straight out of grand opera or *Grimm's Fairy Tales.* For instance, my mother's maternal grandmother, Fannie Cato, about whom my mother was reluctant to speak, was evidently an erratic and terrifying personage who eventually killed herself. My mother's paternal grandmother, Anna Jones, called "The Indian", had nine children, only one of whom was born to either of her two husbands. The other eight were fathered by at least three different men. My mother's uncles were addicted to "firewater" and one of them, Sylvestus, did not *fall* into the path of a subway (actually, it was an elevated train), but deliberately lay in its path. My father's maternal aunts, Mattie and Emma, were "gaiety girls". Mattie ran a notorious "club" and ultimately went to jail for a few days for keeping a "house of ill fame." Worst of all, Frank Kemp, my father's maternal grandfather, after numerous infidelities, seems to have precipitated a final break with his wife by begetting a son on his teenaged cousin.

Having learned these things, I can understand why my questions encountered responses like, "What do you want to know for? And "It's nothing to be proud of." Having written what I have, in darker moments I can almost imagine my parents turning in their graves, but trust that in the other world, their perspective is different from what it was in this. Although, as they said, my ancestors may not all have been people who were "anything to be proud of", they were still my ancestors and in a real sense, a part of me. Through the study of history we come to know ourselves, and history is the story of both the good and the bad.

The subject of white ancestors acutely embarrassed my parents. One afternoon I reduced my father to tears. He sobbed, pounded his breast, and cried, "What devastates me is what devastates most Negro men of my background and complexion: nearly all of my female ancestors were Negro, but nearly all of my male ancestors were white." What lay behind this outburst was his conviction that the racial mixture was a result of rape. He had no evidence that these male ancestors ever gave their mulatto children financial support or even acknowledged them, publicly or privately. Because of this, he insisted that, despite the fact that these men were his *biological ancestors*, they were not ancestors in the *real* sense of the word. Their space, he felt, should be forever left vacant on the mangled family tree.

The attitude of my parents and other relatives is stated beautifully in a letter I received in 1973 or 1974 from Helen Quetrell Dancy, an octogenarian retired school-teacher from Norfolk, Virginia, whose long-dead sister Elsie had married one of my father's first cousins. Mrs. Dancy had grown up with my grandmother and had vivid memories of relatives nobody else alive remembered. When I first telephoned her, she was very cooperative and even invited me to visit her. Just before the planned visit, however, I received a letter from her, withdrawing her invitation on the grounds that my questions had upset her so much that her physician forbade her to see me. She wrote, "Most of the Kemps [were] of white ancestors. You know how it was away back...Please don't ask any more. It would be less embarrassing to you, but don't let it worry you...Don't worry about the past. Keep your apparent aspirations and I think you will be happier." It was the same attitude that my mother's sister Blondine repeated in a maxim drilled into her consciousness by her mother: "Look up, not down. Look forward, not back. Look to the future, not the past."

Needless to say, I failed to take any of this well-intentioned advice. I persisted..

When I was fifteen, about all that I knew of the family of my paternal grandmother was what Daddy had written in the Bible. Granny's name was Blanche Franklin Kemp. Her father was Franklin Kemp and her mother Mary Louisa Sparrow, called "Dodie." Daddy recalled that his grandmother died about 1930. Neither he nor Aunt Elinor had the slightest idea when Franklin Kemp died. I knew, from my father and aunt, that Granny had four sisters and a brother, and I knew that the mother of the senior Franklin Kemp was a slave woman named Lydia. Beyond that, I knew nothing.

Then I sent away for the death certificate of Mary Louisa Sparrow Kemp from the Bureau of Vital Statistics in Washington. I gave her name and stated that she had died in 1930. The document I received described a "white" woman in her sixties who died of a heart attack and was the daughter of Owen McNulty and Mary Doyle, both natives of Ireland. My father believed that this was the death record of his grandmother (whose skin was so fair that she was frequently mistaken for a "white" woman) until he saw that the woman had died on Belmont Street. "Dodie" had died on Vernon Street. Then Aunt Elinor told me that Dodie's surname at death was not Kemp, but Bass. She had been married twice. So I sent another dollar to the Bureau. This time I got the correct record. Mary L. Bass had died May 14, 1929. The informant was Blanche F. Ruffin—Granny. The information given, however, raised more questions than it answered. Dodie's age was given as: "70?" Was Granny ignorant of her mother's precise age? The father was listed as "unknown" and the mother as "Mary Louise Ferguson."

Aunt Elinor was now interested. She revealed that Dodie had told her that a) her father was a German, b) that his name was Greenwood, and c) she was not sure that her mother had any African blood. Dodie, moreover, had said she was not sure where she was born, and thought (erroneously, I was soon to discover) that she hailed from "upstate New York." Dodie's husband, Franklin Kemp, was "the handsomest man in Norfolk", the spoiled and dissolute son of a wealthy white father and a beautiful mulatto slave named Lydia Kemp.

I wrote the Bureau of Vital Statistics in Richmond for the death certificates of Lydia Kemp and Franklin Kemp. They found no record of Franklin's death, but found a record for Lydia. Lydia's death certificate was disappointing in its incompleteness. It gave her age as 79, but did not give a date of birth and listed her parents as "unknown." The informant was "Pinkie Bass." After some thought, my father recalled that "Pinkie" had been his grandmother's nickname.

Using a genealogical handbook from the public library, I decided to write for church and cemetery records--a mainstay of traditional genealogical research. Lydia Kemp's death certificate gave her place of burial as Calvary Cemetery in Norfolk, so I addressed a letter there, but received no answer. My father recalled that the family church was the "Bute Street Presbyterian Church." My letter, addressed there, was never answered nor was it returned, despite the fact that such a church (I later learned) never existed. (My grandmother Blanche Kemp Ruffin was evidently baptized in St. John's Methodist on Bute Street, but later joined First Colored Presbyterian on the corner of Church Street and Princess Anne Road. My father's recollection confused the two churches).

I wrote to Richmond for the marriage license of Franklin Kemp and Mary Sparrow. To my amazement, it was on record, and the document provided an abundance of useful information. Benjamin F. Kemp (so he was *Benjamin Franklin* Kemp!) and Mary L. Sparrow had been married in Norfolk on July 8, 1875. He was then a "servant in an attorney's office". His parents were "William Smith and Lydia Kemp". Hers were "William Greenwood and Martha Sparrow." Benjamin Franklin Kemp was twenty and his bride nineteen[2].

There was a discrepancy between Mary Bass' death certificate and her marriage license: her mother was listed as "Mary Louise Ferguson" on her death certificate and "Martha Sparrow" on her marriage license. Since, however, the information on the death certificate was provided by a daughter while that on the marriage record was provided by Dodie herself, the latter document bore definitive weight. Again, the death certificate seemed to indicate a birth date around 1858-1859, while, according to the marriage license, was born 1855-1856.

It was my aunt Louise who alerted me to the collection of city directories in the Library of Congress. Most major cities in the nineteenth and early twentieth century issued such directories, which were supposed to list all residents of the city, with their occupation and address. There were numerous references to a "colored" Frank Kemp in the Norfolk directories between 1872 and 1895. Moreover, living at the same address were two more Kemps, hitherfore unknown to me: John and Samuel. I assumed at the time that they were Frank's brothers.

I continued to write for information after I went away to college. When I learned that there was a second "colored" cemetery, known as West Point, in Norfolk, I wrote the superintendent there. In contrast to the people in charge of Calvary, who never answered my several letters and who proved gruff and uncooperative in person, the man in charge of West Point was extremely helpful. Although I obtained a great deal of information concerning my Ruffin ancestors, West Point had little information on the Kemps and Sparrows, all of whom apparently repose at Calvary, which apparently preserved hardly any records before the 1920s.

It was during the Christmas holiday during my freshman year that I was able to locate the Kemp family in the census of 1880. Using the "soundex" (indexing according to the *sound* of the name) I was able to locate Franklin and Mary Kemp, who were then living in the household of one Sarah Kemp. The soundex card provided the information for me to find the fully entry in the actual census records. This information proved extremely useful. On June 5, 1880, there were *eighteen* people living under one roof at 59 Fenchurch Street: fourteen family members and four boards. (One wonders how large the house was!) The head of the household was a sixty-eight year old black widow by the name of Sarah Kemp. The census-taker recorded her occupation as "keeps house." She was described as a native of Virginia, unable either to read or write. Living with her were the following persons, all with the surname of Kemp:

> Julia, mulatto, female, age 30, daughter-in-law
> Lydia, mulatto, female, age 45, daughter
> Mary, mulatto, female, age 23, grand-daughter-in-law
> John, mulatto, male, age 40, son
> Samuel, mulatto, male, 34, son
> Franklin, mulatto, male 23, grandson
> William, mulatto, male, age 10, grandson
> Sarah, mulatto, female, age 17, granddaughter
> Elenorah, mulatto, female, age 6, granddaughter
> Callie, mulatto, female, age 4, granddaughter
> Minnie, mulatto, female, age 3, granddaughter
> Mattie, mulatto, age 2, granddaughter
> Benj. F., mulatto, male, age 2 mos., born April, grandson

Everyone except for Sarah, therefore, was described as "mulatto." (How did she feel to be the only "black" among a family of mulattoes?) Only Sarah, her daughter Lydia, and her daughter-in-law Julia were illiterate. John Kemp's occupation was given as "keeps stable." Samuel Kemp was a "clerk in stable." Franklin was a "laborer." William, Sarah, and Elenorah were "at school."

But what was the relationship of the children? Since John was listed as "single", the children whom I did not know previously to be the offspring of Frank and Mary (that is, Elenorah, Callie, Mattie, and Benjamin) must have been the son and daughters of Samuel and Julia Kemp (William, Sarah, and The census-taker, however, failed to distinguish between Sarah's grandchildren and *great*-grandchildren. Elenorah, Callie, Mattie, and Benjamin were the children of Franklin and Mary, Lydia's grandchildren, and Sarah's great-grandchildren. William, Sarah, and Minnie, on the other hand, were evidently children of Samuel and Julia1 and were grandchildren of Sarah. All seven were lumped together by the enumerator as Sarah's "grandchildren."

No copy of the 1890 census has survived, and the 1900 census was not then available to the public. Sarah and Lydia Kemp were in the 1850 and 1860 censuses of Norfolk, which led me to the conclusion that the Kemps were slaves before the Civil War. They first appear in the 1870 census. Under the surname of Kemp:

Sarah, age 60, female, black, washes, born Va.
John, age 25, male, black, laborer, born Va.
Samuel, age 22, male, black   born Va.
Lydia, age 30, female, black   born Va.
B.F., age 15, male, black   born Va.
Raymond, age 15, male, black   born Va.

Now *who* was Raymond Kemp? Was he a twin brother of Frank? For some time I thought that this was the case and that he had died young. Since the 1870 census did not provide family relationships, this was unclear.

There is also a slight discrepancy in the ages when the census of 1870 is compared to the census of 1880. Sarah would have been slightly older and her children slightly younger than the 1880 census described them. Frank was fifteen in 1870 and twenty-three in 1880. The fact that the 1870 census was taken in August and the 1880 enumeration in June does not account for a discrepancy of several years, so, obviously, the information in one or both is not entirely correct. It is also interesting that the entire family is described as "black" by the 1870 enumerator and, with the exception of Sarah, "mulatto" by the 1880 census-taker. The designation was obviously made at the discretion and on the whim of the enumerator.

There still remained the challenge of "finding" the white fathers of Frank Kemp and Mary Sparrow. While many years would pass before a breakthrough occurred on William Smith, the father of Frank Kemp, the search for Mary's father, William Greenwood, quickly bore abundant fruit.

---

1 Later a birth record for Minnie and a marriage record for Sadie were located, both of which confirmed the identity of Samuel R. Kemp as their father. One might assume that William (for whom no other record than the 1880 census has so far been located) was their brother, although he could possibly have been an illegitimate son of John or the offspring of the clan of Sarah's brother Joseph, who will be discussed later)

Then name "William Greenwood" on the marriage license seemed to contradict the tradition that Dodie's father was German. I was unable, in fact, to find *anyone* by that name in the Norfolk city directories then in the Library of Congress, the earliest of which dated to 1866. However, the census of Norfolk City on August 15, 1850 revealed the following family group with the name *Greenwood:*

Martin, male, while, age 52, born Germany

Margaret, female, white, age 54, born Germany

William, male, white, age 29, born Germany

Ellen, female, white, age 16, born Germany

Frederick, male, white, age 13, born Maryland

Martin, male, white, age 20, born Germany

All three adult male Greenwoods were "soap manufacturers." The real estate of Martin, Sr. was listed as worth $2000.00.

The same census also revealed the following *Sparrow* family:

Martha, female, mulatto, age 26, born Virginia

Josephine, female, mulatto, age 8, born Virginia

William H., male, mulatto, age 5, born Virginia

Elenora, female, mulatto, age 8 mos. (born in December), born Virginia

This was clearly the mother of older siblings of the woman known as Dodie. I had never heard of Josephine or of an elder Elenora, but both my father and Elinor had heard of "Uncle Billy", who was a shoemaker. Sure enough, in the 1860 enumeration of Norfolk City, included in the household of Martha Sparrow, along with the three children listed in 1850, are two younger daughters, Missouri, eight, and Mary, six. We will leave the Sparrows for now and direct our attention to the Greenwoods.

I wrote to Cedar Grove Cemetery, the "white" cemetery across the street from West Point in Norfolk, and learned that many members of the Greenwood family were interred there, including Martin, Sr., who died in 1869; Margaret, who lived until 1866; Martin, Jr., who met with a premature death in 1852; and William, whose life ended in 1855. Buried on the same plot, along with two wives and an unmarried son was Charles F. Greenwood, evidently another brother, who lived from 1825 and 1904 and who obviously was married and living in his own household at the time of the 1850 enumeration.

So William Greenwood did not appear in the Norfolk city

directories because he had died before the publication of the earliest existing volume.

There were still two possible complications. First, the census of 1850 did not list relationships. Could I be *certain* that the William Greenwood listed with Martin and Margaret was actually their son? Perhaps he was a nephew or a much younger brother of Martin, Sr. Second, William Greenwood, according to the cemetery records, died August 23, 1855. Although the 1860 census listed Mary Sparrow as six, other records seemed to point to a birth year of 1855 or later. If her birth occurred later than May, 1856, at the very latest, the William Greenwood who lies buried in Cedar Grove Cemetery could not have been her father. However, this was soon clarified. Although births were first recorded by the city of Norfolk in 1853, the early records are scanty, especially for people of color. Amazingly, however, Dodie's birth was registered. The birth of Mary L. Sparrow, "colored", the illegitimate daughter of Martha Sparrow, appears in the birth registers. The date: November 25, 1854—nine months before the death of William Greenwood.

Eventually I perused Norfolk's marriage registers, and found the record of the nuptials of three of Dodie's four siblings[3]. All of them named William Greenwood as their father. William's marriage record is interesting, in that, apparently through a misunderstanding, he gave what were almost certainly the names of his maternal grandparents, Randol and Annie Sparrow, as those of the parents of his bride, Frances Webb[4].

During the summer of 1966 (between my first two years at Bowdoin College) I visited Norfolk. My father's much older cousin, Louise Jackson Elliott, daughter of Aunt Nonie, still lived there. Arriving by bus, I was thrilled to see street signs bearing names that were familiar from the old city directories, even if the actual houses where the Kemps, Sparrows, and Greenwoods had lived had long since given way to offfice buildings, strip malls, and parking lots. Cousin Louise, a former school-teacher then in her seventies, and her husband George, a retired mailman and church musician, received me graciously.

George took me on a walking tour of the Huntersville neighborhood, where the Kemps had lived in the early twentieth century. We saw 1416 O'Keefe Street, where Dodie lived from the 1890s to the 1920s and where my father and his sisters were born. A vacant lot across the street was pointed out as the site of the house of Uncle Billy Sparrow, the mad shoemaker. Around the corner on Johnson Avenue was a house. The lower level, George explained, had once been the grocery store operated by Walter Robinson, Granny Ruffin's first husband. I was introduced to an old lady sitting on her porch, Eloise Jacox, who remembered "Ms. Bass" (Dodie) and other family members. A few blocks away, on Bute Street, was the church attended by Dodie and most of her children: St. John's African Methodist Episcopal Church. A few blocks from that was the First United Presbyterian Church (originally the "First Colored Presbyterian") where Granny Ruffin was a member.

As I went about the city attempting to uncover bits of information, I was struck by the fact that white people tended to be much more cooperative than black. I expected some display of prejudice or disapproval from the white persons of whom I made inquiry, but this was usually not the case. When I stopped in the D.P. Paul jewelry store on Granby Street and asked if the business was the successor to the firm Paul-Gale-Greenwood, the clerk retreated to a back room and returned with the venerable Mr. Paul, who confirmed that this was the case indeed. A grave, authoritative elderly man, Mr. Paul recalled "Mr. Fred" Greenwood (Dodie's father's youngest brother, who lived until 1920) very well.

But many people of color seemed unable then to comprehend my strange hobby. "What do you want to know for? Why would you be interested in that?" There seemed to be little interest in the black community then in preserving records of the past. The son of the director of a black funeral home that flourished early in the century conceded that his father's records ended up in his cousin's garage, where they mildewed and were thrown out. I made several trips, over the years, to one of the churches attended by my colored ancestors, only to be told that no one knew where the records were, until, finally, one lady admitted that there were "some old books" that were kept by the furnace, which were discarded after they deteriorated. The pastor of another church told me that his congregation *still* (in the 1980s) did not keep membership records! The former First Colored Presbyterian Church (now the First United Presbyterian) did have a membership book, maintained by an elderly member, but the information recorded was extremely limited. Moreover, while "white" churches, cemeteries, funeral homes, and schools usually answered my letter, even if they did not have the information I was requesting, similar "black" institutions did not even reply to my letters. Part of this reluctance, it seems, came from the same sense of embarrassment about the past that had affected members of my family. This situation changed somewhat after the publication of Alex Haley's *Roots*, which did a great dal to awaken in persons of color an interest in family history.

This was the first of many trips to Norfolk. Until they entered a nursing home several years later, George and Louise were always gracious hosts, and their home on Barre Street was the base for expeditions to the Court House and other points of interest.

George and Louise provided me with many helpful recollections. Louise confirmed the tradition that Dodie was German with a father named Greenwood, but knew no more than Elinor about that subject. She recalled "Grandma Lydie" as an active, lively little woman who frequently mentioned how kindly she had been treated as a slave. Louise remembered that Lydia recounted how "Young Master" had "taken the door off the hinges" when he went into her room. This fragment of information would many years later prove quite helpful.

I wanted to learn more about the Greenwoods, to trace them back into Germany. I thought they would be easy to tracy, because I had the assumption—erroneous as it turned out to be—that "white" people tend to know a great deal about their families. I tried to track down descendants of William Greenwood's siblings. I found that William's older sister Margaret had married a Joaquin Bayto and his younger sister Ellen had married Louis Curdts. Charles F. Greenwood had a daughter Lizzie who married a Norsworthy. So I looked in the telephone and city directories for the names Bayto, Curdts, and Norsworthy. No one knew anything except for Lizzie Norsworthy's grandson, Sterling Norsworthy Yoder, who invited me to meet him at his home. When he saw me he said, "I *guess* it is the same family." When assured it was, he conceded, "Oh, well, things like that happened." For nearly twenty years he provided invaluable assistance and encouragement, even sending me photographs of Martin and Margaret Greenwood and taking me to see their graves (later desecrated by vandals) in Cedar Grove Cemetery. But he knew only that his great-grandfather, Charles F. Greenwood, came from "Germany," near Frankfurt. He did not know the town or village. Later I was to locate other descendants of the Greenwood siblings. They all knew their ancestors were from Germany, but no one knew *where* in Germany.

So I wrote for death certificates. Martin Greenwood, Jr. and Margaret Greenwood Bayto died before deaths were registered in Norfolk. At the time that William, Margaret, and Martin (Senior)

Greenwood died (in 1855, 1866, and 1869, respectively) Norfolk's death records did not normally list the parents. However, Charles F. Greenwood (d. 1904), Ellen Greenwood Curdts (d. 1915), and Fred Greenwood (d. 1920) died at the time when death certificates were supposed to include not only the birthplace of the decedent, but also the names as well as birth places of the parents. The death records of Charles and Ellen did in fact list their parents, but listed "Germany" as their birthplace and that of their parents. Fred Greenwood's death certificate recorded, in harmony with the census of 1850, that he was born in Reisterstown, Maryland, but gave his parents' birthplace as "Frankfurt."

I looked up obituaries for the Greenwoods. William had no obituary. Ellen had no obituary. Margaret, Martin Sr. and Jr., and Margaret Bayto did, but these did not say where they were born. Charles and Fred Greenwood were well-known businessmen and had fairly long obituaries. One of them mentioned that the family was from "near" Frankfurt am Main. The 1860 census listed Martin and Margaret as natives of "Darmstadt". Darmstadt is in the same general area of Germany as Frankfurt, but there are dozens, if not hundreds of towns and villages nearby.

I decided to write a professional genealogist in Salt Lake City, whose name I obtained from a list in the Family History Center in Annandale, Virginia. The genealogist wrote that it was absolutely necessary to "find the exact location where your immigrant ancestor originated in Germany," going on to point out that "there are so many cities near Frankfurt that a search of all pertinent sources in this area is practically impossible." He suggested that I check the passenger lists on microfilm at the National Archives.

After viewing the first roll of film, which included arrivals at the Port of Baltimore, I was convinced that I had "hit the bullseye." Arriving August 9, 1834 on the ship *Napier* were a group of "farmers" from a place called "Babenhausen". Among them was a family of *Grunewalds*. I compared them with the Greenwoods in the 1850 census. The passenger list included:

Mathae Grunewald, male, age 35 [birthyear c. 1799]
M Grunewald, female, age 37 [birthyear c. 1797]
Wm Grunewald, male, age 13 [birthyear c. 1821]
Ch Grunewald, male, age 9 [birthyear c. 1825]
M Grunewald, male, age 7 [birthyear c. 1827]

Mary Grunewald, female, age 3 [birthyear c. 1831]

The census of 1850 (in which Charles appears in a separate household with his wife):

Martin Greenwood, male, age 52 [birthyear c. 1798]

Margaret Greenwood, female, age 54 [birthyear c. 1796]

William Greenwood, male, age 29 [birthyear c. 1821]

Charles Greenwood, male, age 25 [birthyear c. 1825]

Margaret Greenwood (Bayto), age 23 [birthyear c. 1827]

Martin Greenwood, Jr., male, age 20 [birthyear c. 1830]

Ellen Greenwood, female, age 16 [birthyear c. 1834]

Fred Greenwood, male, age 13 [birthyear c. 1837]

Fred, who was born in America, would not have been on the passenger list. The only problems in linking the family in the 1850 census to that on the passenger list were: 1) Ellen Greenwood does not appear on the passenger list. If she was sixteen in 1850, she could have been born later in the year of arrival. (It turns out that she was already a year old and for unknown reasons was not listed); 2) the second "M Grunewald" on the passenger list should have been listed as "female" if the name were to correspond with that of Margaret Greenwood the younger; and 3) "Mary" Grunewald should have been "Martin" and "male." But such mistakes could easily have been made by hasty and careless immigration authorities.

The genealogist was skeptical. He thought "Mathae" stood for "Matthias", not Martin, and "Ch" for Christina, not Carl (Charles). He wrote: "If you wish to assume that [Mathae Grünewald] is really your third great-grand-father, we must make some effort to prove this connection. I will write a letter to the state archives in Darmstadt, Germany, where an immigration register exists for the province of Hessen".

But I was right after all. After several months the genealogist wrote: "I found a letter waiting from the state archives in Darmstadt, Germany. They found a Martin Grünewald, born 26 March 1799 and married to a Margaretha Koch, born 5 April 1797, who immigrated to the U.S.A. in October, 1833. This date is probably the date they left Darmstadt and not the date they left the port of embarkation".

The archivist also photocopied the birth records of the Grünewald children, and the names and dates corresponded to those I had for the Norfolk Greenwoods.

The Baltimore passenger list is the only document that I have found that records the Greenwood's town of origin. None of the descendants to whom I spoke had ever heard the name of the town from which their ancestors came. Even Martin Greenwood's naturalization papers, which I happened upon several years later among court order papers, reveal only that he had been a subject of the Grand Duke of Hessen-Darmstadt. One is left to wonder whether, for some reason, the first generation of Greenwood *deliberately* refrained from transmitting to their children and grandchildren the town of their origin.

I was now interested in tracing the Greenwoods (or Grünewalds) farther back in time. The genealogist in Salt Lake City advised me that he would write to the pastor of the Babenhausen parish. Parish registers in what became Germany were normally kept as early as the seventeenth century. But the pastor of Babenhausen refused to answer the letters from the genealogist, and, after two years of facing a stone wall, the genealogist gave up and closed my file.

I asked Dr. Ernst C. Helmreich , who had been my advisor and history professor at Bowdoin College, to write a letter to the pastor at Babenhausen. This time I received a reply, but not from the Babenhausen pastor. The letter I received was from one Herr Volp, pastor of the church in the town of Gross-Umstadt, who stated that he had no records of the family. I never learned why the letter addressed to the town pastor of Babenhausen was forwarded to the pastor of another town!

About a month later, Dr. Helmreich wrote, indicating that the wife of Herr Volp had written him to inquire if he had any students who wanted to corrspond with her in English. I volunteered. In the course of our correspondence, Helena Volp told me that the pastor at Babenhausen was a dispirited and embittered old man who spent all his time nursing his invalid brother. She promised to prod him, however, into looking up some of the records I requested. At Christmas time she sent me, as a gift, transcripts of the birth protocols of Martin Grunewald and Margreth Koch. She promised to goad him into doing further research, but shortly after that, she died.

Through the Mormon Family History Center I obtained the addresses of two German genealogical societies. A year after writing both I received, without comment, a six page document from the *Hessische familiengeschichtliche Vereinigung,* which traced the ancestors of Martin and Margreth Grunewald back to 1520. But there were some obvious inaccuracies. One ancestress, Maria Catharina Lemcke, was supposedly born between 1730 and 1740. Her father, Karl

Lemcke, had a 1728 birthdate! There were other inconsistencies, so I decided to write the *Vereinigung* (through a translator), but received no response to this or subsequent letters.

In September, 1978 I was able to visit Babenhausen. I had made arrangements with an American Mormon bishop in Frankfurt to work with two missionaries who would act as interpreters. However, upon my arrival, they informed me that the pastor had gone away for the entire month and that the church records were inaccessible.

I took a walk around the town, the center of which was beautifully preserved and maintained an eighteenth century appearance. I noticed a "Lion Inn." According to the genealogy I had been sent by the *Vereinigung* an ancestor named Paulus Grünewald ran a Lion Inn in the 1600s. Through the interpreters, I questioned various natives. They all replied that the inn had been there as long as anyone remembered, but that they could not say how old it was. The town had at one time been surrounded by a thick, high wall, parts of which were still standing. Within the wall was a large, partly-ruined structure known as the "Witches Tower", where those accused of the black arts were imprisoned in the 1600s. I walked through the city church, which dated to the eleventh century, although most of the current structure was only a few hundred years old--but old enough to have been standing in its present form in the days when Martin and Margaret Grünewald were young. Perhaps they worshipped here. The baptismal font was surely venerable enough to have held the water through which the Sacrament was administered to many of my forebears.

The natives, to tell the truth, were not friendly. Everyone claimed an inability to speak English, despite the fact that most made this statement perfectly in the language of which they professed ignorance. At the Lion Inn, I asked several local men whether there were any Grünewalds or Kochs in Babenhausen. The bartender spoke to my interpreters in German, and they translated his words as, "During the War they all went away and never came back."

I was frustrated for another five years, until, in the early 1980s, the Mormon Church was able to make microfilm copy of the parish registers and I was able to view them at the Family History Center in Annandale, Virginia, not far from my home. With the help of two German ladies, I learned to decipher the old German script well enough to read the entries in the baptismal, marriage, and burial registers. After months of spending interesting Friday nights at the microfilm reader in the library, I was able to trace the line of Martin and Margaret back to the 1580s. Around the same time I found a book on microfilm that had been compiled early in the twentieth century, which traced one branch of the family back to a peasant from the town of Niederzell (north of Franfurt) who flourished in the late 1400s.

It was not until 1990 that I was able to learn about the ancestors of Franklin Kemp. His father was listed, as indicated before, as William Smith. Looking for the appropriate William Smith in Norfolk was like looking for a needle in a haystack. The marriage record, however, stated that Franklin Kemp was born, not in Norfolk, but in Milton, North Carolina. In perusing the 1850 census for Milton I found two William Smiths who were old enough (in the 1850s) to have fathered Frank Kemp. There was William T. Smith, thirty-five in 1850, a childless, unmarried "clerk" who was living with his fifty-five year old mother Martha. Then there was William Smith, fourteen in 1850, who was one of several children of George A. Smith, a merchant whose real estate was appraised at $6000.

Next I consulted the slave census of 1850. Unfortunately, the slaves were listed only by age, sex, and color, but not by name. William T. Smith owned no slaves. However, among the forty-nine slaves of G.A. Smith were a) a woman of forty—the same age as Sarah Kemp, b) a girl of thirteen—the same age, approximately, as Lydia Kemp (according to her death certificate), c) a boy of eleven—the same approximate age as John Kemp, and 4) a boy of eight— just a year or two older than Samuel.

I wrote to the Caswell County clerk for the probate records of George A. Smith. The inventory mentioned one Sarah, two Johns, one Samuel, but no Lydia and no Frank or Franklin. The slave census of 1860 lists slaves of ages generally corresponding to those of Sarah, John, and Samuel but no female whose age approximates Lydia's and no boy of an age similar to Frank. Next door to the Smiths, however, lived brother-in-law Montford McGehee. (I had learned that George Smith had married Adaline McGehee, who, along with Montford, were children of a planter by the name of Thomas M. McGehee.) Among his slaves was a twenty-three year old mulatto woman and a six year old mulatto boy. Lydia would have been about twenty-three, and Frank five or six.

Thus, it seems certain beyond reasonable doubt that the father of Benjamin Franklin Kemp was William Forbes Smith, the teenaged son of a well-to-do tobacco merchant of Milton. Other records indicate a late

1854 or early 1855 birth for Frank. At the time, both William and Lydia would have been about seventeen, which is in keeping with Cousin Louise's recollection of "Grandma Lydie" telling her that Frank's father was "Young Master."

Further research revealed that George A. Smith (whose niece, Alva, married a Vanderbilt) was a native of Dumfries in Prince William County in northern Virginia. His ancestors were from Scotland. The Smith family had, apparently, no connection with Norfolk. It seems as if the Kemps were sold sometime during the late 1840s to middlemen who, in turn, sold them to the Smiths. After the Civil War, they somehow found their way back to Norfolk, where relatives still lived.

I was able to trace Granny Ruffin's white grandfathers back to the 1400s in Germany and to at least to the 1700s in Scotland (a genealogy prepared in the early twentieth century claimed to trace the ancestors of the Smiths back to approximately 1100). It was much harder to trace her mulatto grandmothers. What little I learned about the Kemps came from the censuses of 1870 and 1880 for Norfolk, from the marriage record of Samuel R. Kemp, and from the death records of Sarah, Lydia, Frank, Samuel, and John Kemp. I have been to date unable to learn the identity of their master in Norfolk. Martha Sparrow was evidently born free. Why Granny Ruffin, at the time of her mother's death, gave her grandmother's name as "Mary Louise Ferguson" is still a mystery. The Randol and Annie Sparrow named on the marriage record of Dodie's brother Billy appear in *The Register of Free Negros and Mulattos* for Norfolk County in the entries for the year 1828. Both Randol and Anna declared that they were "born free", giving some credence to Dodie's reported insistence that none of her ancestors were ever slaves.

And so, over a quarter century, I was able to do what my elders warned me not to attempt. I was able to find out who my ancestors were. Before my search began to yield interesting results my mother and father and Aunt Elinor had died. Pleased though I hope they would have been with some of the results, I wonder whether they would have been still extremely uncomfortable with some of the "skeletons" that were released from the closet.

Chapter Three

The sleek high-rise office buildings, the upscale waterfront hotels, the sterile parking lots, the antiseptic low-cost housing projects, and the jammed expressways the assault the eyes of the visitor to Norfolk, Virginia in the 1990s have replaced all but a handful of buildings and obliterated even the pattern of the streets of the nineteenth and early twentieth century, and it is only by an intense effort of the imagination that one can imagine the teeming southeastern Virginia port city in the year 1840.

Norfolk had grown rapidly after the Revolution, during which it had been destroyed by the British. By 1840 the Borough of Norfolk was the home of fewer than 11,000 persons, most of whom lived in wooden houses in a complex of narrow streets that ran north from the Elizabeth River, which flows into Hampton Roads, where the James River meets the Chesapeake and both merge into the Atlantic. The harbor there teemed with tall-masted sailing ships of various types, which maintained a busy commerce with ports all over the world. Across the Elizabeth River was (and still is) the city of Portsmouth. Surrounding the Borough of Norfolk were the fields and farms of rural Norfolk County (now the city of Chesapeake) and Princess Anne County (now the city of Virginia Beach).

In those before satellite, before television, before radio, and even before telegraph, news traveled slowly and was usually relayed by ship's captains, who brought newspapers from other American cities and first-hand accounts of events in those foreign ports from whence they sailed. In order to learn what was transpiring elsewhere, the informed citizen had to study and compare the accounts printed in various newspapers. News of the outside world must have been especially vauge and elusive for that substantial element of the population who were illiterate, and for those in the outlying areas. For them, the world must have consisted of their immediate surroundings.

What were some of the events discussed by citizens of Norfolk in 1840? New Year's Day brought news, through the captain of the brig *Carroll*, of an October revolution in Uruguay. Word was also received of an American expedition to the Antarctic, dispatched to explore "every part of the Southern Ocean, where former navigators have asserted the discovery of new islands...to fix their position or determine their non-existence."[5] News was received of the discovery of a bevy of unpublished works by the recently deceased poet, Johann Wolfgang von Goethe. Citizens buzzed over word of archaeological digs in Central America, which excavated the ruins of amazing pre-Columbia cities built by the "Tultecas." The papers also recounted the visit of former President Andrew Jackson to New Orleans, where "in excellent health" he presided over the twenty-fifth anniversary of his victory there over the British. The local publications also attempted to satisfy public curiosity concerning the upcoming wedding of Britain's young Queen Victoria to her German cousin, Prince Albert, eagerly recounting scandalous details of previous royal marriages and expressing the wish that the young queen would abolish the ancient tradition of inviting "people of quality" to the bedrooms of the royal couple to witness the consummation of their marriage.[6]

News reached the people of Norfolk of continued "Indian murders" in Florida, where the government was in the final stages of deporting the native peoples of the Southeast to barren territories west of the Mississippi, but not without encountering the resistance of the Seminoles. As a result, papers frequently recounted incidents such as the case of a Jacksonville mail carrier who was "shot a few days since and the body found stripped and mangled," and of one Joseph Garcia, who "was killed about the same time and stripped."[7]

Word was received in Norfolk of far-off disasters, such as the fire that destroyed the downtown of Yazoo, Mississippi, as well as the fate of the steamship *Lexington*, which burned in the Atlantic after setting out from New York. The editors of the *Norfolk and Portsmouth Advertiser* published sermons preached on the occasion of the disaster as well as a poem lamenting the loss of life. Poetry—often crude and homespun—was prominent in the lives of the literate. Newspapers generally printed the efforts of local bards almost every day on assorted subjects.

The people of Norfolk—at least those who could read—seemed also intensely interested in politics. Papers published complete accounts of the recent proceedings of the U.S. Congress as well as the state legislature, and described the activities and pronouncements of Henry Clay, John Calhoun, Daniel Webster, Thomas Hart Benton, John Quincy Adams, and other celebrated public men.

A highlight of the year was the celebration of the Fourth of July. That day steamers brought visitors from rural areas who crowded into the city to watch cadets from the local military academy parade and hear the reading of the Declaration of Independence. After this modest entertainment, the steamboats left for the capes in the afternoon, taking people to picnics. By evening the streets were deserted "except for the Negroes" and the police who made sure that they observed the nine o'clock curfew mandated by law.[8]

1840 was a presidential election year, and the papers printed specimens made by the incumbent president, Martin Van Buren, a Democrat mired in an economic recession and weakened by the eclipse of the shadow of his popular predecessar Andrew Jackson. Equal space was given to the Whig challenger, "Old Tippecanoe," General William Henry Harrison.

Election Day was November 2, and that morning the papers published the new "liberalized" voting requirements, still so complex that it would seem that a prospective voter would need the services of an attorney to determine his eligibility. The following white persons over twenty-one were invited to the polls: 1) men possessed of "an estate of freehold in land value of $25"; 2) "tenants in common, joint tenants having an estate freehold of $25, being possessed of an interest or share in interest"; 3)"every person entitled to a reversion-invested remained in fee expectant on an estate for life or lives in land of the value of $50; "every such citizen who shall own and be himself in actual possession of a leasehold estate"; 5) "every such citizen who has for 12 months before the election been a housekeeper and head of a family and shall have been assessed with a part of the revenue of the commonwealth within the preceding year."[9]

Election news trickled in slowly. On November 4, the results from nearby Virginia counties began to materialize. Two days after the election, it was apparent that Harrison, who won 529 votes in Norfolk to Van Buren's 208, was winning overwhelmingly in the Tidewater area. On Friday, results were reported from Baltimore and Philadelphia. By the following Monday there were more Virginia returns, and some from Maryland, Pennsylvania, and New York. Only after a week had passed after the election did it "seem" that Harrison had carried the state of Virginia. It was not until November 26—more than three weeks after most voters cast their ballots, that the editors of the Norfolk papers felt confident enough to announce, "It seems pretty well ascertained that the vote to be given on the first Wednesday in December by the Electoral College will stand 234 for Harrison and Tyler and 60 for Van Buren and whoever Van Buren's electors choose to vote for as Vice-President."[10]

It was a confident age. The literature of the time indicates that the typical American felt that his country was the light of the planet and that America's way of life was the solution for the problems of humanity. The news items relating to other countries nearly always contained an air of condescension that seemed to imply, "What a pity! If only they did things *our* way!" Americans held, in general, the conviction that Fair Columbia was destined for unheard of greatness, glory, and grandeur. The United States of America in 1840 comprised only twenty-six states, but this was the decade of "Manifest Destiny", the idea that it was the obvious destiny of the United States to overspread and possess the entire continent. During the next decade the American Government would, through negotiations with Britain, obtain the "Oregon Country", and, through force of arms, despoil Mexico of approximately half of her territory. Few of the Americans who wrote publicly seemed to entertain serious doubts about the greatness and righteousness of their country.

People seemed to hold few fears of the future. A newspaper editor, noting that the population of the world was then estimated at 900 million, cheerfully predicted that by 1870 the world would contain more than a billion people, and by 1900 more than four billion. This rapid increase was viewed not with dread or alarm, but with the sanguine optimism that things were getting better and better and that mankind could solve all its problems.

This was a time of strict morality. Newspapers reported few instances of crime. Nearly all the incidents reports were (at least by late twentieth century standards) petty. When death records came to be kept in Virginia a decade later, they would reveal that Norfolk averaged then less than one murder a year. When crime did occur, it was reported with a sense of immense moral outrage. Perpetrators of violent acts were seen as diabolical fiends. People tended to a high sense of right and wrong and of personal responsibility. A seaman convicted of an unnamed "wicked was described as "A Specimen of Total Depravity" and " probably as depraved a being and as deeply sunk in degradation and crime as any human creature alive..."[11]

Above all, it was a religious age. The Christian faith permeated all aspects of society to a degree almost unimaginable today. On New Year's Day, *The Norfolk and Portsmouth Daily Advertiser* editorialized: "Christianity herself moves in advance of her own civilization and does not wait the tardy operation of philosophical causes. Conscious of her power over the universal man, she holds the world's destiny in her hands. She has undertaken, as a pacific object and as her own proper sphere, the reclamation—not of provinces or continents, but of all nations—all the millions of humanity, possessed by the grandeur of its conception, every project of ambition, every dream of empire—she has surveyed the enterprise from all its points...Already she is in occupation of the seats of power in every division of the globe and speaks to its swarming multitudes in two hundred languages of the many-tongued earth...[Christianity] will bring light out of darkness and order out of confusion. It will bring into being a new world, more beautiful and glorious than that over which the angels and the answering stars shouted on the morning of creation—a world of harmony and love... in which the spirit of truth will preside to guide into all truth and over which it will reign with a serene and holy domination forever."[12]

This religious character of the people was reflected even in newspaper obituaries, which, unlike today, seldom addressed the cause of death or the career or achievements of the deceased, but rather testified to the character and religious faith of the dead, such as Mrs. Elizabeth Crow of Portsmouth, who died "after a lingering illness of several months" at the age of 43— " an exemplary member of the Methodist Episcopal Church [who]... died in triumph, having obtained the victory over death."[13] Mrs. Leah C.U. Mayo, the wife of a lawyer, who also succumbed at 43, was described by the *Advertiser* as "an accomplished woman" who "displayed throughout her protracted illness a spirit chastened and elevated by the consolations of the Gospel...About two years ago the first symptoms of her disease forewarned her of her coming dissolution, and with the fortitude and resignation of a tried Christian she watched its progress and yielded to its power. Like Job she could say, 'Though He may slay me, yet will I trust in Him.' And till the last hour, not a murmur was heard to escape her lips under her severest pains. And thus she made a good confession."[14]

There was, of course, a dark side to life in Norfolk. By modern standards, at least, it was an extremely unhealthy place. When vital records were first kept in the 1850s, a third of those who died there in a typical year were children under five—and they died mostly of diarrheal disease. Although each year's death register included persons in their eighties and nineties, and occasional centenarians, the average age of the *adults* who died there in the 1850s was only forty-two. Nearly all deaths of persons under sixty were either from gastrointestinal diseases or respiratory infections (most frequently pneumonia and tuberculosis).[15]

Probably the greatest problem that confronted the people of Norfolk (especially if they were its victims) was slavery. More than a third of Norfolk's inhabitants were people of color, most of whom were slaves. Many of them were owned by masters or mistresses who lived in outlying areas and were "hired out" to employers in town.[16] They were either furnished with living quarters (often in attics, basements, or alley dwellings) or allowed to keep a percentage of their wages to rent their own accommodations.

The sale of slaves was advertised along with the sale of corn, tobacco, furniture, "portraits of the Ladies of Victoria's court" and "The Elixir of Love" for "all diseases occasioned by certain secret habits."[17] Along with such advertisements there occasionally appeared notices of "Negroes at Auction", such as this one: "Will be sold before the Court House door Princess Anne County on morning of 3d of February, one negro man named Max, aged 42, also one negro woman named Milla and two children."[18] A slave trader by the name of G.W. Apperson cheerfully ran this ad. for several days: "I will give the highest cash price [for] likely young negroes of both sexes from the age of ten to thirty years. All person [who] have such to dispose of...will be pleased to give me a call, before selling. I can be found at my jail on Reid's Lane, at the Union Hotel, or Gordon's Exchange office on Market Square. I also attend to shipping negroes to the southern states and those entrusted to my care will be shipped free of charge."[19]

Wills contained such callous bequests as that of Mumford McGehee (whom we will meet later), who left his son "one third part of a negro man named 'London', he [that is, the son] being [already] the owner of the other two-thirds, also one third part of the grist mill."[20]

Devout Christians as they tended to be, if the one or two Norfolk newspapers preserved from the 1840s are a true reflection of typical attitudes, many Tidewater whites tended to be ambivalent about slavery. The editors of the *Advertiser* deplored the continued African slave trade, which, though banned officially long ago, persisted alive and well, with American shippers among the most frequent offenders. An editorial lamented: "We regret to learn that the slave trade on the coast of Africa is carried on as brisk as ever in spite of the untiring vigilance of the British cruisers, and it is still more painful to know that the pirates engaged in the traffic are American citizens and their vessels built in this country."[21]

The editors of the *Advertiser* followed sympathetically the plight of a group of captured Africans, destined illegally for slavery in the Caribbean, who seized their vessel, the *Amistad* and tried to sail back to Africa, only to be captured and put on trial in Connecticut. Throughout the year the issue remained to be decided as to whether the Africans were to be freed to return home (as they eventually were) or remanded to their would-be purchasers. It was reported that the "mental powers" of most of the prisoners of the *Amistad* were "fully equal to those of our own race...They all have active minds and are quick, shrewd, and intelligent...They are also uncommonly susceptible of religion impressions."[22]

For many whites, not just in Norfolk, but throughout the nation, the solution to the Negro problem was "colonization" in Liberia. The *Advertiser* frequently published glowing reports about "our colonists." In January, 1840, a sea captain was quoted who described a "thriving religious community" in Liberia. He declared, "It would be impossible to tell from a perusal of the papers that they were issued by a colored population. The records of their marriages and deaths are like ours, and the title of 'Honorable', which, by the way, ought to have been long ago dropped here, is used by the colonists."[23]

Some masters freed slaves in their will only on condition that they emigrate to Liberia, and, over the years, especially after the terrifying Nat Turner slave rebellion in 1831 (which took place in Southampton County, which was a journey of only two days or so to the west) hundreds of blacks had sailed from Norfolk to a new life as "colonists" in Liberia.

If "colonization" was seen by many whites as the solution to the problem of the free Negro, no one could offer any solution to the problem of slavery itself. Although it may have generally been considered brutal and unchristian to impress poor Africans into slavery, few whites in Norfolk seemed to have qualms about holding in involuntary servitude the descendants of previous generations of captured Africans. Many slave holders reasoned that their "people" were better off than they would be in Africa, or even as freedmen, struggling to make ends meet in a environment of hostility.

Among the people of Norfolk in 1840 there were living three individuals who will figure prominently in this our story. This is no known likeness of any of them. About only one is there even the faintest oral tradition. Two of them lie today in graves unknown and unmarked, their dust likely lying beneath the asphalt of freeway or concrete of shopping mall. None of them were considered sufficiently important in their time to merit a newspaper obituary. And none of them were American citizens, the first because she was a slave, the second, because he was an immigrant not yet naturalized, and the third, a free woman, because she was "colored.[24]"

Sarah Kemp was a black woman of 30 who, with her two toddling children, was a slave. William Greenwood, a 19 year old "soap-boiler", had arrived six years before from the Grand Duchy of Hessen-Darmstadt in what would later become Germany. Martha Sparrow, a "mulatto" of 16, had been born free to parents who themselves had never known the chains of bondage. It is around these three people, whose names and almost every record of their being has been very nearly effaced by the years, that our narrative begins.

Chapter Four

The story of Sarah Kemp is like a jigsaw puzzle for which seven pieces out of ten are missing. The last two persons on earth who were able to transmit oral tradition about her could do so only second-hand, through the remembered words of long-dead relatives who had actually known her. According to one great-great granddaughter, Louise Jackson Elliott (1892?-1983), Sarah was always referred to in the family as "Mammy." She recounted, "Mammy was a dark woman. Everybody always said how wonderful she was, how Mammy was so good, how Mammy was so kind."[25] The other great-great granddaughter, Elinor Robinson Waller (1907-1971), stated that she had been told that Sarah Kemp 1) was very dark, almost black, but with European features, 2) that she was part Portuguese, 3) that she had been a house servant who watched her master's children, and 4) that she was a very intelligent and energetic businesswoman.[26] Waller and her half-brother, Bernard Ruffin, Jr. (1914-1972) also knew of a vague tradition that either Sarah or her parents had come from or near Gloucester, Massachusetts.

It seems certain that Sarah was born late in 1809 or early in 1810. Her death certificate gives her age as 87 at the time of her death in May, 1897. According to the U.S. Census of 1870 she was then 60. According to the slave censuses (which, however, do not give names), Sarah's master owned a black female slave who was forty in 1850 and fifty in 1860. Only the U.S. Census of 1880, which gives her age as 68, suggests a birthyear a year or two after 1810.

It also seems certain that Sarah was born in the borough of Norfolk. At least that is what her death certificate states, and there is no evidence to indicate otherwise. The censuses of 1870 and 1880 call only for the state of birth, and in both "Virginia" is indicated.

If Sarah was like most slaves in Virginia's Tidewater region, any tradition of African origins was, at best, very vague. Few slaves were shipped to that area from Africa after the first few decades of the eighteenth century,[27] so most Norfolk blacks of Sarah's generation would have been likely to have not only American-born parents and grandparents, but great-grandparents as well.

What of the Portuguese and Gloucester, Massachusetts traditions? As late as the census of 1880, there were blacks in Massachusetts and Rhode Island who listed the Cape Verde Islands (a Portuguese-owned territory off the coast of Africa), and, occasionally, even Portugal as their place of birth. It was not unheard of for slaves to be sold from Massachusetts to Virginia in the seventeenth and eighteenth century. It is possible that one or more of Sarah's ancestors had been taken from the Cape Verde Islands, been of mixed Portuguese and black African blood, and sold from Massachusetts to Virginia. If the census of 1880 is correct, however, this could have been the case no more recently than the generation of Sarah's grandparents, and it would be extraordinary that in a family in which so little tradition was preserved that this one would have been.

The original for of Sarah's surname is not clear. Throughout the nineteenth century it was spelled alternately *Kemp* and *Camp*. Her death certificate lists her name as *Camp* and gives her parents as William and Lydia *Camp*. Since Sarah was unlettered, she would not have any idea of the correct spelling. The earliest extant family signature is that of Sarah's nephew Alexander, who was asked to sign a signature card when he opened an account in the Freedmen's Bank of Norfolk on March 14, 1872. The clerk who filled out the card wrote the young man's name as Alexander *Camp*, but he actually signed his name Alexander *Kemp*.[28] When Sarah's son John advertised in the Norfolk city directory around the same time, he was listed as John *Camp*. Sarah's other son Samuel is listed in his marriage and death records as *Kemp*. Sarah's grandson Frank is listed as *Camp* in the death register, but as *Kemp* in his marriage register, *Kemp* in the Norfolk city directories (except for one or two years, when he is *Camp*), and all of his children invariably spelled the name *Kemp*.

Contrary to popular opinion, many slaves did, at least in Virginia, have surnames, although these were not legally recognized. When slaves are mentioned in public records, it is usually only by their nicknames ("Bob," "Sally," "Hetty", "Jim," "Betty", etc.) But among themselves they were frequently also known by their surnames, and these were not always those of their current master. There was a white family in Princess Anne County whose name was Kemp, but there is no evidence that Sarah ever belonged to the Kemps of Kempsville. In fact, if *Camp* is the original spelling and the family tradition of Portuguese origins is correct, the name might have been originally *Campos*.

It cannot be determined who Sarah's master was nor who was her husband or the father of her children. Books have been written insisting that slave sales had to be entered in county deed books. This, at least in Virginia, was *not* the case. When a slave was purchased, the new owner seems to have received a certificate, like this one, dated September 6, 1858, handed down by the legitimate Greenwood descendants: "Rec'd of Martin Greenwood [father of William], four hundred dollars being in full for the purchase of one Negro slave named Leander, the right and title of which said slave I warrant and defend against all persons claiming under me in in my fiduciary capacity. Witness my hand and seal.

Wm. H.C. Ellis
Trustee[29]

Such documents were usually kept among the personal papers of the slaveowners, but there was no legal requirement that they be recorded in the courthouse, as transactions of land had to be. Consequently, one finds the sales of slaves recorded in Virginia deed books *only occasionally*.

It is sometimes possible to determine the ownership of a slave by the examination of will books from the appropriate time period. Testators would sometimes mention slaves by name, but just as often would refer collectively to "my slaves", "my Negroes," or "my servants." Only when an inventory was made were slaves listed individually, and then usually only by their nicknames. No wills or inventories of Norfolk Borough, Norfolk County, or Princess Anne County from the first half of the nineteenth century make any mention of Sarah Kemp or her family, or anyone who could reasonably be associated with them.

Although Sarah is listed as a "widow" in the 1880 census and on her death certificate, there is some question whether she was ever married at all. It seems as though Kemp (or Camp) was her maiden name. One would expect to find the name of Sarah's husband in 1) the application for a marriage license made by her children (which, in Norfolk, required the names of both parents), and 2) on the death certificates on her children. Sarah had three children, of whom only one married. In Samuel Kemp's marriage protocol, his parents are given as "_____ and Sarah Kemp."[30] Whoever hurriedly filled out the death certificate of Lydia Kemp omitted the names of both parents. John Kemp's death record lists "Sarah Kemp" as his mother, but "_____ " as his father. Samuel Kemp's death record is more revealing. The youngest of Sarah's children, he was the first to die, and his mother was likely the informant. His parents' names are given as "Russell Kemp and Sarah Bell." This is problematic in that it suggests that Sarah was born a Bell and married a Kemp. However, Sarah's own death certificate, prepared just a year after her son's, for which Lydia or John or both were likely informants, gives

Sarah's parents' names as William and Lydia Camp, and there *was* 72 year old Lydia Camp enumerated in the 1860 census, along with several relatives of Sarah.

The oral tradition received by Sarah's great-granddaughters is that her children were fathered by a white man. The apparent reluctance of Sarah's children to name their father suggests, but by no means proves, illegitimacy. The fact that Sarah, who was described as "very dark" had one child who was brown-skinned (Lydia), one who was white-skinned (John), and one who was olive (Sam) would also suggest a white father.

But who was Russell Kemp? Whoever he was, he was held in sufficient reverence that Samuel Russell Kemp carried his name. Samuel had a grandson, Russell Thomas Kemp, and a great-grandson Russell Julian Kemp. But was the first Russell's surname really *Kemp*? Nobody in or around Norfolk listed in the census, tax records, will books, or deed books had that name. Perhaps he was Russell *Bell*. If so, still no record can be found of a Russell Bell. If, however, he had been a slave who died before emancipation, then there would likely have been no record of him. So, perhaps, he may have been Sarah's slave husband. No information has thus far been uncovered to clarify the matter.

Sarah Kemp had a brother, Joseph[31], who is always referred to as *Camp*—another reason to assume that Kemp/Camp was Sarah's maiden name. Sometime in the mid 1840s Joseph Camp married Minerva Tynes, who had been born free in Isle of Wight County around 1821. Her registration papers describe her as a woman of "black complexion" 5'4½" tall with a scar on her left cheek, and a scar on her wrist. At 21 she was missing an upper front tooth.[32] They had at least six sons (William Franklin, Joseph, Jr., John, Timothy, called "Bud", Alexander, and Raymond) and a short-lived daughter Harriet. According to the U.S. Census of 1860, Minerva and the children were free, as well as Lydia, the mother of Joseph and Lydia, but the head of the household was still evidently a slave.[33]

Sarah had three children: Lydia, born in 1837 (or possibly very early 1838); John, born in 1839 (or early 1840); and Samuel Russell, born in 1844 or a year or so before. There may have been other children (and Sarah's age at the birth of her oldest surviving child—27—seems to suggest this as a possibility) who died young, were sold away, or who have simply failed to appear in existing records. These three offspring would remain, to the end of their lives, the core of a very closely-knit family group.

Before Samuel was four years old, Sarah and her children experienced the catastrophe that all slaves dreaded—sale. Had the Kemps been sold as the result of the death of their owner, they would likely have been listed in a will or inventory, which they were not. There was then a surplus of slaves in the Tidewater area, especially in the cities, and there was a great demand for them, not only in the Deep South, but also on the part of the tobacco planters of the interiors Virginia and North Carolina. Sarah and her children may have been sold because their owners—whoever they were—needed money. Of this experience, no family tradition survived. Lydia Kemp, in old age, was known to assert that she was always well-treated as a slave. This is hard to reconcile with the certainty that she had, as a child, been sold like a bushel of potatoes.

Josephine Smith, a former slave from Norfolk, Virginia, recalled when interviewed in the 1930s, "I remember seeing a heap of slave sales, with a nigger in chains and the speculators selling and buying them off. I...remembers seeing a drove of slaves with nothing on but a rag twixt their two legs being galloped around before the buyers."[34] Could the family of Sarah Kemp have endured such an ordeal? If so, how could Lydia possibly insist to her great-granddaughters that she had never been abused or mistreated?

The situation may have been much less gruesome than that described by Josephine Smith. One of Norfolk's most successful slave-traders, William W. Hall, had, by 1847 or 1848, erected a "magnificent" "Negro Repository." In an advertisement urging Norfolk slave-owners to sell their servants to him, Hall boasted, "The undersigned has at very considerable expense erected and fitted up in a style of comfort and convenience a commodious TWO STORY BUILDING on Union Street, second door east of Church Street, for the safe keeping and accommodation of NEGROES, both male and female (the apartments being entirely separate) which are brought to the market for sale. The building is admirably adapted to the object proposed, having airy and pleasant rooms and every convenience which could be desired, besides large yards, walled in high, a capacious cistern, etc, which while they secure the comfort of the NEGRO, likewise guarantee the most ample security for his safekeeping."[35] The Repository kept descriptions of all the "Negroes for Sale," who were divided into two categories: house hands and field hands.

Slave-owners who wished to unload their unprofitable servants would sell them to Hall, who imprisoned them in his Repository until he could sell them to "speculators" , who bought them to sell them where they could obtain a higher price and thereby make a profit. The slaves kept by Hall at his Repository were evidently not put on the auction block. Potential buyers went there, inspected a list, viewed the slaves in their "apartments", and then bought them like department store merchandise.

The journey from their home to the place where the speculators intended to sell them was ordinarily a terrible and terrifying one for the captive slaves. W.L. Bost, a former slave, recalled seeing, as a boy of 10, speculators pass through his North Carolina hometown with "droves of slaves." He recalled, "They always stayed at our place. The poor critters nearly froze to death. They always came along on the last of December so that the niggers would be ready for sale on the first day of January. Many was the time I saw four or five of them chained together. They never had enough clothes on to keep a cat warm. The women never wore anything but a thin dress and a petticoat and one underwear. I've seen ice balls hanging onto the bottom of their dresses as they ran along, just like sheep in a pasture before they are sheared. They never wore any shoes...They just ran along on the ground, all spewed ice. The speculators always rode on horses and drove the poor niggers. When they got cold, they made them run till they were warm again. The speculators stayed in the hotel and put the niggers in the quarters just like droves of hogs. All through the night I could hear them mourning and praying...The slaves looked just like droves of turkeys running along in front of the horses."[36]

Whether they were placed in a cart or wagon by a relatively humane buyer or savagely driven on foot, the Kemps must have been terrified as they were torn from familiar surroundings into the countryside and conveyed towards the setting sun, over rough and rutted roads, through expanses of farmland. A day went by and then a second, then a third, a fourth, a fifth, a sixth, a seventh. Finally they arrived in the town of Milton, in north central North Carolina, right on the Virginia border.

It is not known whether the family was subjected there to the infamous auction block, described graphically by Bost, who recalled, "I remember when they put them on the block to sell them. The ones between eighteen and thirteen always bring the most money. The auctioneer stood off at a distance and cried them off as they stood on the block...If the one they were going to sell was a young Negro man, this is what he says, 'Now, gentlemen and fellow citizens, here is a big black buck Negro. He's stout as mule. Good for any kind of work and he never gives any trouble. How much am I offered for him?' And then the sale would commence and the nigger would be sold to the highest bidder. If they put up a young nigger woman the auctioneer cried out, 'Here's a young nigger wench, how much am I offered for her?' The poor thing stood on the block a-shivering and a-shaking, nearly froze to death. When they were sold, many of the poor mothers begged the speculators to sell them with their husbands, but the speculators only take what they want. Maybe the poor thing never saw her husband again.[37]

Whether through auction or by some other means, Sarah Kemp and her children found themselves the property of new owners. Intact as a family until then, they were now separated. Sarah and John were purchased by George Alexander Smith, a tobacco merchant of about 40 with a wife and several young children. Lydia and Samuel were bought by Thomas McGehee, an elderly widower who ran a mill in the next county. As she was, no doubt, wrestled away from her screaming children, Sarah Kemp had no idea whether she would ever see them again.

Chapter Five

Sarah soon realized that the separation from Lydia and Samuel was not as disastrous as it seemed, when she learned that the man who purchased her children was the father of her new mistress. Sarah was now in Caswell County in the heart of tobacco country. The county was home to about 12,000 inhabitants, more than a third of whom were slaves and a few hundred were free blacks.

Lydia and Samuel were only a few miles away, just across the Person County line, on the Woodburn Plantation, overlooking the Hyco River. About 8000 people lived in Person County, about a quarter of whom were slaves.

Slavery in North Carolina, as in Virginia, seems to have been somewhat more benign than in the Deep South. In 1937, as one of the many projects of the Works Progress Administration of Franklin Roosevelt's New Deal, scores of interviewers, many of them African American, were dispatched to locate former slaves and take down their recollections. By this time not only Sarah, but her three children as well, had long since partaken of the common lot of humanity; but the reminiscences of those who had been held in bondage in the same vicinity provide some information concerning slavery in Caswell and Person Counties. Although the WPA interviews contacted no one who had been a slave either of Thomas McGehee or George Smith, they did interview several persons who resided in the 1850s in the general vicinity.

Some, like Tempie Herndon Durham, who lived in Chatham County (just to the south) had extremely favorable recollections. For Durham, like many of her contemporaries, white and black, the term "nigger" did not have an unfavorable connotation. At the age of 103 she recalled, "Freedom is all right, but the niggers were better off before surrender, because they were looked after and they didn't get into any trouble fighting and killing like the do these days. Maybe everybody's master and mistress wasn't as good as Master George and Miss Betsey, but they were the same as a mammy and pappy to us niggers."[38]

Durham described how she was married on the front porch of the "Big House": "Marse George killed a shoat and Miss Betsy had Georgianna, the cook, to bake a big wedding cake all iced up white as snow with a bridge and groom standing in the middle, holding hands. The table was set out in the yard under the trees, and you ain't never seed the like of the eats. All the niggers come to the feast and Marse George had a dram for everyone. That was some wedding! I had on a white dress, white shoes, and long white gloves...and Miss Betsy made me a wedding veil...When she played the wedding march on the piano, me and Exeter [the bridegroom] marched down the walk and up the porch to the altar Miss Betsy fixed. That was the prettiest altar I seed. Back against the rose vine that was full of red roses, Miss Betsy done put tables filled with flowers and white candles. She...spread down a bed sheet...for us to stand on, and there was a white pillow to kneel down on. Exeter...made me a wedding ring...out of a big red button.

"Uncle Edmond Kirby married us. He was the nigger preacher that preached at the plantation church...Marse George got to have his little fun: he says, 'Come on, Exeter, you and Tempie got to jump over the broomstick backwards; you got to go that to see which one [is going] to be boss of the house, and if both of them jumps over without touching it, there [would be] no bossing [we would just] be genial."

When Exeter, who had too much to drink, got his feet tangled and fell on the broom, Master George said, "Exeter, you're going to be bossed till you're scared to speak, unless Tempie tells you to speak."[39]

There were several slaveholders in Caswell County who were members of the numerous Graves family. Nancy Williams, living in Norfolk in 1937, grew up on one of the Graves plantations in Caswell County, just a few miles from the Smith and McGehee lands. Her recollections were similar to those of Durham: "I ain't never had nothing to do when I was little except lie around the house and play with the children...I didn't do no work, I just had a good time." She recalled the dances the slaves held in a cabin out in the woods: "Them dances were something!...Every gal had her beau. And such music!...I was out there in the middle of the floor, just a-dancing...dancing with a glass of water on my head...and three boys a-betting on me. I had a great big wreath around my head and a big ribbon bow on each side and I didn't waste a drop of water on neither....One boy won five dollars off'n me." Williams recalled that her father, who was steward of the plantation, had "plenty" of money and described the pretty clothes she bought with money she earned making quilts, which sold for up to ten dollars. She concluded that life with her master's family was a "regular paradise."[40]

Although there were kind and just masters who treated their "people" like members of their family, there were others who were cruel and inhumane. Next to the Graves plantation where Nancy Williams lived was the estate of Thomas Covington. The U.S. Census of 1850 reveals that he was then 44 years old and the owner of real estate value at $2400. He had a wife, three daughters, three sons, and 14 slaves. It is popularly believed that owners of small numbers of slaves tended to be more humane than those who owned large numbers, but this generalization was not true of Tom Covington. According to Nancy Williams, the master of the adjoining plantation was "the meanest man God ever turned loose on this here earth." On Covington's plantation there lived a man known as "Uncle Jimmy" who "used to sing and pray all the time he was walking in the fields." One day, in full view of the Graves slaves an overseer ordered Uncle Jimmy to stop singing, only to be ignored. When Covington was told of this instance of disobedience, he roared, "Kill the nigger if he won't work! Go on down there and kill him! What is a nigger for it he can't work?" According to Williams, "The overseer come on back down the field and took Uncle Jimmy cross the field...He made the poor man dig a hole in the ground with his naked hands. Then they put straw in the bottom of the hole and poured on the tar. Then he chained poor Uncle Jimmy and throwed him into the hole and lit a match to him...Uncle Jimmy say, 'I'm fixing to live again in Christ!' Then he commence to preach and pray. The flames was getting hotter and the last thing poor Uncle Jimmy did was sing:

'God is the spring of all my joy,
The life of my delight!'

As the song faded away, he died. All the time this was going on, we were watching it...through a crack in the fence."[41]

Another brutal slave master was a man named Cash, who lived in Person County. Analiza Foster recalled a heinous crime perpetrated on his plantation: "The woman was pregnant and she fainted in the field at the plow. The driver said that she was putting on that she ought to be beat. The master said that she can be beat, but don't to hurt the baby. The driver...then...digs a hole in the sand and he puts in the woman in the hole—which is nigh about to her armpits, then he covers her up and straps her hands over her head. He takes the long bullwhip and he cuts long gashes all over her shoulders and raised arms, then he walks off and leaves her there for an hour in the hot sun. The flies and the gnats, they worry her, and the sun hurts too and she cries a little, then the driver comes out with a pan of vinegar, salt, and red pepper and washes the gashes. The woman faints and he digs her up, but in a few minutes she is stone dead."[42]

Another slavemaster near the Smith and McGehee lands was Drew Norwood, (whose name does not appear in the 1850 census in that form) who was so cruel that his slaves were always running away. According to David Larson, the son of a pair of his slaves, "if he caught them he beat them near about to death." A woman by the name of Cindy Norwood ran to the home of a nearby planter and begged him to keep her, but the cruel master reclaimed her and whipped her until she was bloody and then put poison in the wounds, so that the poor woman died after three days of convulsions. Eventually, two slaves—David Larson's parents—seized the evil master, tied him up, and killed him by forcing boiling water down his throat. For their act of rebellion the husband and wife were hanged with the same rope with which they had bound their master.[43]

There is little information to reveal whether Thomas Mumford McGehee was a good, evil, or indifferent master. Sixty-four years old and a widower for more than 20 years, McGehee, with his 119 slaves, was one of the greatest landowners of Person County. He was the great-great grandson of William MackGahye, a Scotsman who arrived in York County, Virginia in 1653. MacGahye's descendants claimed that he was born James *McGregor*, but was stripped of his lands and sentenced to death when he had the temerity to support King Charles I, who was defeated and killed at the end of the bloody English Civil War with the Puritan supporters of Oliver Cromwell, who made himself Lord Protector in 1649. McGregor's mother, Marian MacDonald, claimed to be related to the royal houses of both England and Scotland. Forced into hiding, McGregor changed his name to William McEagh , taking a surname meaning "Son of the Mist.[44]" Later, the spelling was modified to MackGahye.

If William MackGahye was in fact James McGregor, he escaped the Puritans only to be killed by Virginia's Indians. One of his sons, Thomas MackGehee settled in King William County, between the Mattaponi and Pamunkey Rivers in east central Virginia, where he died at the age of about 60 around the year 1724. One of his nine children, Edward Macgehee (1702-1771) moved to Cumberland County, some 60 miles to the west, almost in the very center of the present state of Virginia. Edward's wife, Elizabeth DeJarnette, was the daughter of a French immigrant. Mumford, son of Edward and Elizabeth, was born around 1743 and married Sarah Moore of nearby Charlotte County. He lived for a time in Prince Edward County (north of Charlotte and south of Cumberland) before purchasing land in 1776 in North Carolina in what would later become Person County. Shortly afterwards he joined the Continental Army and spent the next winter with Washington at Valley Forge.[45]

Mumford McGehee, who fathered seven children, eventually owned several thousand acres on both sides of the Hyco River, a plantation he named Woodburn. His "manor house", a four story square house with a small front porch and large square columns, painted white with green shutters, stood until burnt by vandals in 1964. On the river below the house McGehee constructed a large mill which made flour from wheat and corn meal from the corn raised by the dozens of slaves he acquired over the years. Near the grist mill the McGehee slaves operated a cotton gin and saw mill. And so, with the help of his slaves, Mumford McGehee, who also bred race horses and livestock, grew prosperous from the sale of cotton, timber, flour, and corn meal. By the time he died at 72 in December, 1815 he was said to own more land and slaves than anyone else in Person County.

Seven months before he died, Mumford McGehee "of sound mind and memory", but "feeling that decline to which advanced age is subject", made out his will. To his 31 year old son Thomas Mumford he left the Woodburn Plantation, as well as "one third part of the negro man called London and a third part of the grist mill." It was understood that Thomas already owned the rest of the mill as well as the rest of London. To Thomas the father also bequeathed "a negro woman named Nancy and her two children Louisa and Locket." Mumford left his son John $200. His slaves Peter, Tom, Aggy, Sicily, Milly, Sidney, Henry, and Henrietta were to be "sold at public sale on a credit of twelve months" and the proceeds were to be distributed to the three McGehee daughters, Elizabeth Moore, Sally Stanfield, and Polly McFarland. As for Mumford's two other sons, Joseph and William, "I have heretofore made provision for [them] by giving them money, negroes, and other property and have nothing to bequeath in this my will."[46]

And so, Thomas M. McGehee and his 20 year old wife, the former Elizabeth Jeffreys, became master and mistress of Woodburn. Thomas became not only a planter, financier, and breeder of race horses like his father, but was a member of the North Carolina General Assembly in 1826 and again from and was a member of the Council of State from 1830 to 1840.[47]

Elizabeth died at 30 in 1825 after bearing Thomas at least six children, four of whom lived to maturity. The older son, Thomas Jeffreys McGehee, a planter like his father, became master of the nearby Burleigh Plantation. The younger, Montford, was a student at the Sorbonne in Paris at the time Lydia and Samuel came to live at Woodburn. He would return to North Carolina to practice law in Milton, as a close neighbor to his sister, Adeline Mildred, the eldest daughter, who in December, 1831, at the age of 18, married the twenty-four year old George Alexander Smith, who had newly arrived in Caswell County from northern Virginia.

At the time that Lydia and Samuel came to live with Thomas McGehee, presumably as house servants with rooms in the garrett at Woodburn, Thomas McGehee had a person estate (mostly slaves) assessed at well over $100,000, and real estate value at more than $60,000. Neighbors later said that "the McGehees looked down on their neigbhors...They held a high head and believed in drawing social barriers."[48]

Exactly what Lydia Kemp and her little brother did at Woodburn is not known. It is not known what she thought of the aging widower who was her master and apparently the only white person living on the plantation. What we do know is from a transaction recorded in the Caswell County deedbook, in which McGehee, on August 23, 1848, sold eight slaves to his son-in-law George A. Smith:

Holcomb, age 45
Moses, age 25
Oliver, age 16
Samuel, age 14
Gabriel, age 13
Isaac, age 14
Melinda, age 13
Lydia, age 11[49]

Samuel Kemp was four, not 14. If the Samuel listed in the deed of sale is in fact the brother of Lydia, it is likely that the copyist simply made a mistake, adding an extra "1" to his age. As far as can be determined, the other slaves were not related to the Kemps. Why Lydia and Samuel were sold cannot be determined from the wording of the document. Did Thomas Mumford McGehee, a humane man perhaps, include the children in the sale when he realized that their mother and brother was owned by his son-in-law? Why were the other slaves sold? There are no documents to cast light upon the matter.

George Smith and his wife "Millie" lived in a large house on the northwest corner of Liberty and Main Streets in Milton, which was then a thriving little village with more than 400 souls. Located close to both the Virginia and Person County lines, Milton was only a few miles from Woodburn. It was here that Lydia would live with her mother and brothers for the next decade. Her remarks to her grandchildren about her benign experience as a slave probably refer to her years with the Smiths. She told her family that she lived with her master and mistress and was treated "just like a member of the family" and that her mistress loved her dearly.[50]

The Smiths were of Scots origins. Master's father was George Smith. Born near Glasgow in 1775, he came to America sometime before 1799, when he married Delia Sterling Forbes. He settled near Dumfries, in Prince William County in northern Virginia. This community, which then had about 1100 people, had been chartered about fifty years earlier by Scots merchants trading in tobacco. Smith bought land just north of the town, at Powell's Creek, where he operated a mill and dealt in wheat and flour. One of his grandchildren would characterize the elder George Smith as "a man of much intelligence and culture."[51]

Delia Sterling Forbes Smith, who was born in Prince William County in 1780, was the daughter of a physician, David Forbes (1752-1789), a native of Pitsfigo, Scotland, who came to America with his wife, the former Margaret Stirling (1754-1806), just before the Revolution. He served as a surgeon in the Continental Army. Both David and Margaret Forbes claimed illustrious ancestry. Although the Forbes family were described (with what justification is not entirely clear) as "one of the oldest families of Scotland," they were not good enough for the family of Margaret Stirling. The orphaned daughter of George Stirling, Laird of Herbertshire, who traced his forbears through the earls of Annandale to Walter De Striuelyng, who received a grant of land at a place called Cambusbarron in 1150 from King David I of Scotland, Margaret, at the age of six, went to live with her aunt Jean, Lady Alva, who disinherited her when she had the audacity as to marry a mere surgeon—a man so base-born that he actually had to *work for a living*!

The elder George Smith died at 47 in August, 1822, leaving his entire estate to his widow, to be divided among their seven young children upon their marriage or majority.

By the 1820s Dumfries was no longer the ideal location for upwardly mobile Americans. The channel on Quantico Creek which emptied into the Potomac and had made the town a prosperous port was now silted up. The seat of county government had been moved. After her husband's death, Delia Smith moved to Fredericksburg. The oldest daughter, Anne Amelia (1811-1864), the wife of James Thornton, was then living at "Fall Hill" near her mother, but then moved with her family, first to Georgia and then to Alabama, where Thornton served for a time as secretary of state. Mary Virginia Smith (1818-1855) married Philip Lewis Lightfoot and became one of the earliest settlers of Green County, Alabama. The youngest Smith daughter, Sallie (1820-1881) and her husband George Willis were wealthy enough to maintain homes both in Orange County, Virginia and Pensacola, Florida. Two of the sons of George and Delia Smith, William Forbes and John Erskine, died, unmarried, in their early 20s[52]. The youngest son, Murray Forbes Smith (1814-c.1875) moved to Mobile, Alabama, where he became a successful cotton dealer. Just before the Civil War he moved his business to New York City, where his fortunes declined. His daughter Alva Erskine Smith (1850-1933)—first cousin to the children of the new master of Sarah Kemp—married, however, as we shall see, into the Vanderbilt and Belmont families.

George Alexander Smith, who was about 14 when his father died, moved, in his early 20s, to Caswell County, North Carolina.. The record of his property transactions from the Caswell County deed books provides the only extant account of the development of his career.

In April, 1834 George bought a storehouse in Milton. The next December, he bought a strip of ground twenty feet long and twenty feet wide on Liberty Street in Milton. In February, 1837 he bought still more land on the same street. Two years later he bought a warehouse from his father-in-law, and the following year was able to purchase still another warehouse. Three years later he obtained a parcel of land along Holding Creek. That same year he bought still more land. In November, 1843, he purchased a house on the northwest corner of Liberty and Main Streets. During the following dozen years he continued to purchased land in and around Milton.

By 1850 George A. Smith was the master of 50 slaves, most of whom lived in six cabins[53], located, probably, on property outside of town. He seems to have acquired Sarah and family shortly after he bought his home. Perhaps he felt the need for a staff of attractive house servants to assist Delila and Ann, who had served him and his wife for some years.

Most of the Smith slaves worked in the fields, growing corn and tobacco and working in the three tobacco warehouses that Smith eventually came to acquire. Sarah, Lydia, John, and Samuel, as well as Delila and Ann, probably had little contact with them.

The inventory of the Smith estate reveals a little of the life of the family. The house, now the site of an overgrown vacant lot, must have been modestly large. Downstairs there seems to have been a kitchen, a parlor, a dining room, and a library. Both the parlor and the dining room had cain-matting carpets. The dining room had three expandable walnut dining tables, and 10 walnut chairs, indicative of the presence of frequent guests. There was a mahogany sideboard in the room and oil-colored shades graced the windows. The Smiths had a "good" set of gilt and white French china and a set of "plain" tableware for ordinary occasions. They owned a set of 23 cut-glass goblets, 10 blown-glass goblets, and 17 wine glasses.

The kitchen contain, among other things, a churn, a sugar bucket, an "old" cooking stove "with furniture", a large oven, one large pot, four common tables, four flat-irons, a furnace "for preserving", a coffee mill, a mortal and pestle, and three wash-tubs.

The parlor had a fireplace and was also illuminated by two "swinging lamps" and candles in two mahogany stands. A "Yankee Clock" kept time. Guests sat on a hair-cloth settee, one of several crimson-cushioned mahogany chairs, or in one of two mahogany rockers. Smith and his cronies—evidently consumers of snuff and chewing tobacco—expectorated into a set of Britannia Parlor Spittons as well as a plain earthenware cuspidor.

The library also had a fireplace, as well as a mahogany safe, mahogany chairs, four mahogany "quartettes", and two mahogany side-tables, as well as mahogany bookcases. Candles set in two-plated candelabrae, a terracotta candelabra, and one single candlestick provided a dim artificial light.

There were several bedrooms upstairs. George and Millie Smith probably slept on the high-posted mahogany bedstead. There was a room for the Smith girls, with two mahogany French bedsteads, and one for the boys, with three walnut bedsteads. There were apparently three rooms for the servants, perhaps located in a garrett. Distributed among the family's sleeping quarters were three walnut wardrobes, a red-stained poplar wardrobe, a mahogany side-table (probably for the master bedroom), and two walnut bureaux and one bureau of mahogany. Each of the three family rooms had a mirror, wash-stand, and chamber pot.

The most revealing part of the Smith inventory is the list of the family's books. The Smiths owned hundreds of volumes. Among them were: a fourteen volume set of *Encyclopedia Americana;* Thomas B. Macaulay's two volume *History of England;* Fuller's two volume *Universal History;* a volume of "obituary addresses" for Henry Clay (who died in 1852); a textbook of chemistry; a *History of the Sandwich Islands* [Hawaii]; *Sketches of North Carolina; Expedition to the Dead Sea;* a volume of Shakespeare's work; two books on the American Revolution; a 14 volume set of the works of Washington Irving; a 17 volume set of *Mrs. Sherwood's Work;* and 27 novels, including Charlotte Bronte's *Jane Eyre.* There was a *Book of Flowers,* a *Young Ladies Own Book,* a *Classical Library of Poetry, Heroes of America,* and a two volume set on the American Revolution. There was also a book by early feminist Mary Wollstonecraft called *The Wrongs of Women.*

Most of the library was religious. The Smiths had one large family Bible and three smaller Bibles. They had a copy of *The Pilgrim's Progress* and two copies of Milton's *Paradise Lost.* There were two copies of the Episcopal *Book of Common Prayer,* a *History of the Reformation,* and such other titles as *Lives of the Martyrs, Life's Discpline, Judah's Lion, Family Prayers, Hannah More on Prayer, Bickersteth on Prayer, Sermons on Morals, Women of Israel, Christian Mothers,* and *Evidence of Christianity.*[54]

It is interesting that nowhere among the books is listed a set of the works of Sir Walter Scott, which, according to popular tradition, were *supposed* to have been in the library of every red-blooded southerner, especially every southerner of Scots descent!

If the inventory of his books is any clue to his character, we might think of George Alexander Smith as a serious, business-like man of severe morality, who was interested in history, science, and literature. Mildred McGehee Smith—more from the Lydia Kemp tradition and the wording of her husband's will,—seems to have been a kind, sweet, and spiritual woman.

The Smiths and their household servants walked a short distance north on Main Street to the Milton Presbyterian Church. There had been no church in the frontier mill town (Milton is a contraction of "mill town") for 23 years after its founding until 1817, when the residents decided it was time to enlist the services of a full-time clergyman. The community met together to decide the type of pastor they wanted to call, since the town was too small to support more than one. Should he be

Methodist? Baptist? Episcopalian? Presbyterian? The citizens of Milton took a vote. The two denominations that finished highest in the polling were the Presbyterians and the Episcopalians. A second ballot was taken, which led to the call of a Presbyterian minister.[55]

The Milton Presbyterian Church, like many houses of worship of the time, had strict rules. All members, black and white, slave and free, were, on paper, on equal footing. But in order to become a member, a candidate had to undergo a meticulous scrutiny by the church elders. The slightest moral infraction resulted in disqualification for membership—or excommunication, if one had already been accepted into the congregation. The minutes of the church provide some interesting stories. One man was dismissed because he went fishing on a Sunday and had the effrontery to insist that his Sabbath-breaking was nobody's "damned business." A woman gave birth to a child long after separation from her husband, and told the elders that she had conceived the baby on a visit to her estranged spouse in Philadelphia. It was determined, however, that this trip had occurred only seven months previous to the child's birth. Thereupon the elders interviewed the midwife and others who had seen the baby shortly after birth, who were convinced that the child was full-term. On the grounds that there was insufficient evidence to prove that that child was premature, the mother was thereby excommunicated![56]

It is no surprise that, of the entire Smith household, only the pious Mildred was received into church membership (on June 21, 1843). George and his brother-in-law Montford McGehee (newly returned from Europe) became trustees in December, 1847, but never members. Although the church did in those days accepted Negro members, Sarah, whose children almost certainly had been born out of wedlock—whatever the circumstances—could never have been received.

The Kemps must have sat upstairs in the balcony with the other slaves. There was, however, one family of color who sat downstairs with the main congregation. This was the family of Thomas Day[57]. Day, born in Virginia in 1801, lived across the street from the Smiths and owned a furniture factory which was said to produce the finest cabinets in North Carolina. It was Day who fashioned the furniture of the church, of which he was an active leader. The church session sometimes met in his home. Day, who had seven hired assistants (six white and one black), had a personal estate (in 1850) of $8000, which included eight slaves[58]

Like most couples of their time, place, and class, George and

Mildred Smith had a large family. The oldest child was Thomas McGehee Smith, born in March, 1834. He finished the Male Academy at Milton and, in the mid-1850s, was studying law. William Forbes, the second son, born in September, 1837, was a student at the Academy, apparently being groomed to become a partner in his father's business. He was followed by Delia Sterling Smith, born in May, 1840. She died as a teenager, probably around June, 1853. The fourth child, Mumford Augustus, born in May, 1842, lived less than three years. The fifth child, Ellen Elizabeth, born in August, 1844, was or would soon be attending Milton's Female Academy. The sixth child, George Alexander Smith, Jr., was born in September, 1847; the seventh, Murray Forbes, in January, 1850, and the eighth and last, Rosa, who lived only three years, in January, 1852. To have five children out of eight live to adulthood was typical—even favorable—for the time and place.

Around the time that little Rosa Smith died it became apparent that 17 year old Lydia was with child and without a husband. When, sometime in the fall of 1854 or early in 1855 she gave birth to a fair-skinned boy, whom she named Benjamin Franklin Kemp, 17 year old William Forbes Smith admitted—or was forced to admit—that he was the father of the infant slave.

Chapter Six

We will leave Lydia Kemp, the teenaged mother, to deal with reactions—lost to history—of the Smith family to the birth of Frank and return to Norfolk and the two other people whose stories are important to this narrative.

Unlike Sarah Kemp, 16 year old Martha Sparrow had never been a slave, nor had her parents. She probably had no idea how or when her ancestors came to be free. In fact, she may have had no idea why, given her European appearance, she was considered a woman "of color," except that she was. Her daughter Dodie would insist that Martha, or "Mattie", had not a single drop of African blood[59] and that the tainted heritage that subjected her to all manner of legal disabilities came from the native Indian peoples of Virginia.

Indeed, in 1705 the Virginia colonial assembly had enacted a "Black Code" which declared all Indians living outside reservations as "free persons of color." Children with one Indian parent were classified as "mulattoes", whether the other parent was white or black.[60] Therefore it is conceivable that Martha Sparrow *was in fact* without African ancestors, but it is unlikely that she knew for your. She did know that as a free woman of color, she could not serve as a witness in court, nor sue a white person, or marry a white man.[61]

No description of Mattie's appearance or any tradition of her personality has been preserved, but we do know what her parents, Randol and Anna Sparrow looked like, thanks to the *Register of Free Negros and Mulattos,* maintained from 1809 to 1852 by Norfolk County. Randol Sparrow, who registered on January 21, 1828, was described as a "free born mulatto, thirty years old, 5'9¾" tall, "of light complexion" with a scar on his right ankle, but " no apparent mark or scar on his head, hands, or face[62]." Anna, then twenty-eight, was 5'2¾" tall, "a mulatto, with full black eyes, long hair...[and] a scar on the right cheek, just below the mouth, occasioned by powder, and one on each arm, from the same cause." Anna had been born free in Warwick County, north of Norfolk, across Hampton Roads.[63]

Of Randol Sparrow we know next to nothing and of his wife we know less. Randaol appears twice in the tax lists of Norfolk County, in 1827 and 1829, when he was living in St. Bride's Parish, across the river from Norfolk City. The Minute Book for Norfolk County covering the years 1832 and 1833 records the fact that Randol Sparrow was taken to court by his landlady, Margaret Callahan, early in 1832, for his failure to pay rent[64]. From this we may conclude that Randol Sparrow was not so much shiftless as poor. It was hard for free blacks to find employment and many whites feared such men as potential troublemakers.

After 1832 there seem t be no records in Norfolk City or County of Randol or Anna Sparrow. They are not in the 1840 census (which lists only heads of households, which they may not have been), nor are they in the 1850 census, which was *supposed* to enumerate all free persons. The fact that Randol and Anna disappear so completely from the public record suggests that they might have died prematurely.

We know nothing of the childhood of Martha Sparrow. If she had siblings, there is no record of them. On the death certificate of her mother, Mary Sparrow Kemp Bass, Blanche Kemp Ruffin had given her grandmother's name as Mary Louisa Ferguson. There is overwhelming documentary evidence that she was Martha Sparrow. But could Martha have also been known as "Ferguson"? Might her mother Anna, after the premature death of her husband Randol, have married a man named Ferguson? It is possible, but there is no record thereof. Of Martha we know only that she was living in (or very near) Norfolk in 1840 or 1841, when she conceived her first child, in her mid-teens, by a 19 or 20 year old German immigrant by the name of William Greenwood[65].

During the spring and summer months of the 1830s, thousands of German immigrants arrived in the port of Baltimore. Most of them had embarked at the port of Bremen on the North Sea on ships with names like *Serene, Ulysses, Dorothea Luise, Lucilla, Cornelia, Copernicus, Jupiter, Hyperion*, and *Napier*. During 1834 81 *ships, brigs*, and *barks* from Bremen docked at Baltimore. One of them was the *Napier*, which docked on August 9, 1834 with 180 passengers. Among them were seventeen men, women, and children from the town Babenhausen in the Grand Duchy of Hessen-Darmstadt, near the free city of Frankfurt. There was John Perschbach, a 20 year old farmer. There were the nine members of the Peter Funk family. And there were the seven members of the Grünewald family, headed by Martin Grünewald, a 37 year old man listed as having no occupation, who arrived with his wife, five small children, and six bundles of possessions.[66]

The town of Babenhausen, which today is almost a suburb of Frankfurt, in 1834 was a community of about three thousand persons, surrounded by an old city wall. With its own city council, law court, and militia, it was subject to the Grand Duke of Hessen-Darmstadt. The ancestors of Martin and Margreth Grünewald had lived in Babenhausen for at least three centuries.

The church registers of Babenhausen record ancestors of Martin Grünewald for seven generations. The earliest was a butcher by the name of Oswald Grünewald, born around 1545. We know nothing about him except that the record of his death in the parish register notes that he was blind the last twenty-four years of his life.[67] At his death in September, 1614, he was survived by at least three sons by his deceased wife Elsa: Hans, Henricus, and Nicolaus.[68]

Nicolaus Grünewald was accorded the style *meister* (master, mister), which indicates that he was near the top of the social pyramid of the town. Most men did not have this appellation in his day. Born in 1568 or 1569, *Meister Nicolaus* was a butcher and a member of the town council. At 33 he married Jacobë Hochsträsser, who died at 50 in 1628 after bearing him seven children. At 63 Nicolaus married again to 35 year old Barbara Kilian, who bore him an eighth child the next year, Anna, called Little *Engen*.[69]

The life of Nicolaus Grünewald came to a tragic end. Central Europe was at that time devastated by what is now known as the Thirty Years War, in which the landgraviate of Hessen-Darmstadt (it did not become a Grand Duchy until the early nineteenth century) was, along with most other Protestant German states, Sweden, the Netherlands, and France fighting Spain and the Catholic states of the Holy Roman Empire. The war left Germany and central Europe ravaged—possibly even more so, if such a thing were actually possible—as World War II would three centuries later, with homes, churches, schools, and other public buildings burnt to the ground and the population decimated by outright violence, disease, and malnutrition.

Babenhausen began to feel the effects of the war in the early 1630s. By late 1634 the Spanish army had converged on the area around Frankfurt. Frantic peasants fled for their lives as their homes and fields were sacked, looted, and burnt. They sought protection within the walls of the little town, swelling the population (which numbered about 1200 at that time) 300% to more than 3500. Early in 1635 the *Pest*—almost certainly bubonic plague—introduced, it was believed, by Spanish troops, took hold among the starving refugees, with the result that during a 12 month period, some 900 people succumbed, including Nicolaus Grünewald and his two brothers. His wife Barbara survived the epidemic, but Little Engen died less than two years later, at the age of four. [cite]

Three children by Meister Nicolaus' first marriage survived, including 27 year old Johann Helfrich Grünewald (1608-1667), who, like his father and grandfather, was a butcher.[70] He married Anna May, from the neighboring village of Altdorf. Anna's first husband, Johannes Kern, had died three weeks after their wedding, and immediately she remarried to Meister Helfrich.[71] (Men and women at that time and place did not remain single long after the death of their spouses). Helfrich and Anna had 10 children, of whom at least five died in infancy or early childhood.

Meister Helfrich's eldest son, Paulus Grünewald, born February 22, 1636, just after the plague subsided, pursued the family vocation, but, in addition to butchering, he opened the Black Lion Inn and served as a city councilman until his death at 66.[72] He married Luise Anna Zollman, daughter of a Lutheran pastor from the territory of Odenwald, and had five children.

Meister Paulus' second son, Johann Ludwig, born in 1664, did not become a butcher, but was apprenticed to a surgeon barber. When he set up shop he performed such functions as bleeding, cautery of wounds, cupping, poulticing, and the setting of simple fractures, augmenting his medical fees by shaving and cutting hair. Most of the villagers received no medical treatment except at the hands of the surgeon barber. Doctors of Medicine, usually found only in universities, wrote and lectured on theoretical matters and seldom treated the sick on a regular basis, and when they did it was for a fee larger than the common person could afford.

Meister Ludwig Grünewald married into a very prominent family when he took to wife Maria Eleonora Lottich, a native of Frankfurt-am-Main. The Lottich family, according to Bernhard Keerner, who researched them in the early twentieth century, had their origins in the village of Niederzell, near the town of Schlüchtern, in northern Hessen. The name was originally *Lotz*, which means "Lotus." The earliest recorded ancestor was Hen Lotz, a peasant who rented land from the monks of the cloister at Schlüchtern. Hen's older sons worked the land, as he did, but the youngest son Peter was sent to the cloisters, where he was educated for the priesthood. Father Peter, who Latinized his surname to *Lotichius* (as was the custom among clergy and scholars in those days) in 1530 at age 29 was appointed Archpriest of the parish of Schlüchtern. At 33 he became abbot of the cloisters, where he founded a school for boys. This was the time of the Reformation, which was sweeping through the German lands. Influenced by his friend Philip Melanchthon (associate of reformer Martin Luther), Lotichius left the Church of Rome for the new religion. Unlike Melanchthon and Luther, he remained faithful, to the end of his life in 1567, to his vows of celibacy, although he worked to further the evangelical faith in the land of Hessen.

Apparently through the influence of Peter Lotichius, most males in subsequent generations of the family became doctors, teachers, or clergymen. Maria Eleonora Grünewald's grandfather, Johannes Lotichius (1600-1649), her great-grandfather, Zacharias Lotichius (1558-1604), and two of her second great-grandfathers, Wilhelm Lotichius (1520-1571) and Johannes Angelus (1542-1608), were Lutheran pastors. Wilhelm Lotichius had studied under his Uncle Peter's friend Melanchthon at the University of Wittenberg during the lifetime of Luther, whom he must have met.[73]

The father of Maria Eleonora Lottich Grünewald was Johann Tobias Lotichius (1635-1666). He, for some reason now unknown, departed from family tradition to become an "imperial notary" for Holy Roman Emperor Leopold I. Tobias died of "fever" at Frankfurt at 30[74], leaving two infant children to be reared by his widow, the former Maria Hellweg, daughter of a beer brewer. Besides Maria Eleonora there was a brother, Johann, who became a barber and "town doctor" in the town of Baldenburg.[75] By the time of her married to Ludwig Grünewald, Maria Eleonora's surname had been Germanized to Lottich (but not the original Lotz!), while her brother Johann went by the differently Latinized family name *Lottigius*.

Maria Eleonora, like her father, died in her early thirties, of unrecorded causes, in 1697. Her husband Ludwig Grünewald, the surgeon-barber, at 33, followed her to the grave four months later.[76] It appears that their five young children were taken in by their paternal uncle, Friedrich Philipp Grünewald (1663-1736).

The oldest son, Johann Georg Grünewald (1690-1766) became a teacher at the local "German School", which instructed pupils in the local vernacular rather than in Latin, and for more than half a century he was administrator of the hospital at Babenhausen.[77] For 54 years Georg was married to Anna Klein (1691-1767), daughter of Georg Ludwig Klein, an innkeeper in the neighboring town of Altheim. Something of Anna Klein Grünewald's personality radiates through the microfilmed pages of the parish register of Altheim, where her eldest surviving son,

Johann Martin Grünewald (1720-1781) served as chief pastor. It was with him that she went to live after her husband's death. When she died at 76 after a long, painful illness, Martin Grünewald used as one of her funeral texts the passage from Isaiah 60:20: "Never again shall your sun set nor your moon withdraw her light, but the Lord shall be your everlasting light and the days of your mourning shall be ended." He wrote in the register how his mother, a saintly Christian, had been severely tested in her life, but suffered her woes in patience and her last illness in anticipation of heaven.[78]

Georg and Anna Grünewald had nine children, most of whom appear to have died young. Other than Martin, they had two other sons who lived to adulthood. The second son, Justus Adolph Grünewald, a brewmaster, died before his parents, at the age of 37. The youngest son, Friedrich Philipp, named for his granduncle, became a merchant and innkeeper and served as a lieutenant in the town militia.[79] He married three times, each time to a pastor's daughter. His first two wives died in childbirth. The third wife, Maria Catharina Lemcke (1735-1808), who worked as a nurse in the orphanage in the nearby city of Hanau, came from a long line of ministers, dating back to Matthias Lemcke, a native of Rehna in Mecklenburg in northern Germany, who served the town of Hochburg before accepting a call in 1678 to the town of Wollbach in Baden (south of Hessen-Darmstadt). Three days after his arrival in Wollbach, before he could preach his first sermon, Herr Lemcke fell down the parsonage steps, and died of his injuries the next day.[80] Misfortune seemed to plague his descendants. His son, Carl Lemcke, after serving as tutor to the children of a local prince, became pastor at Blansingen in Baden, but at 46, seems to have been demoted to "deacon" at Durlach. Three years later he died, leaving 13 children. His son, Carl Lemcke, Jr., the father of Maria Catharina Grünewald, was serving as pastor in Kandern, Baden, when he died at 44 after swallowing arsenic, which he mistook for medicine![81] Maria Catharina was only two at the time.

Before his death at 45 in 1772, Friedrich Philipp Grünewald had 10 children by his three wives. One of his sons by Maria Catharina, Johann Georg Ernst (1765-c. 1847) went to live in London, England, where he became a goldsmith, silversmith, and master jeweler with a shop on 12 Hanway Street.[82] He married an Englishwoman named Mary Frost and had a son, George, Jr., who was also a jeweller.[83]

Friedrich Philipp's son Johann Martin Carl Grünewald (1763-

1825) was the godson of two pastors, his paternal granduncle Johann Martin Grünewald and his maternal uncle Carl Lemcke III. Trained as a silkweaver, Martin Carl manufactured silk stockings, perhaps at his home, until he was in his 40s. This was around the time that upper class men found it fashionable to give up the old-fashioned knee-britches in favor of the trousers that had long been worn by working class men. Martin Carl then became a soap-maker, at trade at which he worked for the rest of his life.

Martin Carl married at 32. His bride was 38 year old Anna Catharina Dickhaut, daughter of a house-painter who had died a few years earlier of lead poisoning. Neither had been married before. They had two sons, Ernst Friedrich and Johann Martin.[84]

In the first decade of the nineteenth century the Napoleonic Wars engulfed Europe. The landgraviate of Hessen-Darmstadt joined Napoleon's Confederation of the Rhine, with the result that Napoleon elevated the territory to the rank of a Grand Duchy—just a step below a kingdom— which it was to maintain even after the fall of the French dictator. Landgrave Ludwig X now became Grand Duke Ludwig I. In 1813 Ludwig joined the Allies against Napoleon.

Martin Grünewald was probably too young to have seen action in the Napoleonic Wars, as he was just 16 at the time of Waterloo, but his older brother might have been old enough to have seen service. It was in 1816, however, a year after the fall of Napoleon, three years after the death of his mother and a year after his father's remarriage to the widow Catharina Kopp Sauerwein that Ernst Friedrich, at the age of twenty, went to London to learn the jewelry business from his Uncle George. Then, in 1825 he left England "for his health" to settle in Edenton, in northeastern North Carolina, where he set up shop as a silversmith.[85]

Martin Grünewald went into business with his father. Like nearly all men of his town, he was a member of the local militia, now called the "war reserve." In 1821, at the age of 22, he fathered his first child, Wilhelm, born out of wedlock to 24 year old Margreth Koch. Three years later, Margreth bore Martin another child, Katharina, who lived only a few days. The next year, when Margreth was heavy with her third child, she and Martin finally married.[86]

Why did Martin wait so long to marry Margreth? It may have been that Martin's father, who came from a line of clergymen, teachers, and tradesmen who were masters in their guilds, may have considered Margreth (despite the fact that she, like nearly everyone else in

Babenhausen, was distantly related) was socially inferior. Her father, Johann Heinrich Koch, who died in 1811 at 58 of a "wasting fever", was a farm laborer and her mother, born Anna Catharina Lang (1760-1826) came from a long line of salt peter miners.

Within weeks of his marriage, Martin's stepmother died. That June his father, Martin Carl, succumbed at 62 to "an inflammation of the chest" and Martin had sole charge of the soap business.

More children followed: Carl Friedrich, born in April, 1825, three months after his parents' wedding, followed, in two year intervals by Margaretha Elisabetha, Friedrich Adam (who died of diarrhea at two months), Johann Martin, Jr., and Magdalena.

When Magdalena was less than two years old her parents Martin and Margreth left Babenhausen for America. It is unclear why they decided to strike out for the new land. By that period many Germans were striking out for America. Perhaps Ernst Friedrich—now married to an Irish immigrant and known as Frederick Greenwood—encouraged his brother to join him in America. Perhaps he convinced Martin that the United States was a land of opportunity.

Martin certainly would have been foolish to remove to the American South, as his brother allegedly had, for "reasons of health." As mentioned above, the average age of *adults* who died in the Norfolk area around that time was only 42. The average age of death for those adults who died in Babenhausen in 1800 was 67. (In the 1600s that average was only 34. By the mid 1750s it had risen to 54, and by the time Martin left, it was almost up to modern standards).[87]

Whatever his reasons, after he notified the appropriate authorities in the city of Darmstadt (the capital of the duchy) that he intended to emigrate, Martin sold most of his possessions, packed his family's remaining possessions in six trunks, most likely put his wife and children in a farm wagon, and, in October, 1833 headed north for the port of Bremen on the North Sea. Sailing ships normally did not contend with the stormy Atlantic during the winter, so the Grünewalds were forced to stay in Bremen or perhaps some outlying town until spring. There is a family tradition that once they boarded a ship, their voyage to America took six months. That seems unlikely. *Six weeks* is a more likely time for a sailing ship, which means that the *Napier*, which normally made two trips per year to America and on which the family arrived in Baltimore in August, may have left Bremen in June. It is possible that Martin and Margreth, because of the huge number of people attempting to get to America, had to wait for months to book passage. No doubt Martin and perhaps Margreth too had to find some temporary work.

The Grünewalds lived in Maryland for six years. Their youngest child, Frederick, was born at Reisterstown, some 30 miles west of Baltimore, in 1837, but when Martin *Greenewald* declared his intention to become an American citizen on July 18, 1840, he was living in the city of Baltimore.[88] Exactly what Martin did for a living between 1834 and 1840 is not clear, since he does not appear in any of Baltimore's city directories for that time period. Perhaps he lived with and worked for a relative or friend.

Late in 1840 the Grünewalds moved again, to Norfolk, Virginia. Why they chose that city is not known. The second son, Carl Friedrich, was sent to his uncle Frederick across the state line in Edenton, to learn the jewelry trade. It seems as if Martin determined that his eldest and third born sons would join him in the soap business.

On November 13, 1841, one Thomas Houghton, a soap and candle manufacturer of Norfolk, agreed to rent his factory on Colbert's Lane and Union Street to Frederick and Martin Greenwood for the annual sum of $100 per year, to be paid in quarterly installments[89]. Martin was evidently too poor to go into business without the help of his brother, but, from that time on, his fortunes seem to have improved. Several years later, still in partnership with his brother, Martin opened a large soap and candle factory at 2 McPhail's Lane, near the Norfolk waterfront. On October 11, 1847, Martin purchased a house at 17 Reid's Lane, on the corner of Union Street, not far from the slave prison[90]. Shortly afterwards he bought another at 36 Church Street, but continued to live in the first.[91] According to the U.S. Census of 1850, Martin Greenwood owned real estate valued at $2000.

His two surviving portraits (a painting and photograph) show Martin as a slight man with a thin face and reddish beard. Her one surviving photograph reveals Margreth as a spent, exhausted-looking woman with a round, wide bony face, huge cheekbones, and tiny, deepset, nearly lifeless eyes. A bonnet covers dark hair (or a wig) parted severely in the middle.

Although two of their sons became Methodists, another an Episcopalian, and one of their daughters a Presbyterian, the elder Greenwoods never seemed to have joined a church. Nothing is known of their churchgoing habits in Babenhausen, where everyone was officially a member of the Evangelical Lutheran Church. There were no Lutheran churches in Norfolk at the time.

On November 29, 1851, Martin Greenwood and his three oldest sons became United States citizens, renouncing all allegiance to the Grand Duke of Hessen-Darmstadt.[92] Since moving to Norfolk —perhaps even earlier—the family had Anglicized their names. They were now Greenwood instead of Grünewald. Wilhelm was now William. Carl Friedrich became Charles Frederick (or simply C.F.). Margaretha Elisabetha was now Margaret Elizabeth. Martin, Jr. did not change his given name except to drop the Johann. Curiously, Magdalena became Ellen.

At that time and place, nearly everyone native to another part of the world took an American name. The naturalization records for Norfolk tell the tale. Some immigrants retained their surname, but nearly all anglicized their given name, as in the case of Peter Joseph Rodriguez (from Minorca), Joseph Surado (from Spain), Francis Marina (from Naples), Henry Proescher (from "Germany"), and Francis Branda (from France). Many new Americans anglicized their entire names, like William Johnson, who had been born Ar Woo (or Ah Woo) in China, John Artow (also from China), John Fay and John Fry (from Rome,) John Kennedy (from Gothenburg, Sweden,) John Pratt (from Spain), William Smith (from Portugal), Matthew Barber (from Germany), Anthony King (from Prussia), John Harrison (from Portugal), and John Mitchell (from Switzerland).[93]

The Greenwoods seem to have assimilated quickly in America. Martin and Margaret seem to have fit comfortably into Norfolk's middle class. There is no indication as to how well they spoke English. A merchant who knew Charles F. Greenwood, who came to America at eight, recalled (in 1966) that the immigrant spoke with "an ordinary southern accent" and the granddaughter of Ellen Greenwood Curdts (who came to the States as an infant) remembered that she had no accent and spoke no German. This *might* suggest that English was spoken in their home.

As the 1840s gave way to the 50s the older Greenwood children, growing into adulthood, seem to have become prosperous, substantial people. Charles, or C.F., who came to Norfolk from Edenton in 1847, set up a jewelry and watchmaking business on 2 Widewater Street. He named his shop "The Casket". On October 18, 1849 he advertised: "C.F. Greenwood would most respectfully inform his customers...that he has just returned from the northern cities with a most splendid assortment of gold and silver watches, jewelry, silverware, and fancy articles, which he offers for as cheap as the cheapest and as good as the best, and would respectfully invite all those in want of any article in his line to give him a call, as they would find it to their interest, before purchasing elsewhere. N.B.—watches, clocks, jewelry, and silverware repaired cheap and warranted. Engraving done at short notice.[94]

Within a year of his arrival in Norfolk, C.F. Greenwood married 16 year old Mary Elizabeth Griffin, daughter of the mayor of Portsmouth. During the next 22 years, she would bear him six daughters and a son. They began attending the Cumberland Street Methodist Church near their home in central Norfolk.

Young Margaret was married on October 19, 1843, at the age of 16, to 25 year old Joaquin Martinez Bayto, a native of Seville who ran a tobacco shop. According to a great-grandson, Bayto fled his native country when his parents tried to force him into a seminary to study for the priesthood.[95] He made his way to Cuba, and from there to Norfolk. Within a few years the Baytos had three daughters: Josephine, Margaret Amelia, and Mary Virginia.

Martin, Jr., who lived at home and worked with his father in the soap factory, seems to have been the favorite son from the few scraps of information that have survived about him. At 17 in 1848 he was attending Sunday School at the Cumberland Street Methodist Church. He applied for membership and was placed on "probation", so that the deacons could scrutinize his character.

William, the oldest son also lived at home and worked at the soap factory. Scarcely any information has survived about his personality or character. The records of Norfolk's Circuit Court record that William Greenwood stood as "security" at the weddings of William Church and Mary Elizabeth Lines on December 16, 1846, of Conrad Lingner and Elizabeth Preeschern on March 13, 1849, and Allan Morrison and Eliza Crozier on October 29, 1849. This seems to indicate that he was respected and trusted citizen and that he had a circle of acquaintances that was not limited to other German immigrants.

What is certain is that shortly after his arrival in Norfolk, William Greenwood met the mulatto girl Mattie Sparrow, who became his common-law wife. It seems to have been customary in the South for lustful white boys of good class, having too much respect for white maidenhood to sully girls of their own social class, to use black and poor white girls as prostitutes. This was evidently *not* the case with William

Greenwood. He never married and neither did Martha. Their children were born over a period of 14 years. Virginia law, until the 1960s, forbade miscegenation, and so the union of William and Martha could never be recognized and in the eyes of the law their children were black bastards.

The oldest child, Josephine, was born late in 1841 or early 1842. William, called "Billy", was born Christmas Day, 1844. Elenora followed in December, 1849, Martha Missouri on August 26, 1852, and Mary Louisa on November 25, 1854. All of them, at least as adults, went by their mother's surname. This does not necessarily indicate that their father did not recognize them, since he was dead before any of them reached their majority.

Chapter Seven

The family of Martin Greenwood seems to have been partaking of the good life of their adopted country. By the late 1840s Frederick seems to have withdrawn from the business and Martin with in partnership with oldest son William in the firm of Martin Greenwood & Son, which was now the largest soap and candle factory in the area. Martin joined the Lafayette Lodge of Odd Fellows and became an active member.[96] In 1850 he bought his first horse and his first slave.[97]

"The Casket", the jewelry business of C.F. Greenwood, where the youngest son Fred was now an apprentice, was also thriving. C.F., like his father, was now the proud owner of one slave.[98] While his father had become an Odd Fellow, he became a Mason In 1850 he and Martin, Jr. were finally admitted to membership in the Cumberland Street Methodist Church.[99].

The oldest daughter, Margaret, the wife of a prosperous "tobacconist", gave birth in 1851 to a son Joaquin Jr. some time in 1851. The little boy took the place of the oldest daughter Josephine, who had died in early childhood, to bring the number of her family once again to three.

On May 15 of that year the younger daughter Ellen became the only member of her family to marry a fellow-German when at 17 she became the bride of 25 year old George Louis Curdts. Born Georg Ludwig Theodor Curdts, the son of a school teacher and church cantor in the village of Fümmelse in the provinces of Brunswick (Braunschweig-Wolfenbüttel), he arrived in New York in 1846, then went to Philadelphia before moving to Norfolk in 1849 to open a jewelry business.[100]

The Personal Property Tax Records for the City of Norfolk reveal that in 1851 Martin Greenwood, the owner of one slave, one horse, and one metallic clock, paid an annual tax of 62 cents. C.F., who owned a slave, a clock, and a piano, paid a tax of $1.08. The next year Martin acquired a second horse and C.F. a second slave. William, who owned $84 worth of metal clocks, was assessed a tax of 39 cents. Martin, Jr. paid a tax of 36 cents. By 1853 Martin, Sr. had acquired his second slave and now paid $2.41 in taxes. By the end of the decade he owned three slaves, two horses, three carriages, and one metallic clock, and paid over $4 in personal property taxes. C.F. also owned three slaves, as well as two watches, one clock, and one piano, and paid $2.24 in annual taxes.

The years brought not only prosperity to the Greenwood family, but sorrow as well. Eighteen fifty-two was a particularly difficult year for Martin and Margaret. On January 20, daughter Margaret Bayto died at 24, leaving six month old Joaquin, three year old Virginia, and four year old Mellie. In an attempt to quiet the distressed baby, the bereaved husband paced the floor for hours on end, night after night, with the child in his arms[101] until in May, the child's lifeless form mingled with the same sod of Elmwood Cemetery that had earlier received all that was mortal of his mother and sister.

That summer Martin Greenwood was the victim of theft. The *Southern Argus* reported on July 6, 1852 in an article headlined "In Soap": "John Copes, who keeps a shop in Barry's Row, near Water Street, was brought up charged with having in his possession a quantity of soap, supposed to have been stolen from the factory of Messrs. Greenwood & Son. Mr. Greenwood believed the soap found in Cope's house to be his, and Cope, failing to give a satisfactory account of how he came by it, was required to give bond in the sum of $300 for his appearance before the Grand Jury, which meets on the fourth Monday of this month." The *Argus* failed to report the outcome of the case.

Perhaps Martin lost interest in prosecuting the case because of a worse calamity which befell him soon afterwards. During the summer an epidemic of yellow fever broke out in Norfolk. This mosquito-borne infection periodically ravaged coastal areas. In 1795 500 people had died of that disease in Norfolk.[102] Seven years later, the pestilence broke out again, to claim more than 100 victims. In 1821 160 Norfolkians lost their lives from the same distemper.[103] The epidemic of 1852 proved relatively minor, but not for the Greenwood family, for on September 18, Martin, Jr., evidently his parents' favorite son and, apparently, a man of sterling character, succumbed to the fever at the age of 21. One of the local newspapers printed his parents' tribute in verse:

"Thou art gone to the grave
But we do not deplore thee,
Whose God was thy ransom,
Thy guardian and guide.
He gave thee and He took thee
And He will restore thee.
Thy death has no sting
For the Saviour has died."[104]

They erected on his grave at Cedar Grove Cemetery, at the city line, across the road from Elmwood a stone enumerating his virtues which stood, virtually illegible, until vandals stole it in the 1980s.

Yellow Fever revisited Norfolk with a vengeance three summers later when, on June 7, the steamer *Ben Franklin*, bound for New York City from the West Indies, was allowed to dock for repairs at the shipyard at Gosport, across the Elizabeth River from Norfolk, even though there were reports that some of the crew were ill. Soon a shipyard worker was stricken with "Yellow Jack" and quickly died. The *Ben Franklin* was evidently infested with infected mosquitoes. That summer of 1855 the epidemic exploded, first through Portsmouth, then through Norfolk, and then the adjacent countryside.[105]

Physicians at the time believed that the origin of the disease was filth: "heat acting on moist animal and vegetable matter [to produce] putrid exhalations.[106] It was only a generation later that a mosquito would be definitively identified as the source of the infection, which was spread, not through human contact, but through the bite of the insect.

An attack of Yellow Fever began with an "unpleasant feeling" in the forehead, which quickly grew into a severe headache. The victim's eyes grew red and he felt "dull, heavy, sleepy." Chills and a loss of appetite ensued, accompanied by weakness and severe pains in the arms, legs, back, and bowels, and a "feeling of oppression" in the chest. More ominous symptoms presented themselves: sores on the face, arms, and hands, bleeding from the nose, mouth, gums, and urinary tract, and the most characteristic symptom of the malady, black vomit and yellow jaundice.[107] Usually 10 to 15 out of every hundred victims died, as a result of internal bleeding or kidney failure, although there were occasionally epidemics in which mortality reached more than 90%![108]

The first people in Norfolk to fall victim to the contagion were residents of Barry's Row, a working class neighborhood near the Greenwoods' factory, which was the home of the soap thief—who may not have survived to stand trial. By mid-August, it was estimated that half of Norfolk's population of 15,000 had fled and the other half were ill. Everything was closed down: shipyards, docks, newspapers, banks, stores, factories, warehouses. An observer noted that through the nearly empty streets there was nonetheless " a perpetual din of carriages, continually passing, from early dawn till a late hour of the night—the physicians' carriages, the hacks conveying nurses and members of the Howard Association [a charitable organization coordinating the relief efforts] and the hearses, and the ever-moving 'sick wagon'—rattling and rumbling to and fro in every direction—there was no sign of wholesome animation.[109]

Curiously, the epidemic seemed to spare the black community. The death register for Norfolk City for the year 1855 (which, in a normal year, recorded between 100 and 120 deaths) listed the names of 444 victims of Yellow Fever, all but 63 of whom were white. Virginia Hayes Shepherd, then a little slave girl, told an interviewer many years later, probably with considerable exaggeration: "During those days the white folks treated the nigger so mean that all the slaves prayed to God to punish their cruel masters. So when the yellow fever came, it killed all the white folks. You almost never heard of a Negro dying from the disease. My mother said it killed most of her white folks. On a lot of plantations every single white person died but not one single slave. The colored people was just having a big time. Everywhere you went the slaves were sitting on the front porches, just a-rocking—white folks all dead. The Negroes said God had sent a sign to the white folks, warning them not to be cruel to the Negroes." Mrs. Shepherd spoke of a "free black undertaker" named Bob Butts, who often deliberately buried sick whites alive: "Once Bob Butts was about to bury some old slave owner and when he got the body to the grave he heard a noise. 'T was the old man in the coffin kicking, had come to. Old Bob said, 'I ain't going to bother about taking him home again.' He just dug a hole and buried him. It's a good way to get even with some of them white folks anyway."[110]

Bodies were piled up "like cord wood," as high as a man could reach, in the Potter's Field, where most victims were quickly interred. There were not enough coffins available, so some corpses had to be enshrouded in the blankets in which their former inhabitants had died.[111]

On August 20, William Greenwood died of Yellow Fever at 34. There is no record as to whether other members of his family became ill and recovered or whether he was the only one stricken. We do not know whether the rest of the family fled the city, as most others did who had the means. Did William remain behind for the sake of Martha and the children, for whom his disapproving family provided no means of escape? Did he agree to attend to business matters while the others sought safety? All that is certain is that William's remains escaped the pits at Potter's Field and were interred beside those of his brother Martin, Jr. In contrast to the long and adulatory epitaph that was carved onto the stone of the younger brother, the granite slab—now vandalized and overthrown—marking the final resting place of William Greenwood bore only his name and dates and the tepid legend, "Rest in Peace."

The Greenwood family seems to have viewed William's common-law marriage to Martha Sparrow with disapproval. During the 1970s I telephoned a 90 year old granddaughter of Margaret Greenwood Bayto. Although she was born long after William's death, her mother (who lived into her 90s) was old enough to remember him. The venerable lady began cheerfully to relate family anecdotes handed down through her mother. She mentioned Charles, Martin (Jr.), and Fred Greenwood, but said nothing about William. When I foolishly asked about him and identified myself as his descendant, she grew silent, and when she spoke again her voice was cold. "I don't have anything more to say," she said. When I tried to contact her a few years later, she refused to speak to me.

I once asked my aunt, Elinor Waller, if her grandmother Dodie had ever spoke of living with the Greenwoods. Elinor replied that Dodie had indeed lived with the Greenwoods "for a while." I asked if she had been well-treated and Elinor, who did not like to talk about unpleasant things, answered simply, "No," and changed the subject.

It *seems* likely that William Greenwood acknowledged his outcaste children. It also seems clear that some or all members of his family considered him—or at least his situation—a disgrace and wanted no dealings with his mistress and bastard children. *Perhaps* in response to a deathbed request, Martin and Margaret took in their mulatto grandchildren, but not for long.

Martha Sparrow was assessed a personal property tax of 22 cents in 1857. This is important because women normally did not pay personal property tax unless they were heads of household *and* had property of some value. Martha's taxable property was a clock. In absence of other information, one easily assumes that this was a legacy from William. Also revealing is the fact that Martha's name does not appear in any subsequent tax lists, although she lived another decade. Starting in 1860 her son William Sparrow (then only 16) is listed as a household head. No clock, in that or any subsequent year, is listed as William's taxable property. It would certain *appear* that the Greenwood family abandoned Martha Sparrow and her children. Perhaps the clock was lost in fire or flood, perhaps Martha was forced to sell it make ends meet.

No document or oral tradition has come to light to reveal the attitude of the William's children to the Greenwood family. All of them went by their mother's surname. There is no evidence that any of William's surviving siblings took any interest in providing for the children's education or financial well-being. The 1860 Census of Norfolk shows that Martha and her eldest daughter Josephine were making their living as cooks and William was apprenticed to a shoemaker.

On the other hand, in the case of little Franklin Kemp, at least one person in his "white family" seems to have showed love and concern—at least, that is the tradition that Lydia handed down to her great-granddaughters. According to "Grandma Lydie" the mistress—evidently Mildred McGehee Smith—loved Lydia and treated her "just like a member of the family".

Elinor Waller believed that she and Frank were freed shortly after the child's birth, but there is no evidence of this. According to the U.S. Slave Census of 1860, in which enumerators asked masters for the number of slaves they had manumitted during the previous decade, no slaves from Caswell County had been freed during the 1850s. In many areas of the South there were laws in force that made it difficult for masters to manumit slaves. Certainly neither William Forbes Smith nor his mother could free Lydia and Franklin for the simple reason that the the two were not their property. They belonged to the master George. It is quite possible, however, that Lydia and Franklin received especially benign treatment, so much so as to generate the tradition that Frank Kemp had grown up a "spoiled child."

The kind mistress seems to have been in failing health for some time. The inventory of the estate of George Alexander Smith (who died suddenly) includes a wheelchair, or "invalid's chair", as such devices were bluntly called in those days. She breathed her last on May 22, 1858, at the age of 44.

It was just before the first Christmas as his wife's death that George Alexander Smith wrote his will. It is a strange document that suggestive of a vain, tyrannical, vindictive, and self-righteous man. "I, George A. Smith of the town of Milton, North Carolina, being of sound mind and body, do make and ordain this my last will and testament...on account of the course my son William Forbes Smith has pursued," he declares. What is going on? Was Master George enraged about William's continuing relationship with Lydia? It is easy to generalize that in the antebellum South it was "acceptable" for young masters to "sow their wild oats," treating slave girls as prostitutes, but the fact is that there were many people who frowned on this practice. It is possible that George Smith might have been among such people. He was closely associated with a church which emphasized moral purity and his library contained many books or a moral or religious nature.

Of course, there are other possibilities for the break between father and son. Given the paucity of information available on either man, the possibilities are infinite. There could have been a falling-out over a business deal. George may have objected not to his dalliance with a slave girl, but with his choice of a bride. The young Smith, probably in 1859, married a 20 year old neighbor, Mary Ellen Huntington, daughter of one of the elders of the Milton Presbyterian Church. The older Smith may have objected for some reason to his daughter-in-law.

Whatever the reason, George Smith was furious with his second son and raged: "In consequence of the course my wayward son William F. Smith has pursued, and says he intends to pursue, setting my wishes at defiance, and heeding none of my advice: acting as he does in open defiance to my known wishes...I am forced to take in the premises he brings upon himself." And so, George Smith orders that all his property that should remain after the payment of his debts is to be be divided among his *four* children: Thomas, Ellen, George, Jr., and Murray. "My beloved daughter Ellen" was to have $1500 more than brother Thomas; George, Jr. was to have $2000 more than Thomas; and Murray was to be given $2200 more than Thomas. All this was because of Thomas' "attitude toward me." Again, the nature of the ill-will between Master George and his eldest son has been lost to history. As for the second son, George declares, "My son William Forbes Smith...is not to inherit on shilling of my property in any way or shape, directly or indirectly and the reason he very well knows and much as I regard the necessity of my thus cutting him off he himself is only to blame and I feel that I am acting right and with a clear conscience."

Master George fills several pages with a bitter diatribe against Williams. He threatens, "I further direct that if any of my children does not agree to and with this my last will and testament and wish to give [William] any part or share in any way", the share of that child in his estate would be conveyed to his (or her) first cousins, the children of Master George's sisters. If the cousins refused, then that share of the estate would be awarded to the Orphan Asylum in Fredericksburg, Virginia, "an institution that my lamented Millie took some interest in during her life."

George gives his "faithful servant" Delila to Thomas, willing the slave $12 "for her to buy her necessaries extra, as I know Thomas will take care of her." "The servant girl Ann", who had been "a faithful servant to my now lamented wife," was left to daughter Ellen.

The will concludes with a final salvo against William: "I hereby appoint my much-esteemed brother-in-law M[ontford] M. McGehee and my son Thomas McGehee Smith my executors to this last will and testament and I wish it to the letter and spirit as regard my wayward son William F. Smith, as I am resolved and do desire he have no interest in my estate, directly or indirectly, painful as it is to me thus to act, as I will know it will to my executors and children. He, my son William, compels me to act, as after my imploring him to act differently, he has trampled on my feelings, spurned my advice, and heeded none of my council [sic], defied my wishes, and, of course, he is not acting as a son should do. I can't act as a father to him, he rejecting all my offers and acting in defiance of my known wishes, all of which have been prompted by that affection I had for him. He has shown by his acts that he has no regard and affection for me and has thus cut himself off from me, not having that affection and regard for a parent which a son should have."[112]

By the spring of 1860 William F. Smith, with his wife, was living in a separate household. There is no evidence that he and his father were ever reconciled. Indeed, there was little time for such developments because on April 7, 1860, George Alexander Smith suffered a heart attack and dropped dead at the age of 52.[113] He was buried in the Milton Cemetery. There is a marker for his wife and other family members, but none for him. Perhaps that is indicative as to the way he was regarded by his children. The records of Caswell County's Superior Court reveal that he died heavily in debt and his possessions were inventoried and put up for sale. In January, 1861 his fifty slaves were divided into four groups, for which the four heirs drew lots. Sarah went to thirteen year old George, Jr.; John went to seventeen year old Ellen; and Samuel went to eleven year old Murray.[114]

What had become of Lydia and Franklin? According to the Slave Census of 1860, none of the servants in the "Estate of G.A. Smith" correspond in age to mother and son. William now owned five slaves (who may have come into his possession through his bride's dowry), but none of them correspond in age to his mistress or his child. Mildred Smith's brother, Montford McGehee, who seems to have lived next door to the Smiths, had several slaves, including a mulatto woman of 23 and a mulatto boy of six. These ages correspond exactly with those of Lydia and Franklin Kemp. Perhaps Master George had sold his slave grandson and his mother to his brother-in-law to in hopes that there they would not be as accessible to his son. Given the bitter hatred toward his son suggested in his will, it is not unreasonable to assume that George Smith might have sold Lydia and Franklin simply to spite his son. Had Lydia been sold far away from her family, she would hardly have told her great-granddaughters that she was never ill-treated. As the property of the brother of her late beloved mistress, living in close proximity to her mother and brothers, Lydia and her son could have continued to live in comfort and security.

Chapter Eight

In November, 1860 Abraham Lincoln of Illinois was elected President of the United States on the Republican ticket. So polarized had the nation become over the issues of slavery and states' rights that the party of the new president had scarcely any support in the South. Convinced that the northern states now had enough power to accomplish the election of a man who, because of his outspoken opposition to the spread of slavery to the territories, was almost universally opposed in the South, many political leaders in the slave states were eager to withdraw from the Union and set up an independent confederacy. Sentiment for secession was especially strong in the Deep South, where seven states seceded from the Union before the new President was inaugurated in March, but feelings in Virginia and North Carolina and other "border states" were less defined. Both in Norfolk and in Caswell County there remained extensive pro-Union sentiment until April, when the federal government responded to the seizure by the Confederates of Fort Sumpter near Charleston, South Carolina. When Lincoln called for volunteers to put down the rebellion, many Virginians and North Carolinians considered themselves the victims of an unconstitutional invasion of their sovereign territory and cast their lot with the Confederate States of America.

In Caswell County, which previously had considerable unionist sentiment, the *Milton Chronicle* editorialized that all hope for "reconstruction" (as the editor called it) of the Union was lost. "It is time to stop watching and waiting and *act*," the paper urged. "Henceforth then," the editorial continued, "we cease to preach from the 'watch and wait' text, believing that it only inspires the Republicans with impudence to insult and disgrace us. They have forced upon us this position, for our love of the old union is deep rooted and hard to unfix, and it is not without a heavy heart that we throw a sod upon our country's grave and raise a cry for secession."[115] This editorial expressed sentiment widespread in the state, for on May 20 North Carolina repealed the ordinance of 1789 by which it had joined the United States of America. She was now part of the Confederate States of America. A "Jeff Davis Club" was formed in Caswell County. Six military companies were recruited from the region. One of them was Company I of the Fifty-Fifth Regiment, made up almost entirely of Caswell men. It was organized at Camp Mangum on the North Carolina Railroad, four miles north of

Raleigh, in the early spring of 1862.[116]

There was no fighting in Caswell County, but there was movement of troops through the region. Comments from former slaves interviewed many years later reveal that many Union troops conducted themselves in such a way as to incur the fear and hatred even of slaves.

Lizzie Williams confessed, "We niggers never knew what it was about. We just go on and work. Never see nothing, never hear nothing, never say nothing, but the war was all around. Every day we hear that the Yankee soldiers [were] coming. The plantations was getting robbed. Everybody kept a-hiding things."[117] Analiza Foster, who lived in Person County during the war, recalled, "The Yankees come through our country and they makes the slaves draw water for the horses all night. Course they stole everything they got their hands on, but that was not what Old Abraham Lincoln told them to do."[118] Willis Cozart, who lived in a nearby county, stated that the Yankee invaders "stole everything they could find."[119] Ben Johnson, in a similar vein, recounted that the Yankees "took what they wanted [then] killed the stock, stole the horses, poured out the molasses, and cut up a lot of meanness."[120] Abner Johnson recalled, "When the war come the Yankees come to the house and asked my mammy where the folks done hid the silver and gold and they say they gwine to kill Mammy if she didn't tell them. But my mammy say she didn't know where they put it and they would just have to kill her...The soldiers stole seven or eight of the horses and found the meat and stole that, but they didn't burn none of the buildings nor hurt any of us slaves."[121]

A Durham newspaper article in the 1950s dealt with efforts to preserve the McGehee mill. It quoted a 1919 interview with one Sam McGehee, a former slave of Thomas McGehee at Woodburn. McGehee recounted that during the war women came day and night with ox-carts full of grain. The mill was so busy that Thomas McGehee sought and obtained permission from local authorities to grind on Sundays. The former slave also recalled that Yankee soldiers, who spared the mill, confiscated mules from the McGehee estate and seized some of his master's "prize horses", exchanging them for worn-out nags. At Danville, however, one of the McGehee horses broke away and led the others home.[122]

We do not know how the war directly affected Sarah Kemp and her family. We do not know whether they shared with many of friends and neighbors, black and white, the negative opinion of the Union Army.

With his older brother Thomas on active duty, the disinherited William Forbes Smith, who had been given a loan of $5000 by his grandfather Thomas McGehee and who bought back many of his family's possessions when they were sold at auction, set himself up as a tobacco dealer and became the head of the Smith family. Although he was then in his mid 20s he did not enlist in the Army.

Like the people of Caswell County, the residents of Norfolk tended towards union sentiment until the firing on Fort Sumter. When Lincoln called for troops, secessionists sentiment became very strong, as it was in other parts of the Old Dominion, which seceded from the Union several weeks before North Carolina.

Except for the inevitable shortages of food and materials that slowly developed as a result of the Union naval blockade, life seems to have gone on fairly normally for the first year of the war. Schools remained open. Newspapers continued to publish. Slaves continued to be bought and sold. The courts continued to register free Negroes. However, some slaves were running away to Fort Monroe, near Hampton, which was under Union control. At first the authorities returned the fugitives to their masters, but in May, 1861 the Government in Washington declared that escaped slaves were to be regarded as "contraband of war", that is, confiscated goods. The "Contraband", as many whites came to refer to former slaves, were frequently put to hard labor by the Union Army, which doled out rations but paid no wages.

Martin Greenwood, bereft now of the two sons who had been his associates, continued—apparently alone—to operate his soap and candle factory. He told census-takers in 1860 that he owned real estate worth $3000 and had a personal estate valued at $1500. He continued to live at 17 Reed's Lane, but all the other houses on that short street were inhabited by blacks. C.F. Greenwood, who made his youngest and only surviving brother his junior partner, continued to make a handsome living as a jeweler. According to the 1860 census, he owned $7200 worth of real estate and had a personal estate (probably including his merchandise) valued at $25,000. On March 4, 1862 he became the father of his sixth daughter Kate, whose middle name, Lee, he bestowed in honor of the popular commander of the Army of Northern Virginia. (Kate Greenwood's middle name led her descendants to the erroneous belief that they were related to the illustrious general.) Days later C.F. took his older girls up to Hampton Roads to watch the ironclad *Virginia* (which was called the *Merrimack* before its capture by the Confederacy) steam out to encounter its Northern equivalent, the *Monitor*.

Then, on May 9, 1862, an army of 5000 men under the command of Major General John E. Wool crossed Hampton Roads, landed on a strip of land called Willoughby Spit, and began marching slowly towards Norfolk. On May 10, the city was in Union hands. While Norfolk's white defenders scrambled to destroy the navy yard (and with it the *Virginia*)so that military supplies would not fall into enemy hands, Norfolk's colored residents, sensing the imminent fall of slavery, poured into the streets, wild with jubilation. All day and all night terrified white residents could hear shouts of "Oh, Lord, too good to be true! Bless the Lord! No more handcuffin' the children now! God bless Abraham Lincoln!"[123] Many slaves immediately walked away from their masters and mistresses and the 9 p.m. curfew for all blacks was ignored. General Wool proclaimed a day of public thanksgiving and prayer for the Negroes of Norfolk. After religious services, over 5000 blacks (and this would have been nearly a third of the entire population of the city of Norfolk) paraded through the streets, singing and waves the Stars and Stripes. After Wool addressed the rally, the celebrants lit bonfires, and all night long could be heard the firing of guns, the ringing of bells, and the sounding of tin horns.[124]

Later that year Lincoln issued the Emancipation Proclamation, which declared slaves free in those areas of the South still resisting Union control. Technically, this did not apply to Norfolk, which had surrendered months before, but, in reality, although some stubborn slaveholders refused to release their people until well after the war, slavery, for most of its victims, ended with the entry of the Union Army. In the minds of most of Norfolk's Negroes the Emancipation Proclamation nailed shut the coffin of slavery in the city. On January 3, 1863 there was a celebration of the order, which had gone into effect two days earlier. A parade of several thousand blacks, carrying Union flags and cheering the downfall of slavery, processed jubilantly through all the major streets of town, accompanied to the Parade Grounds by 500 black troops. There General Egbert Viele, who was then military governor, addressed the crowd, which later roared with delight as Confederate President Jeff Davis was burnt in effigy.[125]

That year General Benjamin Butler succeeded Viele as military governor. Although he had incurred the soubriquet of "The Beast" because of his severity to the resentful rebel population of New Orleans, where he had been stationed earlier, he earned the undying devotion of

Norfolk's blacks. (A grandson of William Greenwood and Martha Sparrow would be named Ben B. Sparrow!) Butler, whom the blacks called "The Benign Father", confiscated lands from rebellious whites, sold them, and used the funds to support the new schools for black children. He declared an end to discrimination in public accommodations. He also recruited black men to serve in the Union Army and organized the Tenth United States Colored Volunteers at Norfolk. Over 200 men enlisted.[126]

Many of Norfolk's whites, understandably, did not take kindly to the attempts of the Yankee invaders to turn their way of life upside down. Predictably, there were episodes of violence and retaliation. The most spectacular occurred on June 17, 1863 when a prominent physician named David M. Wright went berserk when he saw a company of black troops marching by, under the command of a white officer. When he shouted violent invectives and imprecations at the men, the officer, a Lt. Sandborn, ordered Wright arrested. Maddened at the thought of being imprisoned by black soldiers, the doctor shot the officer and killed him. When Wright was subsequently tried and executed for his crime there was a massive outpouring of sympathy from the white population, who honored him as a southern martyr.[127] The presence, however, of General Butler and numerous black troops, who conducted drills in the streets and occasionally arrested white citizens for hostile acts against freed slaves kept the violence in check.[128]

It was perhaps the capture of Norfolk that mobilized the Greenwood family to take an active part in the war. In 1860, Martin and C.F. Greenwood were each the proud owner of three slaves. Now, with their property stripped from them, C.F. and his surviving brother decided to defend the Confederacy. Sending his daughters to a Roman Catholic convent school in Baltimore and leaving the jewelry business in the care of his father, C.F. Greenwood joined Company E of the Fifty-Fourth Virginia Militia, where he served as a private. Fred, who had attended the Norfolk Military Academy, enlisted in an outfit called the Light Artillery Blues, where he too served as a private. Brother-in-law George Louis Curdts, at 36, sent his pregnant wife Ellen (and presumably his children) to Frankfurt, Germany, to live with his relatives, and, joined the same company as C.F.

William Sparrow, who was an apprentice shoemaker in 1860, was in his late teens when General Butler called for black volunteers. There is no record of his enlistment.

Physical conditions in Norfolk grew grim. The former slaves interviewed by the WPA in the 1930s spoke of an influx into the city of liberated or escaping slaves from the countryside, indigent, lacking food and shelter, crowded the streets and lanes. Some estimated that as many as 20,000 freed slaves poured into Norfolk and its environs.[129] A former slave named Charles Grandy recalled, "Nobody owned the niggers, so they all come to Norfolk...hundreds, hungry and without houses to sleep in, was walking around and begging. They army fed a lot of them, but it couldn't feed all. We used to steal bread [from employers]and stuff it in our shirts...When we get out [of work] we would give it to the hungry women and babies...They didn't have no food at all. Women and children used to die two and three a day from being hungry."[130] A woman identified only as "Sister Robinson" recalled that during the war, "People died like sheeps...They died so fast they had to bury them in batches in the vaults."[131]

In early 1864 an epidemic of smallpox broke out in winter. Virginia Hayes Shepherd recalled, "Snow was deep everywhere. White people died so fast and the snow froze the ground so hard that funerals and burying wasn't possible...They couldn't bury the bodies. Bodies was stacked on the snow beside the sidewalk and the gutters." Unlike those who experienced the North Carolina occupation, Shepherd maintained a good opinion of the behavior of the Northern soldier. "I expect everyone would have died ," she declared, "if it hadn't been for the Yankee soldiers taking care of everybody. They gave us plenty of good food and clothes. You could go to them and get anything you needed."[132]

In the spring of 1865 the war ended. Ellen Greenwood Curdts seems to have returned to Norfolk the previous year—by January, 1865 at the latest, because she bore a son, William in early November. Her husband and the Greenwood brothers returned apparently without any major physical ill-effects, but the property tax records of the time suggest that the family was in reduced financial straits. In 1860 Martin Greenwood, then the owner of three slaves, two horses, three carriages, and one clock, paid a tax of $10.23 and C.F., who owned three slaves, two watches, one clock, and one piano, paid $2.24 (despite the fact that the census takers recorded his personal estate as far larger than that of his father). In 1865 both father and son paid a tax of only forty cents. Not only had they lost their slaves, but evidently their horses and watches and clocks as well. Perhaps the animals been confiscated by the Union Army. Perhaps Yankee troops wrecked the jewelry store and soap factory. Perhaps the Northerners pillaged their homes.

The Smith household was affected even more adversely than the Greenwoods. Thomas McGehee Smith, who had been promoted to the rank of major in 1863, was not among those who came home. He had been killed at the bloody battle of Cold Harbor, near Richmond, in the spring of 1864. He was 30 years old and left a childless widow Julia. William Forbes Smith, at 27, now had responsibility not only for his wife and two legitimate children, but also his 20 year old sister Ellen and his teenaged brothers George and Murray, as Caswell County was plunged into the violent maelstrom of that period that came to be known as Reconstruction.

Chapter Nine

The Thirteenth Amendment to the Constitution, which ended slavery, was ratified by Congress in January, 1865, but did not take effect until December, when it was approved by the required number of states. North Carolina's slaves, including the Kemps, were officially freed b order of General John M. Schofield, who headed the Union forces that occupied the state.[133] How the family learned of their freedom, what their reaction was, and what change, if any, it had on their immediate situation is not known, but it does appear that they remained in Caswell County for two years after the war, where the next few years would bring more bloodshed that the war had visited upon it.

As was the case in other parts of the South, there was widespread hunger. A resident named John F. Flintoff wrote in his diary on August 17, 1865, "The people have had scarcely [enough] bread to supply them till harvest fall—they will live on what there is—very little meat anywhere to be had."[134] A former slaveowner, Flintoff declared, "My negroes all stay with me while most of the others are running about from home to home, believing they are free—many of them are killed and dieing [sic] for want of money and protection—poor creatures—I have to ride often after them and arrest them for trial, for their fighting, stealing, and other meanness. They are very troublesome to the white people."[135]

The federal government moved to disqualify from voting most of the men who had served or fought for the Confederacy. Those white males eligible to vote were either newcomers from the North ("Carpetbaggers") or locals who had remained loyal to the Union ("Scalawags"). In addition, shortly after the war the franchise was extended to black males in the state, to the outrage of the former Confederates. Caswell was one of the counties where Negro voters outnumbered whites, who felt especially angry and helpless.

Two violent factions quickly developed there and in many other parts of the South. The Republicans included blacks and their supporters, as well as many poor whites who harbored deep-seated resentment against the old planter aristocracy. The Conservatives, nearly all former Democrats, were comprised largely of the old ruling class, who were determined to crush any bid for political power on the part of Negroes and poor whites. To complicate matters, some Negroes supported the Conservatives. For example, the *Milton Chronicle*, early in the war highlighted a well-to-do black man, Felix Smith, who contributed $20 towards providing equipment and uniforms for Conferate soldiers.[136] After the war there were many blacks who served as informers and lackeys for those who were trying to undermine the influence of the hated federal government. There were instances of blacks who were attacked by other freedmen for voting Conservative and were rescued from lynching by the Ku Klux Klan.[137]

An editorial from the *Danville Bee*, written October 1, 1935, highlights the depth of bitterness felt by the dispossessed ruling class, a bitterness that seemed to have eased little *seven decades* after the conclusion of the war: "Like scores of other communities, Caswell County's inhabitants realized that slavery was over. They did not resent that, for there were still kindly bonds between the white people and the colored. But there was fierce resentment in Caswell over the sending of [officials by the federal government who were perceived to side with the blacks against the white establishment and thus] rubbed salt into the fresh wounds of the war by arraying the colored people against the white people preaching social equality and prodding a race that did not understand its own freedom towards a policy which could never had prevailed."

In Caswell County, the Republicans, some of whom came from the North, were active in organizing blacks into the Union League. According to one outraged slavemaster, they promised Negroes that the government would confiscate the lands of former Confederates and redistribute it so that every freedman received forty acres. Enraged whites complained of the formation of black paramilitary units that intimidated them and kept them awake at night by "drilling...and beating drums."[138]

The most hated Republican leader was a white man named John Walter Stephens, called "Chicken" by enemies who insisted that he was a chicken thief. Stephens, who was 31 at the conclusion of the war, was a poor white who had always been a bitter foe of the planter aristocracy and a strenuous opponent of the Confederacy. Shortly after the war Stephens and Jim Jones, another poor white of similar mindset, were elected justices of the peace in Caswell County. Shortly afterwards Jones not only had the gall to acquit a Negro accused of stealing a hog, but also to warn the white accuser that justices of the peace were bound by law to protect Negro rights. An enraged former slave holder by the name of John G. Lea decided to organize the Klan in Caswell County and quickly formed a "den" in every township. The Klan's first act of terrorism was to flog Jones and drive him out of the county.[139]

"Chicken" Stephens proved more difficult to subdue. He continued to organize blacks, allegedly persuading them to vote in blocs and agitate for land redistribution. The Conservatives were beside themselves with rage when Caswell's black voter majority sent a dark-skinned negro named Wilson Carey to Raleigh as one of the county's two delegates to the State Legislature and elected Stephens as state senator.[140]

The Klan now declared all-out war on the Republicans. In a three year period the hooded terrorists committed at least 16 murders, were responsible for 120 floggings, and burned hundreds of homes and barns.[141] The followers of Stephens responded in kind. Although subsequent investigations would indicate that the violence was perpetrated by a tiny minority of the population, most residents of Caswell and adjoining counties lived in fear. Many, both white and black, felt that it was safer to sleep in the woods because of the prevalence of night raids.[142]

Early in 1870, the hotel in Yanceyville and a row of brick stores, as well as the tobacco crops of two prominent Conservatives were burned. Told by two black informers that the destruction was the work of Stephens and his men, Lea and his Klan gave the senator "a fair trial in absentia" and sentenced him to death. On May 22, Stephens, who for some time had slept in an iron-barreled cage, surrounded by weapons, was lured into a storage room in the Caswell County Courthouse in Yanceyville by a local man whom he mistakenly regarded as a friend. Ten Klansmen burst in on him, garroted him, slit his throat, and stabbed him to the heart.[143]

At this point Governor William Holden, a Republican dispatched over 1000 state militia, mostly from the western hills, under the command of Colonel George W. Kirk to put down the violence in Caswell and neighboring Alamance counties. In Yanceyville the troops made a show of force, marching down the main street, surrounding the courthouse with banners flying and drums thundering. They arrested over 100 men in the two counties on suspicion of subversive activities. No one was convicted because no one was willing to testify against the Klan, and Lea (who later wrote an account of his exploits) was carried with his cronies in triumph on the backs of a cheering crowd. Governor Holden was impeached for acting unconstitutionally and eventually removed from office,[144] and within a few years the planter aristocracy had regained authority in Caswell County and most of the South.

But what role did the Kemps and Smiths have in these tragic events? There is no evidence that William Smith took any side in what became known as the Kirk-Holden War. He continued to run his tobacco business, raise his family of three legitimate children, and, apparently, steer clear of politics. As for Sarah Kemp and her family, they were back in Norfolk by 1868 at the latest, just about the time when the Klan became active.

The circumstances of the Kemp family's return to their native place are unknown. Were they frightened away by the widespread violence? Most likely Sarah was motivated by a desire to see her family. The failure to return to Norfolk for two or three years might possibly been the result that Sarah and her three now-adult children had to scrape together the money to make the journey. Did William Smith show interest in his former mistress Lydia and his natural son? Did he give them money to return to Norfolk? Did he permit them to stay with him after emancipation or were the Kemps dispersed among those Caswell freedpersons who wandered aimless and impoverished through the countryside? There are no answers to these questions. It is unknown whether William Forbes Smith ever saw Lydia and Franklin again—or cared to do so.

Although Norfolk had suffered no damage from fighting, like nearly all southern communities, it was cursed with poverty, hunger, joblessness, and racial strife. The city, which even under more favorable circumstances had been characterized by a northern educator as "dirty, dilapidated, dull, and dead"[145] and which General Butler had described as the filthiest place he had ever seen[146] now teemed with sickly and starving black refugees who found themselves the target of violence by hostile and resentful whites. As soon as "Benign Father" Butler was transferred in early 1865, white mobs began to take out their frustrations in violence against the black community. Returning Confederate soldiers boasted that spring, "We'll kill every nigger or drive 'em out of town!"[147] On June 25 a group of black people on their way to the circus were fired upon by whites. Shortly afterwards an African American man was found hanging from a lamp-post. In the next few days another man of color, on his way home from church, was beaten within an inch of his life by a white mob, and another Negro was shot.[148] That summer northern newspapers reported "a reign of terror in

Norfolk."[149] The *Boston Commnwealth*, for example, reported that blacks were beaten and terrorized every day, as white youths, descending on them, chanted, "Nig! Nig! Nig!"[150]

On April 16, 1866, a full scale race riot occurred. Blacks were celebrating the passage of the Civil Rights Act by holding a parade. The marchers were met by hostile whites throwing bricks and stones. When a drunken off-duty white policeman tried to arrest a black boy, he was charged by the marchers. The officer, William Moseley, fled to the house of a friend, who started shooting at the blacks, only to be shot and killed. The army, which still occupied the city, put down the riot, but violence broke out again that night, with bands of enraged whites roaming the streets, killing and wounding an indeterminate number of blacks.[151] A subsequent federal board of inquiry determined that although Norfolk had been under federal rule for nearly four years, it was "still rebellious and defiant."[152] A colored citizen named Edward W. Williams spoke for most of the Negro community when he complained, "It is a very awkward time in this city and we have to be very careful how we walk and I never go out at night."[153]

Fortunately, not only did federal troops still occupy the city but the Freedmen's Bureau was also active there. Although it failed to bring about land redistribution it did provide important services, it provided such services as encouraging blacks to register to vote and protecting them when they did; providing jobs (mostly manual labor); and setting up a court where freedpersons could redress their wrongs.

Because there had been such resistance to attempts by the government to bring order through legislation throughout the former Confederacy, Congress passed a Reconstruction Act in 1867 that put most of the former Confederate states under military rule. Norfolk became part of Military District I. Many people of color were among the delegates to a constitutional convention which wrote a new constitution for the state which provided the right to vote for all men, regardless of race or color, a uniform tax system, a bill of rights, a public school system, and the election of school trustees by popular vote.[154] When the Virginians who were allowed to vote ratified the new constitution, the state was readmitted to the Union and federal troops were withdrawn.

When Sarah Kemp and her family returned to Norfolk, there was occasion for sadness. Sarah's mother Lydia, who had been freed in the 1850s,[155] had apparently died during the war. Joseph's wife Minerva had died also. Sarah and her family met Joseph's six sons for the first time.

All of them, as well as a short-lived daughter Harriet, had been born during the absence of their relatives. William Franklin, called "Frank", was 20, Joseph, Jr. 18, John 15, Timothy or "Bud" 14, Alexander 12, and Raymond 10.

Most blacks in Norfolk did seasonal labor as dockworkers, oyster shuckers, and farm laborers. The average wage was .75¢ per day for men and .50¢ for women. The census of 1870 reveals that Joseph Kemp, then 48 years old, was a "huckster." Frank was a "waterman." John was a "fisherman" and Bud was a laborer. In 1872, when Alexander opened an account with the Freedmen's Savings Bank, he was described as a man of "black complexion" who worked as an "oysterman" "for Hardy." Raymond, on the other hand, worked "with father in shop."[156] Joe, Sr., who is also described as "huckster, vegetable market" in the Norfolk city directories, must have had shop or stall where he sold produce.

Sarah and her family found accommodations in Norfolk's Fourth Ward, the area most heavily populated by blacks, a place characterized by a former slave as little more than a "hogpath." The house the Kemps rented was on the east side of Fenchurch Street, which was close to downtown and definitely not a "hogpath", but an area inhabited by working class blacks and whites. According to the city directories, the house numbers changed every few years. At first the Kemps lived at Number 51, then Number 61, then Number 59, then Number 57½, but always on Fenchurch Street. The U.S. Census of 1880 shows that their house accommodated not only Sarah Kemp' family of fourteen, but five boarders as well. There were only two houses on the east side of the street between Holt and Cove Streets, so the house must have been quite large. That fact that it had, at one time, the number 57½ suggests that it might have been a two family house.

According Elinor Waller, the Kemps were "set up in business" by "their white relatives." The Norfolk City Personal Property Tax lists for 1868 show that "John Campe" was a "hostler" (stable-keeper) for one W.W. Hall. W.W. Hall was a 70 year old former slave trader. Could he have been the father of Sarah's children?

Within a few years John Kemp went into business for himself. He opened a livery stable at Numbers 78 and 80 Union Street. In 1877 he ran this advertisement in the Norfolk City Directory:

John Camp [sic]
Boarding and Livery Stable

No. 80 Union Street
Board per day, $1.00
Board per month, $15.00
Single feed, 35 cents

Apparently he also had a fleet of carriages for hire, as well.

Samuel Kemp became a barber, but worked at that trade for only a few years before joining his brother's business to work as a "clerk" in the livery stable. Sarah, however, remained the head of the household. In both the censuses of 1870 and 1880 she is listed as the family "head." Her occupation is listed there and in the Norfolk city directories of 1872 and 1874 as "washwoman." According to Waller, her great-great grandmother was no ordinary laundress who "took in" washing, but "had her own private laundry" and employed workers. Lydia worked with her mother. In addition, she made medicine from the jimson weed and her potions were said to have been more efficacious than any concoction obtainable at the office of doctor or shop of apothecary.[157]

We know nothing of the personalities of Joseph Camp or his children or of Sarah's sons John and Samuel. Sarah's family seems to have been very closely-knit. None of the three children ever left their mother. Although Samuel at 28 married Julia Johnson on June 20, 1872, the couple and the three children who eventually were born to them continued to live, along with John and Lydia, neither of whom ever married, under the roof of their mother. One might speculate that Sarah had a powerful, dominating personality. The tradition that has been handed down about her is that she was an intelligent person and a good businesswoman, and that she was very good and kind. In the 1870s and early 1880s the Kemp family seems to have been upwardly mobile. Because they owned neither house, horse, or carriage, John and Samuel Kemp, like most of Norfolk's blacks, paid the minimum property tax. It seems clear, however, that they rose above the lowest class of people into the ranks of the lower middle class.

As for the Greenwood family, C.F. and had quickly recovered economically from the war and formed, with younger brother Fred, the firm of C.F. Greenwood & Brother. Just a year after the war, he opened a new shop of Main Street and ran this advertisement in the *Old Dominion*:

PURE SILVERWARE JUST RECEIVED

Some entirely new styles just out, such as
    sardine forks
    salt and mustard spoons
    sugar and preserve spoons
    pie and cake knives
    berry scoops and spoons
    cream, soup, oyster, gravy, and fruit ladles
    paper cutters, portmonaies
    snuff and tobacco boxes
    fish knives and forks
    crumb scrapers, salt stands
    individual salts, card cases, cups, goblets
    sugar dishes
    new style napkin rings
    table, tea, and dessert spoons
    forks in great variety

      for sale at my NEW STORE No. 27 MAIN STRET, 2nd door from the corner
      of Talbot, where can be found the best assortment of goods in my line in the
      city, at prices to suit the times, and every article warranted as represented.

                     C.F. Greenwood
                     Practical Watchmaker

Soon, according to tradition, C.F. Greenwood & Brother was the largest jewelry in all the South.

     The health of the elder Greenwoods seems to have given way during the war. By the end of the conflict Martin had retired completely and was living with his wife at the home of son Fred at 16 Cumberland Street, with C.F. and family living next door at Number 14. There, on June 6, 1866, Margaret died (according to the Norfolk death register) of "unknown causes." The Norfolk *Day Book* of June 7 recorded: DIED. Last evening at 9 o'clock in this city, MRS. MARGARET GREENWOOD, wife of Mr. Martin Greenwood, age 69 years. The funeral will take place this afternoon at 5 o'clock, at the residence, No.

16 Cumberland Street. The friends and acquaintances of the family are respectfully invited to attend." The same day the *Old Dominion* carried a tribute written by Joaquin Bayto, the former son-in-law who, after the death of his wife Margaret the younger, had remarried to Dolley Harrison. He still regarded Margaret Greenwood with such affection that he wrote, "Mrs. Margaret Greenwood departed this life at 5½ p.m. yesterday evening. Few people leave this world as much regretted and respected as the deceased. She was a pious and upright Christian, a good mother, and leaves three children and sixteen grandchildren to deplore their loss. Her general kindness and geniality endeared her to young and old, and made her a universal favorite in every circle of which she was a member, and her loss will occasion a blank it will take long to refill. One of her sons-in-laws offers this tribute of respect to her good qualities and her memory.

JMB"

    This is the only extant clue to the character of this woman whose crude and shaky signature on her marriage protocol indicates that she was practically illiterate. Most newspaper obituaries printed conventional tributes to the character of the deceased, but Bayto's tribute goes beyond the conventions of the day. Margaret Greenwood was buried beside sons William and Martin, Jr. in the family plot of Cedar Grove.

    Martin's health seems to have failed rapidly after Margaret's death. He seems to have been an invalid during his last years. He made his will July 12, 1869, stipulating that "after the payment of my just debts I desire the residue of my property or the proceeds from the sale thereof to be distributed among my heirs at law and next of kin according to the laws of distribution in the state of Virginia now in force."[158] His death, the day after Christmas 1869, at the age of 70, was attributed to "old age." One of the local papers ran the following rather perfunctory obituary: "DEATH OF AN OLD CITIZEN: Martin Greenwood, Esq., an old and worthy citizen, departed this life Sunday at 1 o'clock at the residence of his son on Cumberland Street, in the 71st year of his age. The deceased was well and favorably known in this city as an enterprising and industrious citizen, and we condole with the afflicted family in their bereavement. His funeral will take place this afternon at 3 o'clock from the residence of his son." More revealing is Martin's epitaph in Cedar Grove Cemetery, which reads: "Mark the perfect man and behold the upright. The end of that man is peace."

The inventory made of Martin Greenwood's estate appraised the value of his personal property at $305.37. His most expensive possession was a "bedstead and bedding" valued at $35.00. Other items listed include:

1 hat rack
1 mahogany table and cover
1 safe
6 cane chairs
1 cane rocking chair
1 large rocking chair
1 bureau
1 secretary
1 wardrobe
1 carpet
1 rug
1 lot [of] books
1 fire screen
1 stove and pipe
2 mirrors
1 fire screen
1 carpet
1 table
1 mirror
1 washstand and basin
1 clock
1 chair, stove, sundries, and closet
1 hair rocking chair
1 gold watch
cash
5 spectacles
1 pistol
3 tables ($1.00)
1 table (.50¢)
1 quilt
1 teacher bed

Margaret's obituary, it will be recalled, listed "sixteen" grandchildren. This number is obviously not meant to include William Greenwood's children, despite a miscount. As of June, 1866, Martin and

Margaret had 15 grandchildren: C.F. and wife Mary Elizabeth had six daughters. Young Margaret was survived by two daughters. Ellen, whose husband George Louis Curdts had founded a bank called the Heptasophian Building and Loan Association, had five children, and Fred Greenwood, who had married Columbia "Lummie" Minter in 1860, had two.

Nothing is known of the experiences of Martha Sparrow and her children during the war. Although tax records show that immediately after the war the family lived on Cumberland Street—the same street as the Greenwoods—it is by no means clear that there was any meaningful contact. By the time of the deaths of the elder Greenwoods, it would appear that all ties with the white family had been cut. Although at least one of the great-granddaughters seems to have known something unfavorable about her granduncle William, for most of the third generation of the legitimate Greenwood descendants—certainly those born after the war—the very existence of the "black cousins" was a skeleton consigned to a carefully guarded closet to disintegrate completely before it could be opened by the following generation, who knew absolutely nothing about it.

Tax records show that by the mid 1860s, Martha's second child and only son William Sparrow, called "Billy", the head of the family, was paying a personal property tax of .90¢. The minimum at the time was .22¢. The city directories show that he was a shoe and boot maker.

The oldest child, Josephine, appears, at nine, in the census of 1850 and at 18 in the 1860 enumeration, in which her occupation is given as "cook." She does not appear in the census of 1870 and there are no records of her dying or marrying in Norfolk or the surrounding cities and counties during the 1860s or 1870s. However, although marriages were recorded in Norfolk during the war years, deaths were unregistered between 1861 and 1865. It is possible that Josephine left the area to "pass for white." There are no records of her appearance, but family tradition about three of her siblings (corroborated by the three surviving photographs of Dodie) holds that were all of stereotypic European appearance. It is also possible that she made no attempt to change her racial identity, but simply moved to a distant city. Whatever her history after 1860, all trace of her has been lost.

Martha died at 43 on September 27, 1867. The Norfolk death register gives the cause as "cholera", which is a violent, infectious form of diarrhea, usually contracted from tainted food or water. Cholera, however, usually occurs in epidemics. Although there had been such an epidemic in 1866, the death register for Norfolk in 1867 does not list any other victims of cholera at the time of Martha's death. Perhaps the term "cholera" was used by the health commissioners loosely to connote any gastrointestinal condition. It is not known where Martha was buried. In the 1860s Norfolk's Negroes were buried either at Cedar Grove, in the "Old Negro Burying Ground", which was bounded by Liberty, Scott, Hawk, and Cumberland Streets[159], or the "Potter's Field", adjoining Elmwood Cemetery across Princess Anne Road from Cedar Grove. She was definitely not buried beside William Greenwood.

Martha's second daughter Elenora was not quite 17 at the time of her mother's death. Norfolk's marriage register shows that in 1869 she married a barber by the name of Jacob Wright. The census of 1870 shows that they were living with his family. She was described as "mulatto", the Wrights as "black." His death is not recorded in the Norfolk death registers from the early 1870s, but when Elenora remarried in 1872 to Frederick Johnson, a middle aged proprietor of a candy store, she was listed as a "widow." There is no record of her having any children by Wright, but, on September 30, 1873 she gave birth to a daughter, Nora. Four days later the mother died, according to the Death Register, as a result of complications from a "premature birth." Fred Johnson survived his wife by only a few years, dying at 52 of cancer in 1877. There is no record of Nora's death or marriage, and her fate has thus far been lost to history.

The second daughter Martha, called "Mattie", worked as a seamstress. She was 14 when she was orphaned. Both Louise Elliott and Elinor Waller described her as a lovely person with blonde hair and blue eyes who looked entirely northern European. At 29 she married a laborer named William Brock—characterized as "black" in census records—and two years later they moved to New York, where Brock worked as a janitor.

The youngest daughter Mary Louisa—afterwards called Dodie— was 11 when her mother died. The census of 1870 which describes William as a shoemaker and Martha as a seamstress describes Mary, who was then 15, simply as "at home." Like her brother and sister, she is listed as being able to read or write, but it is unknown how or when she obtained her education. Elinor Waller recalled, "The white people she worked for called her 'Pinkie' because she had pink cheeks." Everyone who knew her agreed that her complexion was fair. George Elliott, Jr.,

Louise's husband, said, "She was so bright you couldn't tell her from a white woman." A grandnephew, Bernard Ruffin, Jr., recalled that blue veins were evident in her white skin. He insisted that his grandmother's hair was blond and her eyes blue, but his sister Elinor was certain that both hair and eyes were brown. A painting of Dodie executed apparently when she was in her 30s or 40s shows greenish eyes and black hair lightly streaked with gray. Her features were of the type normally associated with northern Europeans and, in fact, her painting shows a striking resemblance to a photograph of her first cousin, Elenora Greenwood Catlin, daughter of C.F. All who survived to recall her agree that she had was intelligent, strong, forceful, and energetic.

Until she was about 20 Dodie and sister Mattie lived with William and his family. In 1865 Billy, then 20, had married 17 year old Frances Webb of Portsmouth. Their oldest child, William, Jr., was born the following year, followed closely by Ben B., who seems to have died as a baby, Martha, who died in early childhood, Gertrude, and Caulbert. Eventually the couple would have 11 children. After Martha's death they moved to New Street, then, shortly afterwards, to 66 Avon, where they lived for some years. Sometime before the summer of 1873, Dodie, then 18, became acquainted with Franklin Kemp, who as also 18, and, as she later told granddaughter Elinor, was "the handsomest man in all of Norfolk."

The traditional handed down about Benjamin Franklin Kemp—from Dodie through Elinor—is that he was a spoiled playboy who had been pampered by his mother Lydia and his "white relatives." According to Elinor, he was given "a job something like a U.S. marshal by his white family." William Smith, however, remained in North Carolina. He never lived in Norfolk nor did his sister or brothers. Perhaps he sent money, but it seems unlikely that he had the contacts in Norfolk to get his son a job. Perhaps if there was any patronage involved, it was through the relations of Lydia's white father, whoever he was. Throughout his life, Franklin Kemp worked at various jobs, but he was never a U.S. Marshal. At the time of his marriage, he gave his occupation as "servant in attorney's office." In the Norfolk directories of the time he is listed as a "driver." Perhaps he was employed by his uncle John Kemp as a hackman. In 1882 he was a "messenger, U.S. Marine Hospital." Around 1883 he became an "assistant jailer" or "turnkey", which was evidently quite a prestigious job for a Negro at that time.

Other than describing him as "handsome", Elinor said nothing about the appearance of the grandfather she never saw. Two people who actually saw Frank Kemp who lived to be interviewed in the late 1960s and early 1970s were Dudley Tucker (1877-1974) and Helen Quetrell Dancy (1886-1973. Tucker, who remembered Kemp when he was about 40, characterized him as a "courtly" or "portly" "old gentleman" with gray hair, who looked entirely white. Dancy said he had "sandy hair" and a "peaches and cream complexion."

On March 6, 1874 Frank Kemp and Mary Sparrow had their first child, a daughter whom they named, apparently, for Dodie's recently deceased sister Elenora. The following year on July 8 the couple was married. Working class couples at that time, both white and black, evidently often delayed a formal wedding until they had one or more children. As we have seen, Martin and Margreth Grünewald married when she was expecting their third child, and Franklin's uncle Samuel Kemp married Julia Johnson when their oldest child was two. It seems as if among the working folk, marriage was rather informal. A couple considered themselves husband and wife when they set up a household together and began having children. The decision to go to a minister or justice of the peace to seek formal recognition of this union seems to have been a legal recourse so that they and the children would have all possible legal benefits. As we shall see later, marriages could apparently be terminated just as informally.

Frank and Mary Kemp, however, did not set up a household of their own. Dodie left the house of her brother to be absorbed in the growing menage on Fenchurch Street, headed by the benevolent matriarch Sarah Kemp. Little Elenora, or "Nonie", joined Samuel and Julia's children William (who was four) and Sarah Jane (who was a year old) as the newest members of the tightly-knit family unit.

Chapter Ten

By the 1880s the trauma of the Civil War and of the Reconstruction period was receding into bitter memory and some people were prospering in what would be called America's "Gilded Age. Among them were the Smith family of Milton. On July 6, 1870 U.S. census-takers found William Forbes Smith in Milton as a "dry goods merchant" with a personal estate valued at $1000 and real estate holdings with a similar value. Milton, however, which had once been the center of a thriving tobacco business, was now drying up, losing both business and population to nearby Danville, Virginia, which had access to the railroad. In the 1880 census, William was again enumerated in Milton, but that year he moved to the tobacco boom town of Winston (which would later unite with Salem) to set up, with his sons Sterling, 20 and Henry 18, the firm of W.F. Smith and Sons, which traded tobacco and manufactured cigarettes. William's sister Ellen, the wife of Preston Roan, a physician from Yanceyville, moved to Winston in the early 1870s, as is attested by her transfer of membership on December 19, 1873 to the Presbyterian Church of Winston. Murray Forbes Smith, the youngest surviving son, after studying at Washington College (now Washington and Lee) in Lexington, Virginia, read law, and after admission to the bar, practiced for a year or so in Greensboro, North Carolina, and then moved to Vicksburg, Mississippi, where he maintained a lucrative law practice. By the 1880s he was serving as attorney for two railroads. Active in politics, over the years he served as delegate to the state assembly of Mississippi, state senator, and delegate to the Democratic National Convention[160].

There seems to have been something wrong with brother George Alexander Smith, Jr., who until the 1880s lived with William. The census of 1880 lists him as having no occupation. The deedbooks of Caswell County and nearby Danville, Virginia throw a curious light on him. On October 16, 1869 George A. Smith purchased, of all things a large "canvas tent" in Danville. There is no clue as to what he used it for. Then in 1883, when several heirs of George A. Smith, Sr.(Murray and his wife Kate; Ellen; Thomas' widow Julia; and George, Jr.) sold their remaining property in Milton for $8000, the residences of each are listed except for George. Was this an oversight? Was he in prison? Was he in a mental hospital? Murray Smith's obituary (in 1909) recounts that he had a brother George who came to live in Vicksburg ten or twelve years before and had died there. Yet the funeral home that had a monopoly on the town's undertaking business at the time and does have record of the burial of Murray and Kate Smith, has no record of the burial of George Smith. Something is strange, something is unusual, but no information has been uncovered to shed light on the matter.

The wealth of William and Murray Smith was, however, dwarfed by that of yet another Smith, their first cousin Alva, whose father, a brother of George Alexander Smith, Sr., was named, like his nephew, Murray Forbes Smith. A lawyer, he moved to Mobile, Alabama, where he became a cotton dealer. The U.S. Census of 1860 records the worth of his personal estate as $300,000. He was rich enough to take extensive vacations in Europe with his wife Phoebe and their five children. However, with the fall of slavery, he was ruined, and moved to New York.

Alva Erskine Smith, according to the census records, was born in 1850. She was even as a young girl, unusually determined, self-assured, and, to many minds, domineering. When she was 25 she married William Kissam Vanderbilt, second vice-president of the New York Central Railroad, a business owned by his colorful grandfather Cornelius "Commodore" Vanderbilt. Despite the wealth of his son-in-law, Alva's father, who died two weeks after her wedding, had some misgivings about the match because the Smiths, who, despite his straitened circumstances, proudly traced their antecedents back to minor Scottish nobility and looked down on the Vanderbilts as *noveaux riches.* Alva later recalled, "The Smiths of Alabama cut me dead for marrying W.K. Vanderbilt because his grandfather peddled vegetables."[161]

Alva Smith Vanderbilt certainly never had to peddle vegetables. During the 1880s she established herself as a leader of New York's high society. At the cost of three million dollars she and her husband constructed a mansion at Fifth Avenue and 52nd Street that took up an entire city block and was characterized as "a fairy tale palace of Indiana limestone."[162] Alva filled it with treasures that she purchased from impecunious European nobility during her shopping expeditions on the continent. She and her husband built a half million dollar yacht which they named the *Alva.* Known to throw parties that cost $250,000, Alva once remarked, "I know of no profession art, or trade, that women are working at today, as taxing on mental resources as being a leader of society."[163] In 1889 Alva began the construction of an eleven million dollar "summer cottage' at Newport, Rhode Island modeled after Louis XIV's palace at Versailles. She called it the "Marble House."

There was apparently little contact between Alva Vanderbilt and the North Carolina Smiths. Perhaps Alva and her high society children (one of whom eventually married Britain's ninth Duke of Marlborough) looked down upon the Mississippi and North Carolina Smiths as poor relations unworthy of any civil consideration. It is almost certain that Alva Smith Vanderbilt knew nothing—nor surely cared to know—of her black cousins in their working class neighborhood in Norfolk. It is also almost certain that the Kemps—at least the children of Frank and Dodie—were unaware of their relationship to her.

Although far below the social status of the Vanderbilts, the Norfolk Greenwoods, like the Smiths of Winston and Vicksburg, were, by the late nineteenth century, among the more prominent citizens of Norfolk. C.F., who built a handsome three-storey home on Freemason Street, was now active not only in the Masons but also the Odd Fellows. A churchman, he helped found the fashionable Epworth Methodist Church in downtown Norfolk. Traditions passed down through C.F.'s descendants are, however, not necessarily complimentary. Sterling Yoder, Sr. (1907-1987), a great-grandson, said that the stories he heard about his ancestor, who died only three years before his birth, were so unpleasant that he would rather not repeat them, but that it would suffice to say that C.F. Greenwood was irritable and hard to get along with. Yoder did mention that C.F. was enraged when his oldest daughter Lizzie married James Rufus Norsworthy, a mere clerk in a dry goods store, and for many years was very cold to her.

C.F.'s second daughter—two years Lizzie's junior—was Laura, born in 1851, who married a railroad freight solicitor named William Joseph Vesey. Elenora Grace, born in 1853, married James Thomas Catlin, an insurance writer, and went to live with him in Danville. Pauline Augusta Greenwood, born in 1855, married a bookkeeper named Frank Peterson. Grace, born in 1860, married another bookkeeper, a man named Alfred Smith Lee, Jr. (no relation to Robert E.). She went to live with him in Baltimore, but died nine months later of "peritonitis," perhaps related to pregnancy. Kate Lee Greenwood, born in 1862, married a merchant named Samuel Swan Stevens. All the Greenwood daughters seem to have been good, substantial Victorian ladies married to men respected in the eyes of the world if not their father, who attended fashionable girls' schools, were active in the church, but never worked for a living. The only son, Charlie, born in 1870, became addicted to alcohol early in life and was never able to hold a steady job, even in his father's firm. The wills of both parents betray their lack of confidence in him. His mother, in particular, seemed obsessed that none of her money find its way into the pockets of any possible illegitimate grandchildren.

Fred Greenwood seems to have been more congenial and outgoing. He served for a time on Norfolk's city council and was its president on three occasions. He also served as Grand Commander of the Pickett-Buchanan Camp of the United Confederate Veterans. Joining the Masons immediately after the war, he attained "The Thirty-Third Degree in the Ancient and Accepted Scottish Rite." [164] While his brothers C.F. and Martin had become Methodists and sister Ellen a Presbyterian, Fred chose the Episcopal Church and served as Sunday School superintendent of St. Paul's Episcopal Church in downtown Norfolk for 25 years and many more as a vestryman. [165]

Meanwhile, the end of Reconstruction did not spell immediate disaster for Norfolk's black community. A government coalition preserved their rights for a while. Although the power of the Republican Party was broken with the re-enfranchisement of most former Confederates, the Conservative Party, which now predominated, split into two factions, the Funders and the Readjustors. The split was essentially over how the state was to pay debts incurred prior to the Civil War. The Funders, who were made up, generally, of businessmen, planters, and white urban workers, wanted to pay the debt. The Readjustors, who wanted to repudiate it, drew support from, among others, blacks and poor whites. This faction dominated the state government in the early 1800s and for a some time maintained a majority in Norfolk. Because they were dependent on black votes, the Readjustors could not afford to alienate their colored constituency entirely. Throughout the 1800s, black men in Norfolk were active in politics and even held some respectable political offices.

Dudley Tucker recalled in a 1969 interview the Norfolk of his boyhood: "Negroes lived in good houses. Some were of brick, others were frame. All were sturdy and substantial. Some people lived in alley dwellings, or courts, which originally had been slave quarters, but these were adequate accommodations and they were kept clean and in excellent repair. I never saw a shack in Norfolk when I was coming up. There wasn't much race discrimination in housing, as proprietors were too eager to have tenants of any kind to be fussy. The only barrier that kept Negroes from the neighborhoods where the more prosperous white people lived was price. Many poor whites lived in the same neighborhood with Negroes. We called them 'poor tabs' or 'poor white trash' and they called us 'niggers.' Gangs of boys from both groups would confront each other with bricks, rocks, balls, and bats, but no trouble of any serious nature ever resulted. We all belonged to gangs. I belonged to the Newton Hill Gang. But race relations, though unequal, were harmonious. There was no Klan in Norfolk. Nevertheless the Negro was at the mercy of his white neighbors. If a white employer struck a colored man, there was nothing the colored man could do and there was no action he could take. If he struck the white man back, he would go to jail. If two colored men happened to quarrel and fight one another and one killed the other, or if a Negro was the victim of assault by another colored man, no legal action was taken, for, as a southern politician said at the time, 'If your horse kills your cow, would you punish him?' The slum area was strictly defined. In a particular area, around Avon Street, there was a red-light district. It was full of saloons, brothels, and other amusements. No child of a respectable family was allowed to stray across Charlotte Street and no prostitute was allowed to cross Charlotte Street into the respectable neighborhoods."[166]

In the early 1870s, many Norfolk Negroes worked at trades other than manual labor. The 1872 Norfolk City Directory lists 12 colored barbers, one boarding-house owner, 10 shoemakers, seven butchers, two caterers, five fish dealers, one fruit dealer, and a man named Thomas Bayne, who was both physician and dentist. The directory of 1883 reveals black representation in all of the above trades and, in addition, two carpenters, one clothier, two confectioners, 15 grocers, an ice dealer, two proprietors of livery stables, and one owner of a "variety store."

As the family of Sarah Kemp grew, that of her brother was rapidly dying out. Joseph Kemp died at 55 on March 14, 1875, of pneumonia, a year after his son Timothy, only 22, succumbed to the same sickness. Joseph C. Kemp, Jr. continued to run the vegetable business. In 1881 he was elected to the Norfolk City Council on the Independent Republican ticket, representing the Third Ward, but, on January 31, 1882 he died at the age of 33, like his father and brother, of pneumonia. Tuberculosis may have run in the family. The Norfolk death register of 1868 lists the passing of five members of the Tynes or Tines family, between the ages of 14 and 40, all of "consumption." Presumably these were relatives of Minerva, whose early death may have been the result of the same cause.

William Franklin, who described himself as a "merchant" when he registered to vote in 1890, seems to have died or left Norfolk within the next year. Alexander Kemp also disappears from the Norfolk directories after 1890. Since there is no record of the death of the two brothers in the death registers for Norfolk City, it is quite possible that they moved out of town. Of the six sons of Joseph and Minerva Kemp, only two were living in Norfolk after 1890, John and Raymond. The city directory usually describes them as "laborers". The census of 1900, however, which lists John as a widower living with Lucy Shepherd, a 40 year old washerwoman and her eight year old daughter Florence at 40 Suffolk Street, describes him as an "oysterman." Of the Kemp brothers, only Joseph, John, and Raymond had children. John had a son Anthony, who at about 21, is listed as a laborer, living on Calvert Street, in the 1895-6 Norfolk directory. Joseph, Jr. left three children by his widow Martha: Christopher, born about 1870, Joseph III, born about 1878, and Frances, born around 1882. Raymond and his wife, the former Mary Johnson, had two sons: Frank, born in 1880, who died of tuberculosis at sixteen, and Raymond, Jr., who died at fourteen months in 1882 of "congenital syphilis.[167]" None of Joseph, Jr.'s children appear as adults in the Norfolk City directories, nor is there record in Norfolk of their death or marriage, so one would have to assume that they moved elsewhere. Likewise Anthony seems to have left the area upon maturity.

By 1888 the Kemp house on Fenchurch Street was the home of 16 persons, nine of whom were children. Sarah, the matriarch, continued to operate her laundry business, assisted by daughter Lydia and daughter-in-law Julia, and, according to family tradition, at least one hired helper. John operated his livery stable and saloon, assisted by Samuel, who, for some reason in 1887 or 1888 decided to strike out on his own to take up again his trade as a barber.[168] Within a year he seems to have been back in his brother's stable.[169] Samuel and his wife Julia (about whom nothing is known except that she was an illiterate mulatto washwoman[170] and a native of Culpeper, Virginia[171]) were the parents of at least six children: William, born in 1870, Sarah Jane, born in 1873, Minerva, or little "Minnie", born in 1878, and Joseph, Caledonia, and Samuel, Jr., who died as babies. Frank and Dodie had seven children, all but the youngest born in neat two year intervals: Elenora, or "Nonie", born in 1874, Caledonia ("Callie), born in 1876, Martha ("Mattie"), born in 1878, Benjamin Franklin, Jr., born in 1880, Emma born in 1882, Blanche

("Beppie"), born in 1884, and Franklin Benjamin ("Frank"), born in 1888. Benjamin died at 15 months of gastroenteritis. Two babies later, it seems evident that the father was desperate to have a child named after him and thus bestowed the name Blanche Franklin on his youngest daughter. When another son was born, unwilling to give him the exact name of the short-lived first son, the parents reversed the given names.

Frank continued to work as an assistant to "Old Man" Colbert at the Norfolk City Jail.[172] Family tradition held that he made a good living and bought fine furnishing for his home (he and his family *must* have had an apartment within in one of the two houses rented by the family) and fine clothing for his wife and children. According to Elinor Waller, Dodie did not have to work and the children had a hired nursemaid.

In 1885 Frank and Dodie moved out of the Fenchurch Street house to rented quarters of their own on 285 Bute Street, which was only a block or so away, where they lived in a home owned by Dodie's brother William Sparrow.

Billy Sparrow, like his uncle C.F. Greenwood, was a talented businessman but an unlikable person. His grandnephew Bernard Ruffin, who never met him, recalled that "Uncle Billy" had a reputation for being "irascible and cantankerous." George Elliott, Jr., who remembered him, recalled that looked entirely "white." Dudley Tucker said, "Mr. Sparrow was one who was colored only because he wanted to be." Elinor Waller, who was a toddler when Billy Sparrow died, understood that while her granduncle had dark hair and moustaches and looked like an Italian. All who remembered him agreed that Billy Sparrow was a very handsome man.

Billy had a shop on the north end of Bank Street (then Norfolk's Negro business district) where he both made and repaired shoes.[173] He was known for the excellent quality of his work as well as for his eccentricity. Sometimes he would lock his shop up for days at a time, to the dismay of customers who could not get their shoes.[174] So violent and ill-natured was he that he was not above taking a shot at complaining customers, like one hapless Tobe Parker, who was presumptuous enough to argue with him.[175] Fortunately Billy Sparrow was not as good a marksman as he was a shoemaker.

In 1881, during the heyday of the Readjustors, he became one of Norfolk's two customs inspectors. The staff at the Customs House at that time included Collector George E. Bowden, Cashier George R. Wilson, Marine Clerk W.T. Webb, Inspectors William H. Sparrow and

R.G. Banks, watchman Thomas Lowry, as well as two janitors and two boatmen. Except for the janitors and boatmen, the entire staff—with the exception of Sparrow—were white.

William H. Sparrow was also involved in real estate. In the mid 1880s he bought lots on Bute Street and erected houses on them. According to Norfolk's deed books, he immediately sold several. He and his family, however, lived at 283 Bute and now his sister and her husband and children came to live in the other.

It has frequently been said that the "Black Church" is the pillar of the "Black Community", but it is not clear what role the church and religion played in the life of the Kemp family. Most of the family attended St. John's African Methodist Episcopal Church. Louise Jackson Elliott remembered Dodie as a "deaconess" there. There is no way of confirming the membership of the Kemp family or what positions of leadership various members may have help because St. John's has preserved no records whatsoever from that period. Old residents of Norfolk recalled St. John's as the church of Norfolk's light-skinned Negro elite at that time. No tradition was handed down about the religious faith or commitment of any of the older members of the Kemp family , except for Lydia Kemp, who was characterized as "very religious."

It seems as if Dodie had some schooling, as all the censuses in which she appears state that she could read and write. Bernard Ruffin and Elinor Waller were in agreement that she was literate. It is not known where she went to school or for how long. All those who remembered her in later years were in agreement that Mary Sparrow Kemp believed in getting a good education and was determined that her children and grandchildren obtain an excellent educational background. Ruffin and Waller were in agreement that the children of Frank and Dodie attended the Norfolk Mission College on Princess Anne Road.

The Mission College was founded in 1883 by the General Assembly of the northern Presbyterian Church, which sought to provide a quality education for boys and girls of color throughout the South. John Richard Custis, Jr.(b. 1914), wrote an unpublished history of the college in the 1970s, based on the recollections of his parents, who were both graduates in the 1890s. A Professor Grove was sent to Norfolk by the Pittsburgh Synod the Church to explore the possibility of opening a school in Norfolk. Canvassing the colored neighborhoods for potential candidates for the school, he was directed to the shop of a barber named

Jackson, who was noted in the community for organizing debates and other constructive activities for black youth. Jackson introduced Grove to several promising students, but to the dismay of the professor, in every instance the parents opposed the idea of the school because nearly all were Baptists and therefore almost congenitally suspicious of Presbyterians. Their negative attitude was encouraged by the black Baptist clergy, who feared that the Presbyterians would "convert" their children and deplete their congregations. Jackson, however, encouraged Grove to go on with the project, suggesting that he visit Mary Ruffin Keeling, a woman very influential in community.

Mary Jane Ruffin (1846-1907) had been born in slavery, but had been freed at the age of two through the will of her mistress. A tiny woman described by Dudley Tucker as a "kind of" hunchback, she was married to William Keeling, who had tried, shortly after the Civil War, to organize a black labor union called the Eureka Laboring Company. The mother of three children, Mary Keeling was very much dedicated to the idea of higher education for blacks. Jackson told Professor Grove, "Mrs. Keeling is so well-respected in the community that if she permits her son to attend, all the other parents will go as well." Keeling received the professor with enthusiasm. Although a Baptist, she immediate enrolled her oldest son William. Together with his first cousin and best friend, Adela Frances Ruffin, Willie Keeling recruited students for "Professor Grove's School", which was quickly organized.

Apparently the land was purchased and the buildings erected through money provided by the Presbyterian Church. Within a year Norfolk Mission College had 96 day students and 64 pupils in the evening. It graduated its first class of 16 boys and girls in 1888. Within a few years the College had an integrated staff of 18 teachers and a student body of nearly 700. It offered 13 years of education divided between a primary department with four grades or "steps", an intermediate department with six grades, and a high school that offered a three year course. Everyone who finished the high school course was trained to teach. Moreover, each female graduate was required "to plan and cook properly the three meals of the day, to be inspected by competent judges of cooking" as well as make her own "graduating clothes."[176] Pupils were taught not only academic subjects but "obedience and piety."[177] Parents were assured that "a careful watch is kept over the habits and moral conducts of the pupils", who were required to attend "Sabbath school" every Sunday at 2 p.m. as well as

Wednesday prayer meetings. The school year began in early September and ended in mid-May, and classes commenced at 8:30 in the morning, with the ringing of the chapel bell, and finished at 2:30 for day students and ran from six to nine for the evening students.

The only one of Dodie's children enrolled at the Mission College at the time the first surviving catalogue was issued in 1899 was young Frank, who was then in the first grade of the intermediate department. The only anecdote handed down in the family concerning the attendance of the Kemps at the Mission College concerns Frank and Dodie's third daughter Mattie, who, according to Elinor Waller, was, even as a child, "the black sheep of the family" and "wayward". All the pupils had to be seated in the chapel by the time the school-bell stopped ringing, but Mattie was habitually late and always subject to discipline.

None of the Kemp children graduated from the Mission College high school. The surviving catalogues reveal that the enrollment at the top level was quite low. For example, in 1900 there were over 300 in both the primary and intermediate departments, but fewer than 50 in the high school. Although Dodie wanted her children educated the fact that the College, which required a tuition of .25¢ for each child in the primary and intermediate levels, charged a dollar a month for the high school course was likely a factor why none of the children obtained the diploma. By the time the oldest of the children was ready for high school, the financial resources available to them had been significantly reduced.

Chapter Eleven

In her autobiography Alva Smith Vanderbilt described the sensation that she made in 1894 when she divorced her "nonentity of a husband": "Women were not supposed to divorce their husbands in those days, whatever their provocation, and social ostracism threatened anyone daring enough, or self-respecting enough, to do it...I was the first woman of prominence to sue for a divorce for adultery, and Society was by turns stunned, horrified, and then savage in its opposition and criticism. For a woman of my social standing to apply for a divorce from one of the richest men in the United States on such grounds, or for any cause, was an unheard of and glaring defiance of custom."[178]

How much easier it was, however, for a person of Mary Sparrow Kemp's standing to rid herself of Alva Smith Vanderbilt's unknown cousin! After ten years, the marriage of Frank and Dodie, if it was ever happy, was showing strains. The move away from the Kemp homes on Fenchurch Street in 1885 may have been an indication that all was not well. Perhaps both husband and wife felt it necessary to escape the domination of Frank's mother and grandmother. But their time away from Fenchurch Street proved as brief as Samuel Kemp's attempt to work apart from his brother. The Norfolk city directory of 1886 shows that Franklin Kemp, "turnkey", was once more living on Fenchurch Street.

"The handsomest man in Norfolk" seems to have been an inveterate philanderer. The version of their troubles that Dodie later recounted to her granddaughter Elinor is that only substantial oral history concerning Franklin Kemp that has survived. According to his wife, Frank was "childish and irresponsible," subject to a "violent temper", and "just *crazy* about the ladies." He was dominated by his mother, who pampered and spoiled him. He was so jealous that he never allowed his wife to leave the house without his permission. Periodically he would give Dodie expensive presents only to destroy them in his violent tantrums.

Dodie told Elinor that one day—and it must have been in the spring of 1891—she resolved to defy her husband and take her children to the circus parade. Unfortunately, the spot where she stood, with little Frank and the five beautiful girls, all dressed in white, carrying balloons, could be observed from one of the windows in the city jail, and when

Frank, looking out, saw his wife and children watching the parade, he rushed out of his office and stormed into their apartment, where, seizing an axe, he smashed a cast-iron stove he had recently given Dodie.

When Dodie returned home and found the broken stove, she made up her mind to leave Frank. This time she had the support of Lydia, who told her something to the effect of, "I don't blame you. Frank is spoiled. We always gave him everything he wanted. You should never have married him." One day, when Frank was at work, Dodie collected her children and, in the words of Elinor Waller, "went to a house she rented on O'Keefe Street in the...suburb of Huntersville. She was soon able to purchase a house on the same street."

This was the version Dodie handed down to her granddaughter. There seems to be more to the story than that. Public documents suggest that in her recollections Dodie was closeting a most hideous skeleton.

First of all, according to the city directories, Dodie went to live at 283 Bute Street in 1891. That was the home of her brother Billy. Second, she never purchased a home on O'Keefe Street.

It is important to note that the break up between Frank and Mary Kemp took place immediately after 18 year old Sarah Jane Kemp, known as "Sadie", who was Samuel' unmarried oldest daughter, gave birth in February, 1891 to a son, Russell Thomas Kemp. The paternity of the child was evidently not a subject discussed in family circles. A friend of the family, however, when questioned in later years, said, "It's better not to know." [179] The fact is that there is strong circumstantial evidence that Russell Kemp's father was none other than his mother's cousin Franklin.

The U.S Census of 1900 found the Kemp clan living in two houses on O'Keefe Street on June 13, 1900. Russell Kemp is living under the same roof as Blanche Kemp, Franklin and Dodie's youngest daughter, and is identified as "brother" to Blanche.

The census record cannot be taken as absolute proof that Russell Kemp was a son of Franklin. In the same census report, Lydia is misnamed "Lillie" and her time of birth recorded as "February, 1832", whereas her birth year was almost certain 1837 or 1838. "Lillie" is identified as a "widow" who had been married 30 years and was the mother of three children, all alive, when in fact she had never been married and then had no living children. Blanche's time of birth is given as February, 1883 when in fact she was born in October, 1884.

A second bit of information supports the theory that Frank was the father of Russell. In an interview in 1969 Dudley Tucker, who was a teenager in the early 1890s, recalled that at the time he knew him, "Old Man Kemp" (then only in his 30s) did not live with his wife but with "his niece who took care of him." Frank, who was an only child, had no biological nieces. Tucker can only be referring to Sadie or Minnie, who were his first cousins. Minnie was only 13 or 14 in 1891. It is perhaps of some significance that Tucker did not say, "Old Man Kemp lived with his mother." He did not say that he lived with his grandmother. Tucker seemed to imply that Frank had a special (though not necessarily immoral) relationship with Sadie.

Third, there is the matter of physical resemblance. The daughter of Russell T. Kemp was quite unable to distinguish a photograph of Franklin Benjamin Kemp from one of her father. The two men throughout life bore an uncanny resemblance to each other—much more than one would expect of second cousins. There is also a striking resemblance, at least in photographs, between Russell T. Kemp and Bernard Ruffin, Jr., Blanche Kemp's son.

Fourth, one would assume that the circus came to town in the spring. By that time Russell (born in February) would have been several months old. Perhaps Frank's insistence that Dodie go nowhere without him came after she threatened to leave him after entertaining suspicions about the paternity of Sadie's baby.

Fifth, it is also curious that while the former residents of Fenchurch Street were split into two households in the 1890s, after the deaths of Samuel and Julia, Sarah, and finally Frank in the mid 90s, Lydia and Minnie were reunited with Dodie and her children on O'Keefe Street while Sadie found lodgings elsewhere in Norfolk—as if she may have been a *persona non grata* on O'Keefe Street.

According to Waller, Frank was heartbroken when Dodie left him and begged her to return to him, but she wanted nothing more to do with him. Within a year she had "married" again, to Armour W.D. Bass, and was living with him at his house on O'Keefe Street. Little is known about Bass, except that he was a native of Pasquotank County, North Carolina and that he was nine years Dodie's junior. His death certificate lists his occupation as "teamster."

The curious fact is Dodie never got a divorce from Frank. She and Armour Bass were married July 10, 1896 at 11 Newton Street in Norfolk by Methodist minister R.W. Dick. They had been living for four years a man and wife. In applying for the license, Dodie stated that she was a "widow."[180] Frank, however, was still living *only blocks away*!

Then, on October 2, 1896—just twelve weeks after the wedding, Armour Bass died at 33 of "unknown causes."[181] Around the time of his marriage he wrote a will, leaving his home on O'Keefe Street to his wife and one dollar to his mother.[182] It seems as if Armour Bass knew that he would soon die. It also seems possible that Bass' mother did not get along with Dodie and that he wanted to be certain that his bride inherited the house after his death. Perhaps this is why the couple went through the formality of a wedding—so that Dodie would be sure to inherit the house in which she and her children had been living.

It does not appear that Dodie and Bass were accused of "living in sin." No one who knew her well ever accused Dodie of being anything but a respected and respectable matron. Perhaps she and Bass regarded themselves a man and wife from the time they first lived together. It seems that in certain places, among the working classes, the concepts of marriage, divorce, and remarriage were quite informal. While Alva Smith Vanderbilt turned high society on its head by divorcing her husband, her cousin's wife seems scarcely to have raised an eyebrow by leaving Frank to become Mrs. Armour Bass several years before they went through a wedding, performed while Franklin Kemp was still alive!

Life seems to have taken a downward turn for the Kemp family after the separation of Frank and Dodie. The 1890s were a period of economic depression and hardship for most Americans, but it was a particularly sad time for people of color, who saw the modest gains they had made during the Reconstruction period eroded away in a tide of racial repression. By 1890 Readjustor movement was a thing of the past and poor whites were firmly within the Democratic camp. The party no longer needed black votes and in Virginia and most other parts of the South state legislatures moved to limit Negro voting by imposing a poll tax. Since this would discourage poor whites as well as poor blacks from voting, anyone was exempted from the tax who was registered to vote before the Civil War or was descended from someone who was.

In 1890, for example, the Norfolk voter registration rolls contain four volumes of black voters. The rolls from 1902 have just one volume of Negro voters that reveals that by that time only 200 men of colored were registered—far too few to be of any political significance.

William Sparrow, Dodie's brother, was a registered voter in 1890 as well as 1902, but it is not clear how the poll tax and grandfather clause affected the Kemp family. In 1890 John, Samuel, and Franklin Kemp were registered to vote, but by 1902 Sam and Frank were dead and John was in the city "almshouse". There were no male descendants of Sarah Kemp in Norfolk old enough to vote and women were not permitted to vote in Virginia until 1920.

With black persons virtually disenfranchised, new, insulting segregation laws were imposed, separating white passengers from black on ships and trolleys, and confining Negro patrons to the "peanut gallery" of theatres. Elinor Waller, growing up during the second decade of the twentieth century, remembered an evening curfew whistle after which people of color were not allowed on the streets[183].

After the breakup of Frank and Dodie the Kemps left Fenchurch and seemed to rent new quarters every year. In 1892 they were at 147 Queen Street. In 1894 they lived at 459 Queen Street, then the next year they moved to 459 Church Street, where they stayed two years before renting a house at 70 James Street in 1897.

It is not clear whether Frank Kemp kept his job at the city jail. The city directory of 1888 lists him as a "laborer", but the recollections of Dudley Tucker as well as strong family tradition indicate that he was still working at the jail at that time. In 1892 he is listed as a "clerk" and in 1894 as an "agent." Family tradition holds that he kept his job until he was stricken by a "creeping paralysis" that started in his legs. Elinor Waller said that she was told that his malady was blamed on years of scrubbing on his knees the cold stone floors of the jail. The disease eventually cost him the use of his arms and hands and for the last two or three years of his life he was confined to a chair in his home. Dudley Tucker remembered "Old Man Kemp" as an "invalid" and his understanding or assumption was that he was the victim of a stroke or strokes. He also recalled that he sat beside a window and, since he could not turn his head, sat looking at a mirror or series of mirrors so that he could see who was passing on the street.

The 1890s took a heavy toll of the family circle. First, Julia Kemp, wife of Samuel, died suddenly of "apoplexy" (perhaps a heart attack) on January 3, 1894, at the age of only 45. The next year Samuel seems to have become disabled, for the city directory lists him as without an occupation. He died at 52 on July 16, 1896 of "intestinal obstruction." The following year marked the passing of Sarah the matriarch, whose death at 87 on May 4, 1897 was attributed to "old age." On September 13 of that same year, Benjamin Franklin Kemp, nursed faithfully through his illness by Sadie, died at 42.[184] He was presumably buried in a plot purchased a few years earlier by his mother and Uncle John. Sarah, Samuel, Julia, and other family members must be there, too, but there is not a single marker on the plot.

It is not known whether William Forbes Smith learned of the death of his natural son. There is no way of knowing whether he maintained any contact, over the years, with Frank and Lydia, or if he even cared about them. By the time of Frank Kemp's death, two of William's three legitimate children were also dead. Julia, the youngest, died at 11 in June, 1877. Henry died at 27 of pneumonia on February 12, 1890. The Winston-Salem *Republican* described him as "one of the youngest buyers upon our market" and "a clever gentleman" who left "a large circle of friends."[185] Shortly after Henry's death, William, who never had any church affiliation, joined the First Presbyterian Church of Winston-Salem, of which his wife and sister Ellen Roan had long been members. On March 27, 1900, he died at 62 at the Phoenix Hotel after a "lingering illness." His newspaper obituary states that he had once done "an extensive leaf business" and had been a cigarette manufacturer, but had been retired for several years from active business.[186] The records of the administration of his estate show that he died without a will and "so far as can be ascertained at the date of this application," and that the value of his estate was "nothing." On May 16, 1900, Sterling Smith, the only surviving son, stated that no funds had passed from the estate of his father into his hands.[187]

There could be two reasons for this state of affairs. During his lengthy illness William could have turned over all his assets to his son Sterling. But he just as easily could have been penniless at the time of his death. According to a local historian, during the boom years of the 1880s many cigarette manufacturers operated in Winston and Salem but within the decade several large companies, most notably R.J. Reynolds, began to buy up smaller competitors. Those manufacturers who refused to sell and insisted on competing with the tobacco giants were ruined. This well have been the fate of William Forbes Smith.

The U.S. Census of 1900 casts a little light on William's plight. By the time the enumerator came to the hotel on Liberty Street where Sterling Smith was living with his mother, William had been dead for more than two months. The occupations given for the twenty other "boarders" in the hotel indicate that it was not the sort of luxurious establishment which cousin Alva was wont to frequent, but the home of people of rather ordinary means. One civil engineer lived there, one reporter, and one bookkeeper, but most of the residents were clerks and salespeople.

After the firm of W.F. Smith and Son folded, Sterling Smith became an employee of the Brown and Williamson Tobacco Company. He may have been his parents' financial support in their latter years. Later he became a director of his company and then left the tobacco business to become a successful hardware dealer.[188] With his death at 57 in August, 1918 in Atlantic City, New Jersey, the legitimate line of William Forbes Smith's descendants came to an end.

Chapter Twelve

With the death of Mammy Sarah, Mary Sparrow Kemp Bass was the new matriarch of the Kemp clan, whom she reunited on O'Keefe Street in what was then the suburb of Huntersville, just north of Princess Anne Road, which then separated Norfolk City from Norfolk County. Dodie lived in the two-story frame house which her husband had willed her. At times she seems to have rented a house next door and another across the street for overflow relatives. In these dwellings lived Dodie and her children, "Grandma" Lydia, now in her sixties, and Samuel's daughter Minnie, who was raising young Russell.

There is no record of what became of William Kemp, the son of Samuel and Julia. He would have been 30 in 1900, but there is no record of him in Norfolk other than the census of 1880. He does not appear in any of Norfolk's death registers. There is no record of his marriage. He does not appear in a single city directory. The most logical conclusion is that William Kemp moved out of town at an early age.

Not much more is known of Minnie Kemp. Her nephew Russell would tell his daughter that it was Minnie who raised him and that she was a beautiful blue eyed woman with blond hair so long that she could sit on it. When Louise Elliott was questioned many years later, she said only that Minnie went to New York. The implication seemed to be that she passed for white.

Sadie, as might be expected, did not live in Dodie's household. Her granddaughter once remembered seeing a picture of her and that she appeared brown-skinned. The census of 1900 reveals that she was living on Queen Street as a "house girl" to 40 year old day laborer John Cotton. According to the Norfolk city directory, by the end of the year she was living at 582 Chapel Street. It is not clear what she did for a living. Louise Elliott seemed to be reluctant to speak of her. Court records show that she married in Norfolk on May 27, 1907 to James Lovitt, who gave his occupation as "musician." The city directory for 1908 gives his occupation as bartender. The following year he was running a pool hall. In 1910 he was listed as a "musician"; in 1911 he was a "driver." The Common Law Order Books of Norfolk show that on December 10, 1908, Lovitt was convicted of conducting a "disorderly house." Barely six months later he was fined five dollars for "breaches of ordinances." It is not clear whether the couple was still together when Sadie died at 40, of pneumonia, in December, 1913. Her son Russell was the informant for the death certificate. Almost immediately afterwards he moved to Chicago, where he became a red-cap at the Dearborn Street Station, married Myrtle Downing, and had two children, Russell Julian and Jayne, both of whomwent on to graduate from college and become professionals. Russell made but one trip back to Norfolk—on his honeymoon in 1915. Through his wife he maintained contact, however, over the years, with his sister Blanche.

John Kemp was also not a part of the new Kemp menage. The end of his life seems to have been sad. In 1898 the directory shows that he was living at 70 James Street and was still working as a "hostler." The previous year he was listed as a "laborer." It is not clear whether he still had his own stable. He had long since given up his saloon. He does not appear in the directories for 1899 and 1900, but the U.S. Census of 1900 reveals that he was then an inmate of the Norfolk City Almshouse in Princess Anne County. The man who in his youth had been an aspiring businessman was now, at sixty, a pauper. One wonders what went wrong in his life. He seems to have tried to extricate himself from his demeaning situation, for in 1901 the city directory describes him as a "driver" for the Norfolk Protestant Hospital, where he resided. Failing health seems to have overwhelmed his attempt to recover his modest fortunes. On January 14, 1904 John Kemp died at 64 of "organic disease of the heart" and "Bright's disease" at the almshouse. His death certificate incorrectly gives his age as 73, perhaps an indication of a raddled appearance. Why he never lived with Dodie is a mystery. She seems to have been willing to take in any number of relatives in need. Perhaps he had sided with Frank in their marital troubles. Like other members of his family, John was interred in an unmarked grave in the family plot in Calvary Cemetery.

Six months later the Norfolk papers prominently featured news of the passing of one of the city's most respected citizens, Charles Frederick Greenwood, who on July 10, at the age of 79, "peacefully fell asleep after a long and painful illness, which he bore without a murmur."[189] It is not known how Dodie reacted to the news of the uncle who most likely wanted nothing to do with her. C.F. Greenwood left a handwritten will, dated January 6, 1895, which, with its misspellings, grammatical errors, and lack of punctuation, seems to have provided a clue to how he must have talked and perhaps how he thought, as well. Mentioning his second wife, Anne[190], he said that she was to inherit a third of his "rearl" and personal estate, stocks, and bonds "during hir life and after hir deth she will have no further use for same and I wish all she airs from me to go back to my children but she is at liberty to distripit the same as she pleases to give them that treat hir best or distripit them as she pleases the rest..." Then, running on, he indicated that after his debts are paid "my rearl and personal estate to be equelly divited amongst my 6 children, Lizzie Norsworthy, Laura Vesey, Ellen Catlin, Pauline Peterson, Kate Stevens, and C.F. Greenwood, Jr. if my son C.F. Greenwood should die before this I desire that his life insurance of $10,000 be equelly divited between my wife and children I mentioned my wife for the reason that she has done so much for him and moore than his owne mother that I wishhir to have hir share.

"I leave my Bro. Fred Greenwood one third of the stock in the store 318 Main St, Store no. 318, tiling, seeling, sandeleurs, beluing to me store fixtures, one third to Bro Fred but it ought to belong to me entirely as we have had no settlement for years of my share of provits ought to bee 3 times as much as they are worth I did this for thie love I have for my brother and I did not wish a fuss I ought to have had a settlement every year.

"I desire the stock in store to be sold to the best advantage debts paid and ballence distripited as aforesaid I desire that store 318 Main St and store 194 Church St not be sold for 5 yrs but rented out and the rent to be devited between my wife and children as their equel potion, as I think the value will be so much moore in 5 yrs. Would be best for all concerned and I desire that my home no. 384 Freemason St not be sold as long as my dear wife lives unless she desires it sold."[191]

C.F. Greenwood's detailed inventory, which records the rooms where the items that were appraised were located, provides a look at the house he had inhabited for more than three decades. It was evidently a narrow three story house. Downstairs there was a parlor with two sofas and six chairs, five rather expensive paintings, and four tables, all resting on a rather costly carpet. There was a dining room with a table and six chairs, a sideboard, a bookcase, a wicker chair, and an upholstered chair. There was a kitchen with a range and tables. There were two bedrooms on the second floor, each with a bed, washstand, bureau, and a clock. In the back bedroom there was a bookcase and a corner book rack. Only the front bedroom seems to have had a carpet. On the third floor there were two bedrooms.

At the time of his death, Greenwood had in his bank the substantial sum of $13,290.28, and he owned ten shares of stock, valued at $1,8000.00 in the National Bank of Commerce as well as 1000 shares of stock, most of which were listed as "worthless", in nine other companies. His interest in the business of C.F. Greenwood & Brother amounted to $5,000.00. There were two stores: the one on Main street was appraised at $25,000 and the one on Church Street was valued at $10,000.[192]

When he wrote his will, nine years before his death, C.F. expressed the concern that his son, who was only in his twenties at the time, might not survive him. C.F., Jr. or "Charlie" had evidently been a hopeless alcoholic from his youth, and developed tuberculosis. At the time of his fathers death Charlie was living in Chambersburg, Pennsylvania. On a note he scribbed his will, which read, "I, C.F. Greenwood, Jr., in the name of God make this my last will in my right mind.

To my dear sister Lizzie I give $50.00

To Pauline, my Diamond Pin

To Little Rufus [unidentified]] my Gold Watch & Chain

To Miss Ann [his stepmother] my Furniture and $50.00

To Little Albert [son of his sister Kate] $20.00

To Sister Ella and Bro. Jimmie [Ella's husband James Catlin] the rest of my Interest in the Estate and all that's coming to me.

I also give $50.00 to the home for consumptives at Baltimore, Md."[193]

On October 21, 1904, at the Home for Consumptives in Baltimore County, Md., Charles Frederick Greenwood, Jr., died at 34, scarcely three months after his father. His body was returned to Norfolk for interment in the family plot in Cedar Grove. According to his newspaper obituary the whole Greenwood clan turned out for his funeral, with male representatives from the family of each of his aunts and uncles (except for William!) serving as pallbearers.

The death of C.F. Greenwood, Sr. left only two his generation, Fred and Ellen. Fred eventually reorganized C.F. Greenwood & Brother, going into partnership with two other businessmen and establishing the firm of Paul-Gale-Greenwood. Fred Greenwood was remembered by the son of one of his partners as about 5'6" tall, 160 pounds, with a big white moustache and "a profusion of white hair." According to Frank Ford, an old Norfolk jeweler, Fred was not a particularly good businessman and spent a great deal of his time at the race track. After Fred's death at 82 in 1920, the firm was reorganized as D.P. Paul, which lasted until the early 1990s, with branches in several cities.

Ellen Greenwood Curdts, who died in 1915 at 81, was recalled by her granddaughter Mildred Curdts Fitzpatrick: "She was a devout Christian, a Presbyterian, and a very sweet-natured, happy person, greatly beloved by us and especially so by my grandfather, who spoiled her outrageously...She was a very stout woman. She wore a wig because she didn't have much hair and she used to go to New York to get her wigs and that was quite a trip in those days. She was very happy-natured and full of fun. Grandfather spoiled her to death. He would send her off for the day and when she returned she would find that he put a new carpet down for her or got some other present. As I said, she was an extremely heavy woman with a very large stomach. She used to sit in a big chair and we children would climb up on her shoulders and slide down to the floor [apparently using her bust and belly as a sliding board]. She'd make all kinds of pies and cakes and crawlers. My mother loved lemon pies and Grandmother would make her one every week, all for herself."[194]

The lifestyle of the family of Mary Bass was somewhat more severe than that of her white relatives. Evidently she did tell her children that they were related to the Greenwoods, but it is uncertain how much of that knowledge filtered down to the next generation. Louise Elliott recalled an incident that happened when she was a student at St. Frances de Sales High School near Richmond. One day one of her teachers, a German nun, studied Louise closely and asked her, "Are you German?" When she had the opportunity, Louise asked her mother Elenora, who replied, "*Of course* you're German!" But more she did not say.

Billy Sparrow around 1905, moved into the little house directly across from his sister. With the fall of the Readjustor faction, he had lost his job as customs inspector. Instead of reopening his shoe shop, he opened a butcher shop. Like other members of the family, he seems to have fallen on hard times. He sold his house and other properties on Bute Street and moved into rented quarters on Brewer Street. He left the butchering business to take up again his old trade of making and repairing shoes. His final years were tragic. Little was handed down in the family about his wife Frances, who died July 22, 1902, at 54, of "debility and internal hemorrhaging."[195] By then Billy was alienated from nearly all his children.[196] He had 11, of whom three—Ben, Martha, and Franklin—had died young. The others scattered away from Norfolk and most apparently did not even associate with each other. William, Jr. and Van Buren (Vannie) became a printers in New York City. Gertrude (Gertie), a milliner, went to Philadelphia and married William Glass Williams, an eccentric upholsterer. Caulbert Sparrow also went to New York. Ophelia lived for a time in Philadelphia. Only daughters Estelle and Lillian remained in the Norfolk area. Estelle in 1902 married a black banker named Thomas Jefferson Harris, but died three years later, at 25, shortly after the birth of a daughter.[197] Lillian married William Henry Ballentine, who ran a cleaning and pressing business, and went to live across the river at Portsmouth. The Ballentines were evidently relatively prosperous and were able to send at least two of their three children to college. "Miss Lil" has been described as a "pert" woman of aristocratic bearing who "looked just like white."[198]

After the death of his wife, William H. Sparrow moved into what has been described as a "shack" across the street from Dodie, where he set up his shop as well as his home. His behavior grew bizarre. One day he deliberately set his shack on fire, but neighbors extinguished the blaze before any major damage was done. By then the old shoemaker was wont to go about town dressed only in his nightshirt and a top hat, carrying over one should a string on which he dragged behind him a tin can.[199] Indeed, according to a grandniece, "Poor Uncle Billy lost his mind." His niece Blanche Kemp, who was one of the few people who could get along with him told her son that Uncle Billy suffered to "locomotor ataxia", a type of paralysis often associated with the late stages of syphilis[200] Elinor Robinson Waller insisted that Uncle Billy most likely had Parkinson's Disease. Eventually Dodie moved Billy across the street to her home, where she nursed him until he died in 1908 or 1909.[201] He was about 64.

Dodie was left with but one remaining sibling, Martha Brock, who had lived in New York City for many years. Elinor Waller insisted that Martha, or "Mattie", and her husband "Uncle Brock" were very well off and that he managed several white apartment buildings. The census of 1900 identifies William H. Brock as a "janitor" and indicates that he and wife Martha lived in the all-white residence that he tended. The couple was childless, and, unlike most women of her class and generation, Martha apparently did not work for a living. Waller recalled family tradition—probably received from her grandmother, that Martha was devoted to her husband, who was secretly unfaithful. When she finally learned the truth, she was so devastated that she wasted away to "die of a broken heart." (Her death certificate states that her demise occurred January 29, 1910, at 151 W. 133d Street and gives the cause as "chronic nephritis, uremic coma, and exhaustion," after a two month illness.) She was 57 (although her death certificate gives her age as 49). After a funeral at St. Mark's African Methodist Episcopal Church in Harlem, the body was shipped back to Norfolk and placed in an unmarked grave at Calvary.

Dodie was now the head of a growing family that, by 1900 included five grandchildren and by 1910 eight. Since separating from Frank, she worked as a washwoman, taking in laundry, assisted by her daughters, who came to be known in the community as "The Five Beautiful Girls."

The oldest was Elenora Virginia, who as a teenager changed her name to "Eleanor" and then, in old age, to "Elnora", was called "Nonie." According to family tradition she was "the most beautiful girl in Norfolk." She had black hair and skin so fair that he could "pass" if she so desired, and possessed a beautiful soprano voice. Although she never graduated from high school, she impressed most of those who met her as highly educated. Nephew Bernard Ruffin was sure that she was a college graduate. As a young woman she modeled for a cigarette card. (In those days tobacco companies often enclosed photographs of pretty girls as well as baseball players in their cigarette packages.) In 1969, 92 year old Dudley Tucker recalled that Nonie was shown in a long skirt with a basket under her arm and her foot on a drum. Waller similarly recounted that "Aunt Nonie was so pretty that they put her on baseball cards." One wonders if the tobacco company that featured Nonie was the one owned by her grandfather, which was probably still in operation in the early 1890s.

While still in her teens, Nonie married Samuel Joseph Jackson, the 20 year old son of a Charleston, South Carolina caterer. Their first child, Mary Louise, named after her grandmother, was born the next year. She was followed two years later by Allan and three years after that by Florence.[202] The Jacksons went to live in New York, where they worked as servants in a private home. Samuel Jackson seems to have been improvident and irresponsible and the children seemed to have spent most of their time in Norfolk with their grandmother. Shortly after the turn of the century Nonie was separated, perhaps divorced, from Jackson, and moved back to Norfolk, renting an apartment on Princess Anne Road in Norfolk, a few blocks from her mother. From time to time, various family members, including "Grandma Lydie" would live with Nonie.

Samuel Jackson remained in New York. His daughter Louise had only one memory of her him, and that was not pleasant. She remembered a dandified brown-skinned man who did not want her to sit on his lap, for fear she would spoil his clothes. She also recalled how her mother once directed her to write her father for money for shoes, who answered his daughter that he would send the funds "when the good times come."[203]

The second Kemp daughter, Caledonia, was first called "Callie" and then, later in life, "Carrie." She also went to New York, where, in March, 1896, she married Benjamin James, Jr. Caledonia worked as a stewardess on the Old Dominion Line of steamboats,[204] which conveyed passengers between New York and the cities of Tidewater Virginia and seems to have spent part of the year at an apartment at 42. W. 135th Street and part at home. She had three sons, who seem to have been born in Norfolk and raised by their grandmother. Only one of them, William, seems to have lived to adulthood..[205] No anecdotes about Caledonia's personality survive. Louise Elliott recalled her as tall, stout, regal woman, magnificently dressed. The only surviving photograph shoes a buxom young woman clad a low-cut dress unusually revealing for the 1890s.

It is not clear whether Benjamin James died or whether there was a separation or divorce, but, according to Elinor Waller and Bernard Ruffin, Jr., Caledonia married again to a waiter on a ship named Jim Jones, allegedly a very fat man who "ate himself to death." There was at least one child, James D. Jones, born to this union.[206] According to both Louise Elliott Carrie "was really married to a white man." Since her marriage license to James states that he was "colored", the "white husband" must have been Jones. No record of that wedding has as yet been uncovered. Carrie died between 1906 and 1910. According to Waller, who never saw her, "Aunt Carrie" was very large and grew "so big and fat that her kidneys failed." Both Waller and Elliott insisted that Caledonia died in New York, but the five boroughs of that city, which were keeping fairly complete records by the early 1900s, have no record of that event.

The third daughter, Mattie, was regarded as the "black sheep of the family." According to Waller Mattie was "wayward" from childhood. Louise Elliott and Bernard Ruffin described Mattie as light in complexion. Waller said that Mattie's skin was "yellowish" and George Elliott insisted that alone of her family, she "wasn't very pretty." Dudley Tucker, who dated Mattie when they were teenagers, recalled that at the time she was a "beautiful girl" who "looked just like white," but that when he saw her many years later she had become "as big as all outdoors."

Mattie's marital history is virtually impossible to trace. At various times she was known as Mattie Smith, Mattie Brock, and Mattie Young, but when her marriage to John Anderson was recorded in Norfolk when she was nearly 40, she is described as "single." It is not clear whether she was ever married to Joseph Walton Brock, a man six years her junior, by whom she had her only child, a girl named Janice Meredith, who was raised by her grandmother and variously known under the surnames of Kemp, Brock, and Young before her marriage to Harry Ogburn in the 1930s.

The U.S. Census of 1910 lists one Mattie Smith as "the keeping of a boarding house" at 106 Mayo Street in Richmond. Her lodgers, who include her sister, Emma Kemp, were all young women in their teens and '20s.[207]

Mattie Kemp was constantly in trouble with the law. In response to an inquiry in the 1960s, the Norfolk Police Department stated that their books recorded "numerous" arrests for Mattie Kemp, a.k.a. Mattie Anderson, between 1908 and 1923, but "because of the old way of keeping records" the offenses for which she was arrested were not recorded.[208] Bernard Ruffin insisted that she was continually arrested for prostitution and petty larceny. When questioned, Waller and the Elliotts maintained a stony silence.

Norfolk's Common Law Order Books list only two arrests which ended in a trial. Early in 1908 30 year old Mattie Kemp "stood charged with robbery from the person" and was "duly recognized in the sum of five hundred dollars with Mary L. Bass, surety, who justified her sufficiency on oath, conditioned for the appearance of the aforesaid Mattie Kemp in the Corporation Court" on March 2.[209] Indicted on charges of grand larceny, however, Mattie was found not guilty. She was not so lucky in January, 1921, when she was charged with "not being of good fame and keeping a house of prostitution." She was sentenced to one month in jail and a fifty dollar fine.[210]

Marian Elliott Bess, whose brother George married Nonie's daughter Louise and who knew the family well, recalled that Mattie was "coarse and rough" with "an Italian complexion" and "very fat." She danced at a club— "and you know what kind of club that was!"— located "near the cemetery" in Norfolk that was frequented with sailors. Mattie, whose hair fell to her feet, used to dance completely naked on top of the tables, covering the intimate parts of her body with her tresses,

Bess recalled.[211]

Louise Elliott recalled that shortly after her marriage in 1917 she took off her diamond ring to do some household chores. Mattie, who was then living with her husband John Anderson in the apartment above George and Louise on Lexington Avenue came to see her niece. Louise had taken her ring from her finger and left it in the living room in full view of Mattie, whom she left for a few minutes. When she returned, both Mattie and the ring were gone. Several weeks later Mattie staggered in, "drunk, of course," slobbering that she had sold the ring. "I'm sorry, I'm sorry," she said, "I just needed the money." Louise informed her aunt severely, "Aunt Mattie, I know you're my aunt, but I don't want you to set foot in my home again!"[212] "Mattie was the worst child Dodie ever had," Louise Elliott declared. "I hope she called on the Lord for mercy before she died." [213]

The fourth daughter, Emma Maud Kemp, on her eighteenth birthday married a 29 year old fisherman and bartender named George William Gatling. Marian Bess remembered that Dodie, who encouraged her daughters to seek white partners, disliked her brown-skinned son-in-law. The U.S. Census of 1900 shows the newlyweds George and Emma Gatling living in an apartment a few doors away from Dodie. A few years later, Emma returned to her mother's house, where, according to Bess, Dodie periodically allowed Gatling to "visit" her. According to Louise Elliott Emma moved to West Virginia and married a second time. "At least she *told me* she was married." No record has been located of the marriage. After her return to Norfolk, Emma once again became the nominal wife of George Gatling. According to Elliott, Emma, a beautiful girl, could not resist the advances of the white men who corrupted her.

Unlike her siblings, Emma was brown-skinned. According to her grandniece, Dorothy Goude Bryant (b. 1919), Emma's complexion was "a beautiful, smooth, red brown." Everyone who remembered her recalled Emma's hair as long, straight, and black— "flat-straight, Japanese hair," as nephew Ruffin put it. He also described Aunt Emma as an extremely fat woman with unusually large legs, "a rough-talking woman, constantly smoking." George Elliott likewise recalled Emma as a prodigious smoker, like her sister Blanche. Marian Elliott Bess' recollections were: "Emma was a very beautiful woman. She was short and very fat in late years. She was very Italian. She danced naked when she was young. In later years she did nothing."

Louise Elliott recalled that later in life, Emma, who had led "a public life", was "converted" and afterwards led a blameless, respectable existence. Whereas she and her husband remembered Mattie with disgust, Elliott had fond memories of Aunt Emma, who was jolly, friendly, and extremely fond of children.

Blanche, or "Beppie", was just 13 when her father died. Smaller and slighter than her sisters, according to Helen Ogle Atkins (b.1908) family friend, "she had a bright physical beauty and looked just like a gypsy."[214] Another friend, Sara Davis Taylor (1898-1993) insisted that Beppie "looked just like an Indian."[215] She had a broad face and her black almond-shaped eyes, which her son called "sloe eyes", led some to mistake her for an Asian. Her soft black hair with just the trace of a curl, contrasted with the severely straight hair of sister Emma.

When Beppie Kemp was 14 she was the object of the romantic attentions of Walter Scott Robinson, a 22 year old white grocer who lived on the corner of Johnson Avenue, which intersected O'Keefe near the Kemp-Bass home. Little is known of Robinson. His daughter Elinor was convinced that he was born in Edinburgh, Scotland, but the censuses of 1900 and 1920 give his place of birth as "Virginia." In 1900 he was the head of a large household which included his widowed mother Elizabeth, also a Virginia native, two younger brothers, George and William, and several sisters. According to the census, Walter's father was born in England. Ruffin once said that Robinson was a Jew, but later denied it.

Unlike the men who exploited Mattie and Emma, Walter Robinson (who was single as late as 1920) truly loved Beppie and, at least according to their daughter, considered her his wife—according to Marian Bess, "He kept her good." On September 5, 1899 Beppie gave birth to a daughter Viola, whom she named for a popular actress. Robinson acknowledged her. Although Viola is listed as "Kemp" in the 1910 census, she and her younger sister always used their father's surname. According to Waller, her mother and Robinson never lived together, but he made frequent trips to the house and provided financially for his children.

Beppie worked as a seamstress and lived at home until she was in her late twenties. No doubt she learned her trade at the Mission College, which she evidently attended until her pregnancy. According to her daughter, she was an intelligent woman, dignified, and a lover fine clothing and the theatre. Waller recounted how her mother, dressed like a great lady with a stylish cape in a dress of taffeta trimmed with lace, would ride on the back of the trolley to one of Norfolk's theatres, there to sit in the upstairs "peanut gallery" reserved for persons of color, to watch the plays and operettas she loved so well.

Franklin Benjamin Kemp, the youngest child and only surviving son, was entirely European in appearance, with white skin and green eyes. No anecdotes have survived about his personality as a boy or young man. His appearance, as she shall see, would shape the course of his life.

Chapter Thirteen

There is no record as to how Dodie and her family reacted to the events of the day. There is no indication as to what they thought about the Spanish-American War, the assassination of President McKinley, the administration of Theodore Roosevelt, or the worsening of the racial situation. No diaries, letters, or papers survive. What is known for certain, thanks to the recollections of Elinor Waller and Louise Elliott, is Dodie's devotion to her grandchildren. Four of them made their permanent home with her: William James (Caledonia's son), born in 1896; Viola and Elinor Robinson (Beppie's daughters), born in 1899 and 1907; and Janice (Mattie's daughter), born in 1903. Dodie seems to have reared Nonie's children for a while, but since Nonie's return to Norfolk, Louise, Allan, and Florence lived with their mother a few blocks away.

Waller insisted, "Dodie had high ambitions for her grandchildren. She was determined that we were going to have a nice home. She was determined that we were going to succeed in life. She was determined that we were going to get an education. She saw to it that we had reading materials and study periods. She even set up a little classroom with a blackboard and desks."[216]

Waller described the house on O'Keefe Street as "small" but "well-kept" and "well-furnished." Her brother, Bernard Ruffin recalled that 1416 O'Keefe Street was wired for electricity on the ground floor, but not upstairs. Although he once said that his aunts "sat on cracker barrels", according to Waller the house was full of "fine Victorian furniture, satin draperies, china, painting, and bric-a-brac." There was fine silverware and numerous family portraits, some of which sat on easels in the parlor. Recalling her childhood, she continued: "We children had adequate backyard place space. We always had pet dogs and cats. The children and family trained them to do tricks. We had one cat we taught to walk the clothesline. We had a goat named Billy whom we taught to pull us around in a little cart. We rigged up a shoot-the-shoot, a little roller-coaster, on the woodshed. I had a dollhouse there in the woodshed. We always had lovely toys. My sister Viola was given piano lessons. We dressed well because our mother sewed and made most of our clothes. We were also exposed to the theatre, as they call stage plays in those days, but we had to sit in the peanut gallery."

On race relations, Waller recalled, "Parents did not discuss race at all. If you asked questions about segregation, you would be shut up and told you would understand some day. We were never deprived. There was always plenty of food and clothing. We had a happy life. Everything was segregated. We could not go to the restaurants. In the theatres, if there was no peanut gallery, we could not go in. The street cars were segregated. Negroes could not try on clothes in the best stores. That is why my mother made so many of our clothes. But Negroes were by no means bitter. They accepted it. They took it as their lot. They had to. They had no choice. They could do nothing about it. They were not unhappy. The white people for whom the Negroes worked were usually very kind. If any Negro in the community got into trouble, his white employers would always go to the judge and pay his fine and get him out."

Dodie's brood apparently did not socialize much in the community. As mulattoes or "yellow niggers" they were not entirely accepted by the general "black community." In appearance, in manners, in speech, in culture, they had more in common with the whites who shunned them. Marian Bess recalled that "black" children would curse "yellow" and pelt them with stones. Her brother, George Elliott, who worked as a letter carrier for many years, recalled being accosted once by a dark-skinned man who snarled at him, denouncing him as "a yellow nigger", adding, "I hate yellow niggers!" Perhaps this led to the intense dislike of black people that characterized Dodie in later years.

Elinor's feelings about her father were different from those of her elder sister did. Viola, she said, hated Robinson. Whereas Vie seemed unwelcome in the store, her father received Elinor with great affection.

According to Waller, around 1912 Walter Robinson asked Blanche to accompany him to New York, where they could be legally man and wife. For some reason she refused. Marian Bess recalled, "He wanted to marry her, but she was unwilling." One day Elinor went to the store to see her father and he was not there, nor was he at home. Nobody seemed to know where he was. The five year old was in a daze. She set off looking in vain for her father through the streets of Norfolk. She stopped eating. For a time Dodie and Beppie feared for the child's life. Elinor neither saw her father nor heard from him for the rest of her life.

She later learned that her father had gone to New York, but was never able or willing to track him down. The census of 1920, which became public long after Waller's death, reveals that Walter S. Robinson, still single, was indeed living with relatives in New York, at 107 Henry Street in Brooklyn. No subsequent record of his life has surfaced. He seems to have made no effort to re-establish contact with his colored family.

Exactly why Blanche chose to break off her relationship with Walter Robinson is unclear. It seems fairly certain, however, that by the time of her break with him, Blanche Kemp was in love with Caulbert Bernard Ruffin, a former neighbor, five years her senior.

"Mr. Ruffin" (nobody except his oldest friends addressed him familiarly) was one of Norfolk's Negro aristocracy. His family was more educated and more influential than the Kemps. His paternal aunt, Mary Ruffin Keeling, helped in the foundation of the Norfolk Mission College. His mother's brother, Richard L. (Tobe) Langley was the proprietor of a saloon, and his brick house and carriage marked him as one of Norfolk's most prosperous blacks.[217] A first cousin, Lemuel (Lem) Bright, owned an ocean side hotel where such nationally prominent Negroes as Booker T. Washington stayed when they were in the Norfolk area.[218] Caulbert Ruffin's sister, Adela Frances Ruffin was a prominent educator who, from 1899 until around 1912 served as teacher and "Lady Principal" at the Slater Industrial State and Normal School (now Winston-Salem State University) in Winston-Salem, North Carolina.

Ruffin's paternal grandmother, Elizabeth Cornick Ruffin was the slave of a Norfolk attorney, John Camp and his wife, the former Ann Cornick (the original owner of Elizabeth's grandmother Hannah Cornick). When the widow Ann Camp died in August, 1848 she left a will in which she manumitted her dozen or so slaves as well as directed that all her assets be sold so that each of the women would be guaranteed a small annual income for life.[219] Among the newly freed Camp slaves were Elizabeth Ruffin and her three children, William Henry, age four, Mary Jane, age 2, and Ottaway Francis, Jr., age six months.

According to the register of free Negroes, Elizabeth Ruffin was of "black" complexion and only 4'9" tall.[220] According to family tradition, she was one of the organizers of what later became Norfolk's Bank Street Memorial Baptist Church.[221] Elizabeth became active in the Underground Railroad, hiding slaves escaping from the South in her apartment until they could be smuggled aboard ships headed for Canada.[222] Her husband, Ottaway Francis Ruffin, Sr., who according to family tradition was a Powhatan Indian nearly seven feet tall,[223] never served the Cornick-Camp family. He is not listed with his wife and children in the censuses of 1850 and 1860, which suggests that he was a slave who belonged to another owner or a free man who escaped the notice of the census enumerator. He appears in the 1870 census as a "black" laborer.

Ottaway Ruffin, Jr. was said to have been "the most peculiar man who ever lived,"[224] a man who hated children, stayed to himself, associated only with "a few old-timey friends," and did not attend church or even believe in God.[225] Dudley Tucker remembered him as a handsome, heavily built man with a severely trimmed moustache. A relative of his wife remembered him as a short, heavy, dark-brown-skinned man.[226] Both Ottaway and his brother William were trained as barbers, but during the Readjustor period Ottaway worked as a clerk in the post office. In later years he gave up or lost his post office job and, according to Dudley Tucker, became a "sporting man", moving from Norfolk City across Princess Anne Road to Norfolk County, to operate a "policy game", which was legal there at the time.

Ottaway and his wife, Elizabeth Langley, never had a home of their own and always lived with relatives, first in a multiple-family household (similar to that of the Kemps on Fenchurch Street) on Cumberland Street with his parents, his aunt, his sister, Mary Keeling, and her husband and three children. After about 1880 he lived with his wife's sister, Louisa (Lula) Langley Reed and her husband William Jefferson Reed.

Ottaway's wife and Caulbert's mother, Annie Elizabeth Langley, described as a "mulatto" in the 1870 census in contrast to her "black" husband, was described by a niece as warm, outgoing, sweet-natured intelligent, sociable, and a devout member of St. John's AME Church.[227]

After attending the Cumberland Street Grammar School, "Collie" Ruffin went to college. Where is not entirely certain. Bernard, Jr. once said that his father was a graduate of "Knox College." Knox College in Illinois has no record of a Caulbert Bernard Ruffin; neither does Knoxville College in Knoxville, Tennessee, which, unlike Knox College in Illinois, was founded to offer education to Negro students. Another time Bernard, Jr. said his father went to Kittrell College, a now-defunct black school in North Carolina which offered both high school and college curricula. Caulbert's first cousin, Lula Norris, taught there at the time. According to the North Carolina State Archives, there is likewise no record of Caulbert Bernard Ruffin attending either the college or high school. However, their records for the college prior to the 1950s "are very incomplete" and non-existent before 1898.[228] . So it is quite possible that Caulbert was a graduate of Kittrell. He is listed in the Norfolk city directories without an occupation between 1898 and 1901, and this quite possibly indicates that he was in fact in school somewhere at the time. There is also a strong tradition that he studied for the ministry. Dudley Tucker said that he went away to Hattiesville, Georgia to study for the Baptist ministry and remembered seeing him in his ministerial robes. Bernard, Jr. said that his father studied for the Presbyterian ministry, which would seem likely in light of Adela's denominational affiliation and the fact that Tucker recalled that it was she, a woman "as religious as they come", who pressed her brother to enter the ministry. Neither Bernard, Jr. nor anyone else was certain of the name of the place where he studied for the ministry. Perhaps Kittrell College offered a ministerial course at the time.

According to Tucker, just before his planned ordination, "Something happened." Just what this was, no one seemed to know. Tucker believed that his friend simply lost his faith. Ruffin's stepdaughter, Elinor Waller, recalled him saying, "I realized I was too big of a devil to go into the ministry." Certainly, in later life, according to his son, C.B. Ruffin was "irreligious." Tucker recalled that he would sometimes attack the Bible as a collection of inconsistent myths and remembered a conversation in which he ridiculed the account of Creation in Genesis.

C.B. Ruffin's hostility to Christianity set him apart from most people in his community. According to George Elliott, during his boyhood there were just two colored people in Norfolk who openly denied the existence of God: Caulbert Ruffin and his uncle, Tobe Langley. To that list Ruffin's cousin Margaret Saunders Manning (1887-1987) added a third: Ottaway Ruffin.

Cousin Margaret, interviewed in her 101st year, remembered that both Caulbert and his father were strange individuals who did not work for a living. That is not entirely true, because Ottaway evidently made a living through the "numbers" business, and Caulbert, after about 1902, at least part-time, tended bar for his uncle, Tobe Langley and at an establishment owned by "Carmine and Creekmore." Much of his time, however, according to Cousin Mag, he spent reading and playing chess, a game at which he was so proficient that he was in Washington later known as "The Colored People's Champion."

Caulbert Ruffin, Sr. or C. Bernard Ruffin, as he sometimes called himself, was about 5'10" tall, with a complexion that has been variously described as "yellow", "light," "tan", and "red" with a sharp, pointed nose, grey eyes, and reddish hair which his son characterized as "so bad it carried pistols." In his prime he weighed about 230 pounds, with a large abdomen and thin legs. Foul mouthed—his stepdaughter said he "swore like a sailor"—he, like his father, associated with a handful of cronies. Few who remembered him liked him and most thought of him as cold, unsocial, and eccentric. The son of a friend, observed, however, "He wasn't eccentric, he was just *different*."

Blanche Kemp had apparently known Caulbert Ruffin for many years. She and her family had already been living on O'Keefe Street when, shortly after the death of his mother, fourteen year old Caulbert and his father moved in with William and Louisa Reed around the corner in a rented house at 15 Washington Avenue.

It is not clear how Caulbert and Blanche became romantically involved. Tucker recalled that his friends were shocked, because until then Ruffin had shown little interest in women. At that time, Tucker, recalled, his normally serious friend grew cheerful and even penned little verses, two of which he recalled after an interval of nearly six decades:
"I rescued a maid from a villain's clutch
The maiden thanked me very much."
"I do not care to claim elation
The incident happened at Union Station."

Ottaway Ruffin had died at 59 on October 15, 1907, of pleurisy, which he allegedly contracted from watching a baseball game in the rain, and Caulbert continued to live at the house on Washington Avenue with his aunt and uncle. In 1912, shortly after Aunt Lula died, Caulbert obtained a job with the federal government as a railway mail clerk. Considered one of the very best jobs then available to persons of color, it involved the sorting of mail on trains. It also necessitated a move to Washington. It was here that Blanche joined him, probably in the autumn of 1912, just before the two were married there on October 23, 1912.

Two years after their marriage, Blanche presented her husband with his first and only and her third and last child, Caulbert Bernard Ruffin, Jr., always known as Bernard (with the emphasis on the first syllable). Blanche returned to Norfolk to give birth at 1416 O'Keefe, where his birth was registered with the Norfolk Department of Health as "Caulbert Ruffin, Jr." When he was five weeks old she returned to Washington with the baby.

Chapter Fourteen

Until now we have traced the fortunes of all of Dodie's six children except for the youngest, Franklin Benjamin, who had an interesting fate. Frank, as he was called, had, like his siblings, attended Norfolk Mission College, probably through the eighth grade. He was a handsome man, six feet two inches in height and never weighing more than a trim 185, with absolutely no features usually associated with negritude. Like his sisters Nonie and Caledonia he went to New York to work. There nobody assumed that he was anything other than white. He worked as a chauffeur and soon was hired long-term by wealthy families to drive their limousines, often when they vacationed in different areas of the country. Later he became a truck mechanic, opening his own garage on the West Side of Manhattan.

Late in 1914 Frank's white girlfriend, Maud Cornell, became pregnant, and in April he married her. There was one complication: he had never informed her that he was "colored" and her family were evidently intense negrophobes. And thus, quite by accident, Frank Kemp was forced to "pass" for white and avoid almost all contact with his family.

Up to that point, Frank had made regular trips to Norfolk to see his family. After that he was able to return only once. Marian Bess recalled that Frank brought his wife to Norfolk and introduced her to every member of her family without arousing in her any suspicion of his Negro blood. That account seems unlikely, even if Frank introduced Maud only to the lighter members of his family, because Frank's family lived in a neighborhood that was then predominantly "colored." Louise Elliott insisted that Frank came alone. When he sat down at his mother's table, Elliott recalled, he burst into tears, said he never intended to "pass", and lamented his terrible situation.

According to Elinor Waller, "Only Aunt Nonie was able to go up to see Uncle Frank, because she was the only one able to pass for white." Apparently there must have been some contact—at least by mail—with Blanche as well. Elinor, whose appearance was entirely northern European, once said, "Uncle Frank asked my mother [Blanche] if I could go up to live with him, but she said, 'No.'" Frank's daughter, Eleanor Virginia, never remembered seeing any of her father's relatives. However, when Frank came to die, his widow knew at once who to contact.

Although Nonie had white skin and straight black hair, her features were not as aquiline as those of her brother, and her visits may have been the occasion of a remark that Frank recounted during his visit to Norfolk. During a family dinner a brother of his wife violently denounced the Negro race, then turned to Frank and glowered as he held up a carving knife and said with frightening malice, "I'm glad there's no colored blood in *our* family. If I thought there was any colored blood in my family, I would take a knife and let that blood out!"[229]

Chapter Fifteen

Caulbert Ruffin evidently did not believe in remaining at the same address for longer than a year or two, and, shortly after Bernard was born he and Blanche rented a house at 1754 T Street, N.W. The following year they moved to 922 Westminister Street, N.W[230]., which they shared with Cousin Gertie Williams and her family.

Gertrude Lillian Sparrow (1871-1944) was the daughter of William Sparrow, Dodie's brother and was thirteen years older than Blanche. Gertie told her daughter-in-law Marie Madden Williams Ford (1901-1997) that she left home at an early age. According to Ford, Gertie, who was "short and plump" and "neither light nor dark", her brothers were so light and handsome that she felt that there was no place for her at home—whatever that meant. So she left home, never to return, at an early age, and by 1893 she was living at 1318 Carpenter Street in Philadelphia, working as a milliner, or hat-maker, and married to an upholsterer by the name of William Glass Williams (1871-1941), who was as eccentric as her father.

Williams was born in Stonington, Connecticut, the son of a laborer by the name of Daniel Williams, who gave his place of birth at various times as Virginia, Maryland, and Pennsylvania, and his wife, the former Harriet Simons, who was a native of Connecticut[231]. In later years, William G. Williams would claim that his family were whalers from the island of Tristan da Cunha, in the Atlantic. According the census records of 1880, the parents of both Daniel (c.1854-1900) and Harriet Williams (c.1857-1908) were born in the United States.

Around the time that Harriet's father, Russell Simons, a 65 year old day laborer, was found horribly and fatally burned in his bed in March, 1888, Daniel and Harriet Williams and their children moved from Stonington to Philadelphia. For some strange reason, they changed their names. Daniel took the name Robert Armstrong Williams and Harriet changed her name to Eliza![232]

William and Gertie had three sons: William Glass (1894-1907), Oswald Sparrow (1897-1957), and Robert Armstrong Williams (1899-1974). Around 1907, 13 year old William, on a family excursion to the zoo, was run over by a streetcar, which severed his legs and killed him. The family immediately left Philadelphia for Washington. The parents never spoke of the child and the accident again.

The Williamses had been Episcopalian, but Gertie became a Christian Science practitioner, who was reputed to have cured many patients, accepting little in the way of remuneration. Daughter-in- law Marie Madden Ford said, "She had a pleasant countenance and a subtle smile, and there was nothing about her that wasn't faith, sweetness, and light." Her husband, William, on the other hand, she described as an "infuriating" man with a violent temper, who made his wife permanently lame by throwing her down a flight of stairs.

The combined Ruffin-Williams family unit, with the two eccentric fathers, did not work out well, and Gertie's son Robert blamed this on Ruffin, whom he characterized as impossible to live with. Shortly afterwards Gertie ran away to Chicago with a student from Howard University who had been a classmate of one of her sons.[233]

Bernard Ruffin, Jr. told his son that his parents separated when he was a young boy and his mother took him back to Norfolk. This must have been in late 1916 or early 1917, for, on March 3, 1917 Blanche joined the First United Presbyterian Church of Norfolk[234], which had been organized by the same people who ran the Mission College and which stood on the college grounds. It is not known whether Blanche had been active in any church before, but, since she was not baptized at First United Presbyterian, one would assume that she had been christened as a child at St. John's AME.

It is not clear how long Blanche stayed in Norfolk. It was probably not for long. The Mission College had recently closed and Blanche, unimpressed with Norfolk's segregated schools, brought her two daughters to Washington, where the elder, Viola or "Sissie" attended Dunbar High School, from which she was graduated in 1918. Because it seems likely that she would have completed at least a year there, it would seem likely that Blanche and Vie and probably Bernard were back in Washington by the fall of 1917. Elinor, on the other hand, was still living in Norfolk in November, 1917.

Blanche continued to spend summers at Norfolk, not only at the home or her mother but also at the residence of her sister Elenora (Nonie) at Garden City, near Hampton. At about the age of 30, Nonie had become interested in the Roman Catholic Church. Although she never became a Catholic, in 1907 she had her oldest daughter Louise, then a teenager, baptized at the Church of St. Joseph in Norfolk and then sent her to the St. Francis de Sales boarding school for Negro girls at Rock Castle, Virginia. Shortly afterwards, however, Nonie, became a

Seventh Day Adventist, and would observe zealously the tenets of that communion for the rest of her life. Louise remained a devout Catholic, but Allan and Florence, Nonie's younger children, to their mother's great disappointment, displayed little if any interest in any sort of religion.

Nonie, probably after the death of her first husband Samuel Jackson in 1914, married a steam engineer at the Newport News Shipyards by the name of George H. Manners and the two moved into a large country house on Shell Road, near Garden City. Blanche and her children considered Nonie's place their summer home. Despite a ten year age difference, Nonie and Blanche were extremely close, closer to each other than either were to the middle sisters Mattie and Emma.

Still part of the family circle was "Grandma Lydie" Kemp, who lived next door to Dodie. Although he was only three when she died, Bernard Ruffin, Jr. retained throughout life a vivid image of his great-grandmother, the "oldest and darkest" person he had ever seen, who made delicious sponge cakes called "lady-fingers." Elinor Waller recalled Lydia as "fine-looking mulatto woman", short and petite. "She looked like an East Indian, with a lovely creole complexion and long, soft, black hair." Louise Elliott remembered her as lively and energetic, always enthusiastic and full of life. "Grandma Lydie" worked as a maid for a private family on "The P'int", or Point, a section of Norfolk, formally known as Ghent, where well-to-do white citizens (including many Greenwood descendants) lived. Lydia still experimented with medicines she made from the jimson weed, and Waller recalled that there was talk of patenting one of her concoctions. A devout member of St. John's, she spent a good part of her day distributed Bibles and tracts and cornering passersby on street corners in an attempt to persuade them to give their lives to Christ as Saviour. Still active and vigorous at 80, she was evangelizing in front of a little church on Johnson Avenue, around the corner from her home, when, one warm November morning in 1917, she suffered a heart attack or stroke and died. Great-granddaughter Elinor was passing by on the other side of the street when she saw a crowd of people gathering. Someone told her, "Your grandmother is very sick."

America was now at war with Germany. Bernard Ruffin remembered soldiers marching (probably during the summer of 1918) down Shell Road, past Aunt Nonie's house, headed for ships that would take them to the battlefields of Europe. Only single men were subject to the draft and the only family member affected was Nonie's son Allan Jackson, who served as a cook in the Navy. While serving on a ship at the Norfolk Naval Base, he jumped overboard to rescue a white sailor who had fallen into the water. and was drowning.[235] According to his sister Louise, he was deeply embittered that the Navy failed to recognize his act of heroism.

By the fall of 1918 Blanche and Caulbert were renting a house at 140 Seaton Street, N.W. in Washington, where they would continue to live for two years. All three children were apparently with her. Viola, after graduation from high school, enrolled at the Minor Normal School, which, for six dollars a semester or less[236], offered a two year course which certified colored women to teach in the D.C. Public Schools.

Around the time the war ended, the District, like nearly every other city or town in the world, was gripped by an epidemic of an especially virulent strain of influenza known as the "Spanish Flu". Schools and businesses were closed. Bernard, Jr. recalled one local theatre which remain opened and tried to attract patrons by quoting public health officers who warned people to avoid crowded places, adding that their theatre was the place to go to follow such advice, because, "There's nobody here!" Helen Irene Ogle Atkins (b. 1908), who would become Elinor's best friend, recalled, " We all wore those little asafoetida bags around our neck and they stunk like I don't know what. I don't know what it was. It was something supposed to ward off germs. They smelled like the devil! I don't know how the teachers stood it! I remember Louise Whitehead in my class—her brother died from it. I think I had it but the old people didn't take you to the doctor then unless you were dying. They dosed you up and rubbed you down. I remember my cousin's wife said her mother was a so-called nurse and she got more work than she could do, working with these white people. She just said, "Just have a lot of whiskey." She kept them rubbed down and made them toddies and things and she didn't lose a patient. I wasn't scared. I didn't have sense enough to be scared!"[237] As far as is known, nobody in the Kemp clan was seriously affected by the flu.

The next summer race riots broke out in more than 20 cities, including Chicago, Omaha, Nebraska, Knoxville—and Washington, D.C. Racial tensions were high. They were not eased by President Woodrow Wilson, who replaced with white men African American government officials appointed by the previous Republican administrations and segregated all government lunch rooms and the toilets and working spaces of many federal offices.[238] News of Ku Klux Klan activities in Maryland and Virginia (a few years later the priest at the church in Norfolk where

Louise Elliott and her husband George were members was kidnapped and beaten by the Klan) and numerous lynchings of black citizens throughout the South added to the racial tension in Washington, which was exacerbated by some local newspapers, which, during the early summer of 1919 featured stories which repeated unfounded rumors of assaults on white women by black men. On Saturday July 19, 1919 a mob of white thugs stormed a black working class enclave southwest of the Capitol, near the waterfront, where they attacked any colored person who dared to cross their path. Joseph L. Drew (1909-1991), a native Washingtonian later a friend of Bernard Ruffin, Jr. recalled, "I remember the riot a little. The worst part was around 7th and Florida Avenue, where the Negroes got themselves together. A lot of them had guns...The 7th Street Streetcar line ran through there...and they turned over a couple of streetcars with people in them. There was a fight somewhere down near the Navy Yard. Then it spread up through Southwest and over to Foggy Bottom and that way and then up town. They were fighting about something. I don't know exactly what. The people were hungry, I guess. The soldiers...had come back and they got no respect. I think this was the bottom of it. They were still being called 'niggers' ...by the poor whites and I have an idea that this is more or less what kicked it off."[239]

Sunday saw more violence in several areas of the city. A furious mob of whites surged north on Seventh Street, N.W., towards the neighborhood around Howard University where affluent Negroes—as well as Blanche and her family—lived. Joe Drew recalled , "Georgia Avenue and 7th Street at Florida Avenue [7th Street turns into Georgia Avenue north of Florida], that's where they set up the barricade and told the white people, "Come across here if you want to. Don't come through here....Now my Dad was a fiery guy...He wanted to go out and my mother just put her foot down. She said, 'You stay right here!...Don't you go out!' He was ready to go."[240] There near Griffith Stadium, the old ball park at Seventh Street a force of more than 100 blacks hurled the mob back.[241] According to some reports, some Negro veterans mounted a machine gun atop Brown's Corner clothing store at 7th and T and fired on the rioters when they approached the barricades.[242]. Bernard remembered the barricades and said that his mother went there, perhaps to provide food and refreshment to the men who were making a successful defense of their neighborhood. After three days and the loss more than 40 lives, Wilson dispatched 2000 troops to take control of the city.

Drew recalled, "There were no winners, but I think the Negroes were a bit more respected because I thought they got the better of it."[243]

Chapter Sixteen

At the time that the Ruffins moved there, Washington, D.C. was considered the capital of America's "Negro Elite", the center, as one journalist put it, of "Negro 'bluebloods' and aristocrats."[244] Most of these people, who were sometimes referred to as the "Black 400" (after the Four Hundred of New York high society, over which Blanche's cousin Alva Smith Vanderbilt Belmont had for many years been queen), lived in handsome brick homes, often surrounded by books, paintings, fine furniture, and musical instruments and summered at exclusive Highland Beach, on the Chesapeake, near Annapolis, where they had elegant summer cottages.[245] These aristocrats, many of whom were doctors, lawyers, and business people, comprised but a tiny percent of Washington's colored population of about 100,000, most of whom worked as laborers, cooks, maids, janitors, laundry workers, or servants.

Helen Atkins recalled, "Beppie [Blanche] had her friends...but I don't think they were the ones who called themselves 'Society', but they were nice, respectable middle-class people. They weren't any riffraff."[246] Caulbert, on the other hand, was not a social person, and, according to Elinor, had only about "six or eight" friends. Although not a member of the "Elite", he had a very good job. He worked as a railway mail clerk, one of only about 300 black government "clerks" at a time when the overwhelming majority of African American federal employees were messengers and laborers.[247] According to Atkins, "The railway mail clerks made good money in those days, one of the best salaries a colored man could make. The railway mail clerks made more than the postmen."[248] Caulbert did not believe that women should work[249] and Blanche was now a housewife.

While Caulbert did not attend church, Blanche and her children attended the prestigious Fifteenth Street Presbyterian Church, which Viola joined in 1921. While not one of Washington's largest black congregations, Fifteenth Street Church, with about 350 members, was one of the most prestigious, the place (along with St. Luke's Episcopal and the Nineteenth Street Baptist) where the Negro intelligentsia worshipped. According to Marie Louise Taylor Primas (b. 1912), daughter of one of the pastors there, recalled, "The church was a large red building with winding steps that led up both sides of the building the [nave]...As you faced the front of the church, there was a big inscription,

'I was glad when they said unto me, Let us go into the House of the Lord.' That was up there in big, bold letters and it was very impressive."[250] The black newspaper, the *Washington Bee* claimed that the first step a socially ambitious newcomer to the Washington scene had to take was to seek membership there.[251] One observer noted, "The people dress, look, and behave precisely like nice white people, only some are black, and others shaded off from white."[252] A white visitor was startled to find in the congregation "women with lorgnettes", men with "pointed beards and button-hole bouquets" and youths "dressed like the best dressed young men on Fifth Avenue."[253]

Pastor for more than 40 years was the scholarly and forbidding graduate of Lincoln University and Princeton Theological Seminary, Francis James Grimké (1850-1937), the son of a slave and a wealthy Charleston, South Carolina planter. A small light-skinned, blue-eyed man with pince-nez spectacles Dr. Grimké gave learned sermons, often spiced with Latin, Greek, and Hebrew. Primas, recalled, "Dr. Grimké was sort of taciturn, stiff, and formal, not much of a 'hale-fellow-well-met.' I remember him in his black suit, black overcoat, and black umbrella as he came in and sat down. He looked like one of the other race with his narrow, pointed face."[254] Waller recalled that his sermons were so learned "that a lot of the people didn't understand what he was talking about." Although Grimké sometimes shook his fist when emphasizing a point and frequently warned of eternal perdition (Bernard said that the burden of most of his sermons was "If you sin you're going to hell and burn up" and Primas said he frequently spoke against the evils of strong drink) he never shouted or roared like the stereotypic "black" preacher. At Fifteenth Street shouting, clapping, swaying, and extravagant physical gestures were strongly discouraged. Although Bernard remembered one—and only one—old lady who used to wring her hands and ejaculate, "Oh, yes, Jesus, my Jesus!", he agreed with others who recalled that if someone had the bad manners to shout in Fifteenth Street Presbyterian Church, he or she would be quietly asked to leave.

In 1925 the Rev. Dr. Halley Blanton Taylor (1879-1965), a 46 year old native of Newburn, NC, who had earned his collegiate and divinity degrees at what was later Johnson Smith University, was called to Fifteenth Street Church. Although he performed all pastoral duties, he was accorded the title and pay of "Associate Pastor", while Dr. Grimké, who gave up all involvement except leading a Bible class and preaching every fourth Sunday, continued as "Pastor" until his death in 1937, by which time age and illness had long since made it impossible for him to attend at all.

Dr. Taylor, a fair-skinned man, had numerous freckles, and Bernard Ruffin., who was given to bestowing nicknames on everybody he knew, spoke of him as "One Freck." His sermons, based on Scriptural verses, focused on current affairs and the focus of his ministry was to fight racial segregation in the city, beginning with meetings of the local presbytery, which had frequently been held in hotels and institutions closed to blacks. His daughter said, "The presbytery had a habit of having meetings at hotels that did not cater to our folks at that time...My father let the Presbyterian ministers know that it was really wrong—absolutely wrong—to have meetings where all of their members were not welcome. So he changed those things...Papa fought segregation every step of the way."[255]

Blanche and her family lived comfortably in the 1920s. Helen Ogle met Elinor in 1921, the year both entered high school. More than seven decades later she recalled, "Elinor and I kind of took to each other. You know how when you meet somebody you kind of fit in? We became *the best of friends.*" She also remembered, "I used to go to Elinor's house and Elinor's mother was a good cook and a beautiful housekeeper and they would want me to stay for dinner and I wouldn't stay because in those days you were taught, 'You don't eat in anybody's house; you come home and get your dinner.' But one day Bepie took hold of me and and said, 'Sit down, Helen, at eat this dinner. You act like you think my food is dirty.' They knew I didn't have any mother—my mother had died when I was a baby—and they just took me in. They were always so nice and warm to me."[256] At the time she met Elinor, Viola, or "Sissie" was an adult, teaching, and Bernard was "a handsome little boy" who used "to meddle with our games, knock over things and get on our nerves."[257]

Atkins' recollections of Caulbert Ruffin were not so pleasant. "Mr. Ruffin was very silent," she declared. "He didn't talk much. You'd go in there and he would just bow to you and he didn't say anything and then he disappeared. He never talked to me. He was a kind of a light bronzed person. You know how fair people turn bronze-like when they get older? He didn't have much hair. If I remember, he was tall and kind of big—not fat, but broad, with big shoulders...He never said anything to me."[258] The family situation was not a particularly happy one because of Caulbert Ruffin's hostility toward his stepdaughters. While Bernard had all the clothing he wanted, until Viola was graduated from Miner in 1920 and started earning money as a teacher, Elinor had to wear "hand-me-down" dresses.

Elinor remembered her stepfather as an evil, menacing man with "gimlet eyes" who "swore like a sailor." Another friend of the family remembered him as a "sour" and "unfriendly." Sarah Davis Taylor, a friend of Viola and Elinor, recalled that Ruffin frequent put his meek wife down in front of their son, and privately spoke of her so as to destroy the boy's respect for his mother.

Caulbert Ruffin took his son to plays and concerts at the Belasco Theatre, across from the White House, which was one of the few downtown theatres (perhaps at that time the only one) which admitted blacks. Bernard remembered attending concerts by John McCormack, the Irish tenor, and Madame Ernest Schumann-Heink, the German contralto. On the other hand, Elinor recalled, "My stepfather never took me *anywhere* or did *anything* for me."

Caulbert instilled in Bernard a love of baseball, taking him frequently to Griffith Stadium to see the Washington Senators. In those days there was a close interaction between players and fans. Bernard recalled that relief pitchers used to warm up in the corridors under the stands. He came to talk to such standouts as Walter Johnson, Goose Goslin, and Joe Cronin. The latter—later the president of the American League— he said, believed it good luck to rub the head of a Negro boy and often asked his young black fans for that privilege. Bernard did not say whether he himself ever obliged him, but he did insist that he was in the stands on the October day in 1924 when Washington won its first and only World Series.

Caulbert Ruffin did not like to remain long at one address. In 1920 the family moved from Seaton Place to 1624 Swann Street, N.W. The following year they were at 729 Fairmont Street, then they moved to 243 N Street, behind Dunbar High School. They had to move from that home because the school bought the property to construct a stadium. Next they were on the 1000 block of Euclid Street, near Howard University, then in 1927 at 152 W Street, N.W., near the ball park. Caulbert always rented pleasant homes in pleasant areas in the Northwest quadrant of the city, where affluent Negroes lived, but he could not or would not purchase a home.

He hated wrist watches (he kept an old-fashioned railroad pocket watch), safety razors (he used an old-fashioned straight razor), and never paid bills until the day they were due, because he said, his son remembered, "I might die and not have to pay them." He did not believe in dancing, because that was a "niggerism." He did not want Bernard to play with dark-skinned children, whom he referred to as "boodaddies," and whipped him if he did. He did not believe in observing Christmas and permitted neither tree nor presents in his home. Bernard recalled, "The only thing I ever remember getting for Christmas was a yellow pencil." After Christmas, when stores had sales, he would take his son downtown and buy him whatever he wanted and the two would come back loaded with gifts—for themselves and Blanche. The girls got nothing.

Caulbert had a violent temper. His daughter-in-law recalled that one day, dressing, he became so enraged that he flung his pants so high in the air that they caught on a light fixture. Now berserk with fury, he tore the fixture right out of the ceiling. One day he bought Bernard a flexible flyer sled and went out to play with him in the snow, pushing him down an incline. He caught a ring in the rungs of the sled and dislocated his finger. According to one version of the story, he smashed the sled. According to another, he merely cursed furiously. Bernard, Jr. asked for a rabbit and obtained one only to have it bite him on the finger. In a towering rage, he grabbed the animal and flung it over the back fence to its death. He was certainly not an easy man to live with.

Despite being ignored by their stepfather, Blanche's daughters successfully pursued their education. Viola was graduated from Miner Normal School in 1920, second in her class. At that time graduates were considered for positions in the D.C. Negro schools on the basis of their ranking, so Sissie did not have trouble obtaining employment as a teacher, and three months after her graduation was hired at Briggs School. [259] Elinor—and later Bernard— went to Dunbar High School. At that time there were only two black high schools in the District: Armstrong, which emphasized a vocational curriculum, and Dunbar, which was "academic." Maxine Reynolds Baker, who attended a few years later, reminisced, "Dunbar was a sophisticated, top of the notch school. Anybody who was anybody went to Dunbar. The other schools were for the other folks."[260]

The principal, since 1921 was Walter L. Smith (c.1875-1943), a former math teacher who was a native of Illinois and a graduate of Howard. According to Joseph Drew, who attended Dunbar from 1923 to 1927, "We used to call him "Fatty" Smith. He didn't have any hair and you could spot him coming down the hall a block away! But we was a fine principal, very fine."[261] Mary Jones Nightengale Carter (1902-1994), who taught at Dunbar in the 1930s described Smith as "an educator, strictly an educator. He was a big man with a bald head—completely bald—and he was very strict. He had good discipline. He was, of course, very conservative. At the assemblies the students marched in quietly and Mr. Smith would bring his guest down the aisle and up on the platform. As soon as he hit the auditorium, there was complete silence. You could hear a pin drop. There was no rustling nor laughing nor anything. When he walked through the halls, they would be just as quiet."[262] Julia Brooks, daughter of the longtime pastor of Nineteenth Street Baptist Church, was assistant principal. "Boy, she could have been one of those old-fashioned college deans of women!" Drew observed. "Boys couldn't even speak to the girls! She was pretty rough!"[263] Carter said basically the same thing: "Miss Brooks, the assistant lady principal for girls, was very strict and hardly allowed the girls to speak to the boys in the hall." She added, however, "One of her students...said she never respected her because she found out something about her that showed that her actions at school and her home life were two different things!"[264]

As for the teachers, Carter explained, "At that time there were many good teachers...They were graduates from outstanding colleges, but at that time there was no work for them in the white universities...They were excellent teachers...They had a system of teaching that I guess was old fashioned, but they taught the children to speak well and write well and read...They prided themselves on their education. They didn't have to be *real* good teachers, because the students wanted to learn and they had the ability to learn and they came with the attitude to learn. Dunbar was no problem with discipline. You'd go into the classroom and the children would immediately stop talking and get ready for their assignment"[265]

"It was amazing to see how [new] students.. would, within a few months, absorb the air of culture that prevailed at Dunbar at the time. It was really a pleasurable school in which to teach."[266]

Grace Ridgeley Drew (b. 1910), who was graduated in 1928, commented, "One of the most interesting things about Dunbar was that we were addressed at 'Miss.' You were not addressed by your first name. You became 'Miss Ridgeley.' And the boys were addressed as 'Mister' by most of the teachers, I think, except [ones] like Mr. Bassett and Cat Thomas. They would call them peculiar things...It made you feel very grownup to be addressed as 'Miss" and everybody was very polite."[267]

However, as Carter insisted, "Dunbar was *hinkty.* Certain groups ran the school. They had a whole group of girls with long hair down their back and they ran the school, these fair girls with long brown hair."[268] Joseph Drew conceded, "There were, I have to admit it, some select groups that *may* have got a little more attention than the whole. But the opportunities were there for everyone.   But these teachers did concentrate, more or less, on the more outstanding students."[269] Grace Drew added, "There *was* a select group.   There was no two ways about it, those kids who came from certain families who were known to the other families. I wouldn't say they were given any *special* treatment, but we were given some advantages that the other kids were *not* given. I wouldn't say there was *discrimination* against the others."[270] Atkins also recalled, "There was a group there that thought they were better than anybody else." After recalling a few names, she added, "There were a number of them. They had a little group and they didn't take anybody in it. ..They *did think* they were better than anybody else....But some of those fellows liked Elinor!"[271]

Elinor was described by Helen Atkins as "a pretty blond with dark eyes... She was brilliant. She was a very bright girl. She could cook and sew and she played tennis, she swam, and played basketball. She was an all-around girl."[272] who was a good student as well as a good athlete who excelled in tennis.[273] When her little brother got into scrapes in the neighborhood, it was she who intervened, even it if meant subduing boys twice her size with her firsts.. Elinor was characterized in her yearbook as "shy, gentle, brilliant" and was President of the Players Guild, Secretary of the Fleur-de-Lis Club, President of the French Club, and a member of the basketball team.[274]   Helen Atkins recalled, "Jennings Newsom who taught at high school was crazy about Elinor. He was a teacher and she was a student. She was *crazy* about her—till it made talk! He just worshipped her! I was kind of an innocent child. I don't know how he could have managed to do that. I don't know whether Elinor was trying to push him away all the time or she wasn't." And I guess it was kind of hard for her."[275]Marie Taylor Primas recalled that when she came to Washington in 1925, the year Elinor was graduated, "I used to see Elinor occasionally riding in the car with the top down with Mr. Newsom. He was my first Latin teacher."[276]

Viola, called "Sissy", who graduated second in a class of twenty from Miner seemed to be her mother's favorite. Beautiful and intelligent, she was vivacious and religious. Elinor recalled that Blanche made sure that Vie never had to do housework, so as not to interfere with her studies. That job was left to the younger sister, who loved Sissie so that she did not resent it. Sissie, in turned, helped pay Elinor's tuition at Miner.

Viola was considered an excellent teacher who loved children. She was selected in 1925 by the School Board to be a "demonstration teacher" at Garrison School. There she established a reputation "as a companion, teacher, and scholar."[277] Both regular and student teachers were sent to observe Miss Viola Robinson just how first grade should be taught[278].

Helen Atkins recalled, "Vie was very sweet. She looked like a little Jap. She had tiny, tiny feet. She wore a size two shoe, which is about the smallest shoe you can get. She was kind of short. She might have been about Elinor's height[2], but she was a smaller person than Elinor. Elinor wasn't big but Sissie was tiny. Her hair was dark like Beppie's and straight like like a Japanese...She was very kind and understanding and very nice to Elinor and Elinor's friends. I can think of two examples: Elinor said, 'Let's get up a club.' So we got up a club. In those days you had a sponsor and Vie sponsored us. She came to all our meetings and that was nice for a young woman in her twenties. ..Then when we went to Normal School we gave [the club] up because we had to study. You came out by numbers. The one with the highest score was Number One and the next was Number Two. Nobody would tell you anything. Nobody would help anybody. But Elinor would call me up and say, 'Helen, come on over to my house and make your charts. Sissie's got enough material for you and me.' I guess Sissie would bring it from school."[279] Then there was another time we were at Normal School and I guess a girl had a miscarriage. Sissie came home and said, 'I heard a girl up at the Normal School had a miscarriage in the class room. What do you know about that?' We said, 'We don't know anything about it.' Sissie said, 'What do you mean, you don't know anything?' We said, 'A girl got up and she dropped a lot of blood and we just thought she was menstruating too heavy and had to go out.' We were innocent. 'You two little monkeys!' she said, 'You're the dumbest two!'

---

[2] 5'2"

Sissie went downtown and bought a book and brought it to Elinor and said, 'Elinor, you read this book and get Helen and read this together.'" Then I came over to see Elinor the day before Sissie was married and Elinor wasn't home. Sissie said, 'I've got to go downtown. Come on downtown with me. I'll pay your car fare.' She knew I was just a student and didn't have anything."[280]

Sissie was also active at church. Whereas Elinor claimed that she could never understand the Bible and never joined the church, she conceded that Viola "believed every word in the Bible." She headed the Christian Youth Fellowship at Fifteenth Street, which met at 5 on Sunday evenings. Primas recalled, "She organized the program...and we young people, teenagers and all, would come back to church for our third service on Sunday. We'd start with Sunday School about 9:30, then church at 11. Then the Christian Fellowship at 5. We would sing and listen to violin solos and we'd talk about certain things that pertained to life."[281]

Chapter Seventeen

Every summer Blanche and her three children went to the Wharves on Maine Avenue, S.W. to board one of the paddle-wheeled steamers which set out in late afternoon or early evening down the Potomac and Chesapeake down to arrive the next morning in Norfolk. The ticket agents would not sell state room tickets to black passengers, who thus had to spend the night on the deck. Blanche solved this problem by sending the fair-skinned, silken-haired Elinor to purchase the reservations. Even though Blanche, Vie, and Bernard, Jr. were not so fair as she nobody challenged them once they had the reservations in hand. However, the family acquiesced to the segregated dining arrangements. In later years Bernard spoke about the fact that Negro patrons were not admitted into the dining room until white customers had been served, and expressed bitterness that his mother never showed the slightest resentment at what he considered a gross humiliation.

In January, 1921 Blanche pulled Bernard and Elinor out of school for an emergency trip home when Mattie was jailed for a month. Bernard, Jr., six at the time, for the rest of his life resented being taken into a jail to see this unpleasant aunt, old and ravaged far beyond her 42 years, a bloated, pale, haggard woman with tattoos on her arms. A child, he said many years later, should not have been taken into a jail or been forced to meet so unsavory a relative.

Most of the summers seem to have been spent at Nonie's house at Garden City. Dorothy Goude Bryant, one of Nonie's granddaughters, recalled, "Granny had a beautiful house in Garden City, a big house with a great side porch. There was a fence around it and Granny used to plant sweet peas all along it. I know it was one of the first houses in Garden City with indoor plumbing. I remember especially the brass door-knocker. Big Daddy [George Manners] used to polish it every Sunday morning.

Sunday mornings at Granny's usually began when the paperboy knocked. It was time for his collection. Big Daddy was still in bed and he would swear, 'John Brown it! It's that damned paperboy!' Granny, offended by his swearing, would cluck, 'Tsk! Tsk!' and shake her head. Then Big Daddy would get up and pay the boy and then he would lovingly and meticulously shine the brass door knocker."

"Big Daddy" Manners was a favorite with all the children in the family. Audrey Elliott Vagner, Louise's daughter, later recalled, "He was a wonderful person. Children loved him and flocked around him. I remember running to him when he stopped off the streetcar returning from work. He was like the pied-piper. Children were always following him." Dorothy Goude Bryant recalled: "Big Daddy was a stocky man with crinkly hair parted right dab down the middle. He limped a little, as one of his legs was shorter than the other. He wasn't religious at all and he used to make wine—purple grape and white grape—and I used to help him. Big Daddy had a good job at the shipyards and we never lacked for anything while he was alive. He was such a sweetheart."

Dorothy Bryant declared of her grandmother (whom Bernard Ruffin, who seldom complimented anyone, characterized as a "saint"): "Granny was the sweetest thing that ever wore shoes. Only she had such bad taste in men. She and Mom [Florence] didn't get alone, but Granny was so patient. She was very religious—a saint, really. She was a Seventh Day Adventist and whenever the doors of the church were open, she was there. She went to church Friday at sundown, came back at night, then went again Saturday morning and stayed till they closed the doors that evening. Bright and early she used to take me to church Saturday morning in Newport News...We took lunch and stayed all day. I remember Granny taking me to camp meetings in the summer time in the fields around Hampton and Newport News...As soon as the tent went up, Granny was there. Granny had me learn and recite great chunks of the Bible. She pounded religion into me so much that I lost interest...I used to say to her, 'There's going to be nobody in heaven but you, St. Peter, and God.' When I was first allowed to have boyfriends, whenever a boy came to our home, I took him into the living room, where Granny held forth...like a queen. I would introduce the boy to her and she would ask, 'Are you a Christian, son?' The poor guy didn't know what to do. Granny wouldn't eat pork, shellfish, or mackerel, nothing without both fins and scales. Nor would she wear jewelry, powder, or rouge. [Nevertheless] she looked like a movie star—gorgeous. She was about 5'5" tall, a little heavy, and very fair in complexion. Her hair was very thin and its darkness contrasted with the paleness of her scalp. She was almost completely bald on top and I remember how white her scalp looked. Granny had a beautiful soprano voice, but she refused to sing opera; she sang only religious music. She was an elegant, dignified lady. She was very proud. She was very well set-up. She starched everything—even her handkerchiefs. She read the Bible constantly, but not much else, maybe sometimes a newspaper. She gave the impression of being highly educated, but I don't think she was. She suffered from insomnia and went to bed with lettuce leaves, which she munched during the night...When I made up her bed in the morning I would always find wilted lettuce leaves in the bed."

Blanche and her children also spent time with Dodie. The U.S. Census of 1920 reveals that on January 13 of that year Mary L. Bass, a widowed mulatto laundress of 62 (she was actually 65) was the head of a household on 1416 O'Keefe Street that included a daughter Emma "Gatlin', age 28 (she was actually 37!), who was also a "laundress"; granddaughter Janice Young (Mattie's daughter), who at 17 as neither employed nor at school during the past year; also grandson Allan Jackson and his wife Florence. Allan's age was given as 23 and his occupation as "steward on steamship." His wife was a native of Pennsylvania and worked as a "nurse in private family." Allan ultimately married twice. According to his death certificate, his second wife was "Elnora" and therefore it is interesting that he chose marital partners with the same names as his sister and mother!)

Marion Bess remembered "Mrs. Bass" as a magnificent woman, very large, "as wide as the doorway", always dressed in black velvet or black satin, with a majestic, queenly bearing, who "hated black people and didn't want her daughters to have anything to do with colored men." Bernard Ruffin's recollections are not so appealing. He recalled a wrinkled "but not dried up" blond, blue-eyed woman with an almost transparent white skin that showed a multitude of blue veins, with huge legs and an immense, pendulous belly that hung nearly to the ground. Although she had no teeth, her gums were so tough that she could eat steak. According to him Dodie "talked like a poor white" and "split her verbs." Elinor recalled that her grandmother had brown hair and eyes and because of hair loss, wore a bun on top of her head.

Nearly every day Dodie walked to the home of her granddaughter Louise, who recalled, "Now my little Allan used to sleep with Dodie and Dodie was so big and heavy that the side of the bed she slept on would go down almost to the floor and my little Allan would slide down against her like he was on a sliding board. 'Now don't you squash my little Allan!' I used to joke."

Louise Elliott also remembered Dodie's apparent disaffection toward black people: "One day Dodie and I were sitting on my front porch when a black lady walked by and said, 'How do, Ms. Bass!' Dodie said, 'What's that black nigger doing, speaking to me?' 'Oh, Dodie!' I said, 'you don't *really mean that*!" Dodie said, 'She black, ain't she?' 'Oh, Dodie,' I said, 'who do you think you are?' She said, '*I ain't black!*' Poor Dodie thought she was white."

In August, 1921, Dodie suffered a stroke. Elinor remembered that she was sent to the beach to gather sand for the bags which the doctor attached to the sick woman's limbs, apparently to prevent paralysis. A big, strong woman who had never been sick, Dodie hated the confinement and was so impatient to be well that she tried to walk too soon, fell, and broke a hip. Elinor declared, "That finished her." After that she hobbled about on a cane painfully—Bernard said, "She could just barely move around"— and was never the same emotionally.

A major deterrent to Dodie's full recovery was the action of her grandson William James, the only surviving child of Caledonia, who, by then was 25 and married to the former Elsie Lillian Quetrell, a school-teacher. Like Big Daddy, William worked at the shipyards. Most people remembered him as a handsome, genial, pleasant man. He was an active member of the First United Presbyterian Church. Bernard Ruffin recalled that he was a "hustler." George Elliott said that he speculated in real estate. Shortly after Dodie's stroke, William persuaded her to sell her house to him for ten dollars. The deed of sale was accompanied, however, by a clause that read, "The grantee shall have and enjoy quiet possession of said land free from all encumbrance."[282] When Dodie got better and realized what she had done, she insisted that she was delirious at the time and, denying all knowledge of the transaction, she accused William of cheating his own grandmother. At that point, Elinor was sure, "something went out of her."

Dodie's old age must surely have been made bitter by the passing of prodigal daughters Mattie and Emma. Waller, without discussing their questionable means of livelihood, described them as fat, lazy, spoiled, improvident women who leeched away their mother's meager substance. "Both of them came home to die," she added. Early in 1924 Mattie, apparently suffering from liver cancer (her death certificate gives the cause as "tumma" of the liver), came home to die. When she breathed her last on February 18, daughter Janice sent a telegram to Blanche in Washington: "COME AT ONCE MOTHER IS DEAD." Apparently they knew (or cared) nothing of Mattie's illness, and, since Janice usually called Dodie "Mother" and her own mother Mattie by her given name,

Blanche assumed that it was Dodie who had died and immediately Blanche, with Bernard and possibly Elinor and Viola too, took the boat to Norfolk and hastened to 1416 O'Keefe, to find Dodie, if not well, alive, and Mattie laid out. "If we had known that it was Aunt Mattie who had died," Bernard recounted, "we probably would not have gone to Norfolk."[283]

Emma had gone to New York, where Nonie's son Allan and her daughter Florence were living at the time. Florence's daughter Dorothy Goude Bryant recalled Emma as "a big brown, beautiful, lusty, earthy woman, part of the fun-loving, high-balling crowd. She used to drink pretty good. Mom and Aunt Emma had awful arguments, especially when Emma was drunk." Bryant recalled that Emma had the peculiar habit of using the kitchen sink as a chamber pot when she was feeling no pain. She also recalled, "I found a ten dollar bill on the street one day. We needed the money for food and clothing, but Aunt Emma, Uncle Allan, and Mom took the money and spent it all on booze."

Yet everyone who knew her agreed that Emma Kemp, who reverted to her maiden name in late years after two failed marriages, was a jolly, vivacious person who was kind and good. In 1925 she began to lose weight rapidly and vomit blood and came home to die. At the Norfolk Protestant Hospital, she begged her niece Louise to bring her two little children, Allan and Audrey Elliott. "Louise," she said, "did you bring the children?" When Louise told her that the children were there, Amy said, "I can't see them." "In a moment's time," recounted George Elliott, "she was dead."[284] Family members were indignant that Emma's doctors attributed her demise to syphilis. Elinor Waller was convinced that white doctors flagrantly attributed any long illness in a Negro patient to that undignified cause. She thought Emma died of a heart attack. Bernard Ruffin believed that Emma had lung cancer.

In the fall of 1926 Dodie's grandson William James defaulted on a loan for a real estate transaction for which he had given as security the O'Keefe Street house that he had purchased from his grandmother. He lost the property. According to Elinor Waller, William and wife Elsie rushed to plunder the house of all its contents and put his ailing, 71 year old grandmother out literally on the street. George and Louise Elliott did remember how Dodie lost her house—or said they did not—and maintained that William was a nice person and that the affair must have been connected to his real estate speculations.

Dodie ended up living at Garden City with Nonie, where

granddaughter Dorothy Goude Bryant recalled she spent most of her time in a rocking chair, "Rocking, rocking, rocking, like she was going to rock right out of the world." She became increasingly sullen and irritable. Florence had returned from New York and was living with her mother with seven year old daughter Dorothy, or "Dot" and two year old son George. According to Dorothy, Dodie would not let the brown-skinned George near her. Whenever he approached, she yelled, "Get that little black varmint away from me!"

Just before Christmas that year Big Daddy's streetcar delivered him to the shipyards a few minutes late. His boss, who was a close friend, was also late, and but, as Dorothy Bryant put, "Just to cut a funny," Big Daddy, who had suffered from angina pains for some time and was supposed to avoid sudden exertions, decided to race his boss to the door. He reached the threshold and fell at his boss' feet, dead at 53.

After the death of Big Daddy, Nonie left the Garden City house in the care of daughter Florence and her current husband and moved to New York to live with son Allan. Dodie went to Washington to live with Blanche.

Caulbert Ruffin was furious that his wife had agreed to take her mother in. It was time for the annual move, and this time he rented a small house at 1030 Euclid Street, N.W. It was large enough for him, Blanche, and Bernard but for no one else. Blanche was not about to abandon her mother or daughters and so the marriage was over. Although they never got a divorce, Blanche and Caulbert Ruffin apparently never spoke to each other again.[285]

Blanche went to work again as a seamstress. Elinor said that she worked for a "Mrs. Thom", whose husband was a railroad president or executive. Washington city directories reveal an Alf P. Thom, Jr., who was the general solicitor of the Association of Railway Executives who had a wife named Rosalie and lived on Cathedral Avenue. Mrs. Thom took Blanche on many of the trips she made around the country, where she insisted that Blanche share her first class accommodations. According to Elinor, once, in Georgia, hotel personnel, recognizing her as a Negro, tried to force Blanche to use the service elevator. Blanche held her ground and summoned Mrs. Thom, who made it clear to the hotel management that if they desired her business they would offer her companion the same first-class facilities made available to her.

After spending some time in New York, Nonie returned to Garden City where she discovered that Florence and her husband were making and selling liquor in the house. She closed up the house and made Florence and her children move north with her.[286]

In January, 1928, Nonie, who was living at 173 Decatur Street in Brooklyn, went to the altar a third time. The groom was 54 year old Norfolk native James Frederic Renshaw Wilson, a musician and lifelong bachelor. Elinor believed that it was out of a mutual love of music that they married. Indeed "Fess" seems to have been a talented musician, although there is no record of the instrument he played. Evidently made his living giving music lessons to wealthy white children in New York. Nobody in the family seems to have liked him and everyone commented on his ugly, simian appearance. Louise Elliott remembered, "He looked just like a park ape!" Dorothy Bryant said, "He looked like a spider or a gnarled piece of wood." She gave a graphic account of life with Nonie and Fess: "He was as grotesque as one can be and still be human. He looked like a horrible-looking little black monkey. He was a hunchback with one leg shorter and he walked sideways, tip-toed, in an attempt to minimize his limp. He was literally as black as coal and was five feet tall or less. What kind of ape is it, a chimpanzee or an orangutan, that has a big round flat face and a big huge nostrils and immense protruding lips? That's what he looked like. Granny called him 'Park Ape' to his face. Whenever he and Granny went outside all the passersby stopped and stared at what appeared to be a fashionable, well-turned-out white lady leading a black monkey by the hand! Our neighbors used to call them 'Beauty and the Beast.' Fess was *mean*. Oh, he was very brilliant and highly educated, but he was too damned pompous for his own good. He gave music lessons to white children, but whenever the parents politely asked him to use the side door, as was customary in those days, Fess wouldn't go anymore. He was the kind of educated idiot who looked down on everyone, including Granny. I don't see what Granny saw in him. He was many years older than she[287]....Fess was a mean, hateful, evil man and he used to beat Granny up. Mom, who was working as a singing waitress, hated him and never called him anything other than 'Old Black Bastard.' Once, after Fess beat Granny, Mom picked up a pan of boiling grease and hurled it at his face. Unfortunately it missed and splattered all over the place. (I had to clean it up.). Fess ran. He was scared to death."

Nonie divorced Fess Wilson and moved with Florence to Philadelphia, then, after a short time moved to Norfolk to live with daughter Louise.

Chapter Eighteen

Dodie's last years were not happy ones. Dorothy Bryant who remembered Dodie's brief stay at Garden City, remembered her as "an immense woman who couldn't walk well." She had three striking characteristics: her corpulence, her whiteness, and her temper. "She was so white!" Bryant recalled. "I have never seen a human so white! Her skin looked as if you could see through it. She used to sit in a rocking chair and rock and doze and rock and doze. She hated black people [and] she was as mean as hell!" Bernard Ruffin remembered a senile, ill-tempered woman who walked with crutches which she would periodically fling at family members.

Unfortunately, those people who wrote or taped their recollections of Dodie knew her only when she was old and ill and life had turned irrecoverably sour for her. She could look back on seventy years of suffering. She had lost her father before she was old enough to know him and had been rejected by his German family as a black bastard. She had lost her mother when she was twelve or thirteen. Her first marriage was a disaster. Her second husband died young. All but three of her seven children were dead, and Frank might as well have been, passing for white as he was. She had outlived her siblings. She had worked hard so that her six surviving children could have a better life than she had enjoyed. None of them had gone on to a higher education and before they died Mattie and Emma had been the cause of untold heartache. She struggled to make a home for her grandchildren and encouraged them to obtain an education. Although she had reason to be proud of Louise, Viola, and Elinor, Janice, Allan, and Florence were alcoholic failures, and William had cheated her out of her home and possessions. Old and crippled in Washington, she could do nothing but sit and think of her shattered life.

Elinor, who dearly loved her grandmother recalled, "She had lost her faith." When asked if she had lost her faith in God, Elinor replied, "Perhaps not in God, but certainly in man. Sometimes I think she lost her faith in God, too." During her last years she never went out and demanded, over and over, to be taken back to her home in Norfolk.

Most of those who knew her in her later years remember Dodie as "senile." Sarah Davis Taylor, a friend of Vie's, said that Dodie was "just like a baby," speechless and mindless, and had to be dressed, bathed, and hand-fed. Bernard described his grandmother as completely deprived of her mental faculties. Elinor, however, insisted that Dodie was not senile and quite capable of conversation on those rare occasions when she desired it. Helen Ogle Atkins, lifelong friend of Elinor, was also able to get Dodie to respond. "I loved Dodie and she loved me," Atkins recalled. "She had quite a sense of humor. Whenever I came to visit Elinor, Dodie would say, 'Move the rocking chair. Here comes Helen.' Dodie was a very stout woman, not really fat, but wide and massive. She was very handsome. She had beautiful gray hair which she wore brushed straight back." Atkins also said, "Dodie was nice-looking, but Dodie was big. We used to laugh, you know. Elinor and her mother didn't want Dodie to eat too much because she wasn't doing anything and they didn't want her to get *too* fat, and Sissie was feeding her. Anything that was left in the dish, she would say, 'Dodie, don't you want the rest of this rice here? Here's some more chicken?' And Elinor and her mother could have thrown it out the window. They weren't begrudging people about food, but they just didn't want Dodie to get *too* fat, doing nothing, you know."[288]

There was still one more blow in store for Mary Sparrow Kemp Bass before release from earthly trials. Granddaughter Viola was said to have been "the one who was always trying to keep the family together."[289] Bernard characterized his older sister as a "spendthrift" who ran up huge bills and was hopelessly in debt. But friends insisted that she bought not so much for herself, but her family, especially her mother. Atkins recalled, "She catered to her mother's every whim. She always told me, 'Beppie wants the most expensive thing in the store."

One letter survives from Viola's pen, written to Elinor ("Little Sissie") on August 2, 1927 from the home of Louise Elliott in Norfolk and it gives a vivid picture of her vivacious personality: "Dearest Little Sissie, I am sure that you thought I had forgotten all about your birthday. But I didn't, Sissie. I have felt very badly because I have such a little to send and the little I have is late reaching you. You see, I went to [Buckroe] Beach Friday Friday and it has stormed dreadfully ever since Saturday morning. That has kept me from going down town earlier. What I am sending you is very little, but you know nothing is too much ortoo good if I only had it. Please write and tell me all about the pretty things that you got....

"My stay in Norfolk has been very pleasant thus far and I really think that the remaining time is going to be rather nice. Dr.[Frank]

Coppage [a dentist] carried me out one evening and really showed me quite a swell time. He carried me for a long drive all through Virginia Beach and then we topped the evening with a too bad supper. Melvin has been very steady, but he is out on his run at present. He carried Louise and myself to Buckroe [Beach] Friday and some day we had, too! Really, Sissie, Melvin spent $15.00 or $20.00 that day. No stone was left unturned—from the taxi to and from the ferry on up to the room he hired at Buckroe for Louise and I to rest ourselves in. Oh, he was just too <u>terrific</u>!! He is taking us again one day next week. And, Sissie, he tries to make me believe he worships me.

"Why, we even went crabbing last Wednesday and had a most thrilling day. Every thing went well until it became necessary for Louise and I to save a little white boy from drowning. He tripped over his net and fell right into the channel. I got to him first with our crabbing net but in my haste I knocked my head against an iron girder and knocked myself completely out. I actually thought for a while that my skull was fractured. It made me sick. Any way Louise laid on her stomach while I held her feet and succeeded in reaching the boy after he had gone down once. Then the two of us pulled him in. It was some experience!! When it was all over, of course, I got fainty and had a crying spell. Jut like foolish me! Wasn't that a thrilling experience?

"Now about 'Sam'. There really isn't much to tell as he can come over just once a week—Sundays. See, the first time I saw him was on a Monday. Then I got a letter that Thursday. He came over again Sunday but I didn't see him until <u>9</u> o'clock that night, because we had an <u>awful</u> electrical storm that lasted all day and all night. When he did come he was soaking wet, and Sissie, he had been drinking rather heavy. See, he really doesn't love me after all. If he did he would at least lay off that stuff the one day in the whole week that he is to see me. Now, don't <u>you</u> think so, too? But, Sissie, he is rather pitiful. I see, though, that 'Sam' will never make me happy. On the other hand, he keeps me miserable.

"Albert [Burgess] has been wonderful. I get a letter nearly every day. He has sent me a package already. He has sent me a package already and also papers and magazines. And, hold your breath!!! He has called me up <u>twice</u> already. Can you beat it? Now, why <u>can't</u> I be crazy about him?

"I have lots to tell you when I see you and that will be soon. Poor Bep seems so worried. Gee! I wish I <u>could</u> do something. [This was written at the time her mother's marriage was crumbling]. I have been as restless today as a maniac—wondering what is happening there.

"Give my love to everybody, and Sissie, please special your old bathing suit to me. Will you? Tell Dodie that Janice is no sicker than she has been for the last year or so. She has just left here.

"Love to Ma, Dodie, and Bernard, but keep most for yourself. I do hope that you will like this little package. Kiss Jennings [Newsom] for me. Hear?

Lovingly,

'Sis'

You! Hoo!"

"Melvin" and "Sam" are not identified, but it was "Albert"—Albert Anderson Burgess, a high school teacher, printer, and musician—that Vie finally chose to marry, on May 30, 1928.

In the meantime Elinor, who had finished ninth in her class at Miner in 1927, got her first teaching job on February 17, 1928, when she was assigned to Wilson School to place a Mrs. M.B. Conrad, who had died.

Early in December Vie confided to her best friend, Kathryn Carr, "I'm pregnant, but Beppie's upset. She's afraid there won't be any money if there's a new baby in the family. She wants me to do something about it."[290]

Abortion, at least in Washington, DC, was commonplace in those days, even though it was technically against the law. Mary Jones Nightengale Carter, former wife of a physician and a long-time teacher and Washington resident, recalled, "Abortion was a way of life. Abortions were easy to get. My husband did not perform them, but there were *certain* Washington doctors who did. Nobody ever said anything about it being wrong. Nobody ever said anything about it being a sin in those days. Everybody did it." Carter stated that the "certain doctors" made a fortune from aborting the pregnancies of Washington school teachers. Another contemporary, Mary Gibson Brewer Hundley, another teacher, said in an interview in the 1980s that female teachers could not afford to have children because they would have to resign once the pregnancy became obvious. Then, after the birth of the child, they would have to apply for a position over again, having lost all seniority.

On December 28, during her Christmas vacation, Viola was to see Kathryn that evening. At six she went to her doctor. At eight she came home and went to bed. She told Katherine, who had come to her house on 219 S Street, N.W., "It's just cramps. I'll be all right." Kathryn stayed with Vie until 10:30. "These cramps are so bad!" she complained. Now I'm passing blood." "Can you eat salt?" Kathryn asked. "No," replied Vie. "The doctor just said to stay in bed." Kathryn went home.

At two the phone rang. It was Blanche. Carr recounted, "Beppie screamed, 'Sissie's *DEAD*!!!' 'She *can't* be,' I cried. 'Oh, *yes—she—is!*' screamed Beppie. I went to the house and entered a scene of utter chaos. Elinor was sitting as if she was in a daze. 'What did she tell you? What did she tell you?' Beppie demanded. 'She didn't tell me anything,' I answered. 'Are you *sure*?' insisted Beppie. I was convinced that there was no doctor in attendance that night. They had a family doctor, I forget his name, and he signed the death certificate, but there was no autopsy. All of us were convinced that Sissie died as the result of an abortion. She was a horrible corpse...*horrible*...*HORRIBLE*...*absolutely HORRIBLE!!!*...She was black, black, *absolutely black*! It all happened between 10:30 and 2!" Marie Madden Williams Ford (1901-1997), who married Coustin Gertie Sparrow William's oldest son, attended the wake and commented, "Everybody knew it was an abortion. She was the most horrible corpse I've ever seen in all my life. It was black...*hideous.*"

Elinor refused to discuss Viola's death with even her closest friends. Helen Ogle had been visiting her grandmother in Ithaca, New York. "We didn't have a phone [my sister] Mary called a neighbor and told me. She told me that Sissie had died suddenly. So then I came back...Elinor was so upset she was almost like in a stupor. She and Sissie were *crazy* about each other and she was almost insane when Sissie died! They said Sissie had a heart attack. Others said it was an abortion. That's what they said. Elinor didn't tell *me* that. Maybe Elinor didn't know it. That's what people said. I *do* remember Sissie have some little trouble with her heart. Elinor and I were the dearest friends. But she just told me Vie died of a heart attack and I said, "Oh, I remember Vie had a little trouble with her heart." She said, 'Yeah, *you* remember, Helen, don't you?' Like she was so glad I said that. I guess all of us have secrets, don't we? She may have known it or suspected it. Beppie was a good woman but I guess she was in her children's business too much. Sissie had a husband! She must have felt *terrible* about that. I *do* know this: Elinor was *very mad* with Vie's husband after this happened and that must have been why.

She maybe felt that he was the cause of it. But she didn't talk about it. It hurt her so."[291]

There was always a sinister mystery about her passing, in the way it was discussed in the family. The author once asked his mother how Aunt Viola died, and received the reply, "Heart trouble, *I guess.* But that must have been forty years ago. You needn't think about it now." Bernard, Jr., in response to a similar question, answered, "She died *just like that.* She came home one evening and was dead before the next morning. I wasn't with her when she died. Only Elinor and Granny [Blanche] were with her." (Where was the husband?) Bernard once stated that Vie had died from a "coronary embolism, " but a few days before he died, recounting the deaths of various family members and their cause, he said that Viola had succumbed to "septic poisoning", but commented no more.

Viola's death certificate was signed by Simeon Carson (1882-1954), who was evidently the "family friend" Carr identified but could not name. Carson, a native of North Carolina and the son of former slaves, was a graduate of the medical school of the University of Michigan who operated a Carson's Private Hospital near Howard University. He gave the cause of death as "endocarditis chronic (rheumatic)with "dilatitation—acute" as the "contributory cause." Bernard always referred to Dr. Carson as "The Butcher."

Elinor and Beppie never recovered fully from Viola's death. In later years she recalled, "I cannot see how God would let someone so young and so good be taken away like Sissie was. If there is a God, how could he let that happen?" Burgess remarried within the year. Elinor, Blanche, Bernard, and Dodie immediately moved from S Street into an apartment at 1822 Vernon Street. Helen Atkins recalled, "I remember the day we moved Dodie. Not only was she very stout, but she was feeble as well. She was wearing a little short black coat. Trying to get her in the cab, we pushed and shoved, but Dodie got stuck half way in and half way out. She just wouldn't go. I was a young girl then and started giggling. Dodie laughed, 'Damn you, Helen, you're laughing at me!' Finally we got Dodie in the same some way. I think they had to ease her in sideways[292]."

Shortly after the move to Vernon Street, the wife, mother-in-law, and children of Russell Kemp (Blanche's half-brother) came from Chicago to see the Hoover Inauguration on March 4. Elinor had maintained contact with Russell through his wife Myrtle by letter, but this was the first physical contact between the Chicago and Washington families. For some reason, Russell did not accompnay his family, perhaps to save the feelings of Dodie relative to the apparent circumstances of his birth.

Jayne Kemp Taylor (b. 1919), the daughter, in later years recalled the visit. "They lived on Vernon Street in a large apartment, sparsely furnished like they hadn't lived there too long. Elinor was the friendliest. She played the role of gracious hostess. She was a very pretty young woman, very fair, with straight light hair, dark blond maybe. She treated us well, but she didn't take us around. We had to take cabs and the weather was very chilly. Elinor and her family didn't go to the parade with us.

"I still see only the back of Blanche, Elinor's mother, at the kitchen sink. I don't remember her saying anything to us. She was very distant. She seemed to hover in the background, not saying much. She was tall, reddish-brown, with straight black hair. I think she smoked. She looked like an Indian. We ate at the dining room table or buffet.

"I thought Bernard was very handsome. He was tall and had a light complexion and large lips. He was tolerant of young kids, like my brother and I, but he did not seem to be a happy young man. He had his own bedroom and he had his own things and he let Russell and me look at them. I don't remember what they were. He seemed most interested in asking us about Al Capone. He thought there was a machine gun on every corner in Chicago. He didn't join us for meals. He seemed to hole up in his bedroom in the evening. He felt pressured by his sister. Elinor was constantly after him to do this and do that and he was a typical teenager. I didn't think their relationship was a warm one. She was mothering him too much, perhaps.

"Then there was an older woman they called Dodie. She was very fair, but not as fair as Elinor. She didn't have grey hair. It was dark. Maybe it was a wig. She was very, very heavy—*huge*—and she did not move around. She sat at the table and had nothing to say. She was at the table for a long, long time, eating, eating, and eating. Elinor said, "You don't want to eat so much." She didn't see to take much interest in us." [293]

Two months after the visit from the Chicago Kemps, Elinor went into Dodie's room to dress her grandmother and help her to the kitchen to feed her. Dodie, perfectly lucid, said calmly, "Elinor, I don't feel so well today. I think I'll just have breakfast in bed. I think I'll stay in bed all day. I'll be all right." When Elinor came home from school that afternoon, she found her 74 year old grandmother dead in bed. "We didn't want any autopsy," she recalled. "We got a doctor to sign the death certificate saying that she'd died from a stroke." There is no record as to whether the funeral was in Washington or Norfolk. More than likely it was in Norfolk, where Mary Sparrow Kemp Bass was laid to rest in a markerless grave in the markerless family plot at Calvary Cemetery.

Mary Ogle Wilson, sister of Helen and a friend of Elinor, recalled in 1965 that the summer before Sissie's death, Elinor had consulted a gypsy, who told her fortune and warned her that she was going to have "a very bad year."

Less than a year after Dodie's death, on February 18, 1930, Blanche received word from New York that her brother Frank was dead at 41. He had opened a garage on the west side of Manhattan which had been demolished in the mid '20s when the West Side Highway as constructed. After that he became a foreman of a garage in the Bronx that serviced trucks. His daughter remembered him as a very quiet, gentle man, a devout Methodist, tall and thin, who wore glasses and smoked a pipe. On a very cold winter's morning he left his apartment at 424 E. 65th Street and went to work. Later that morning told his boss that the fumes from the trucks were making him sick. "I'm very sick," he said, and collapsed. Rushed to nearby Lincoln Hospital, he was pronounced dead. Although an autopsy attributed his death to a heart attack brought on by "coronary artery disease, fibrosis of the myocardium, and chronic purulent congestion of the lungs," his wife and children insisted to the end of their lives that he had been poisoned by the truck emissions.

After Frank was buried in a single, unmarked grave in St. Michael's Cemetery in Queens, his widow Maud, according to Elinor Waller, contacted Blanche and told her that she was so upset by her husband's death that she wanted her two children to go to Washington and stay "for awhile" with their aunt there "so she could get herself together." Blanche told Maud that there was sickness in the family. Maud apparently made several pleas, and then all contact was lost with the family. Bernard recalled that Frank's widow wanted her children to go to school in Washington and asked Blanche what school her son attended. He. felt that she learned that the children would be going to Dunbar, and learned (or surmised) that Dunbar was a "colored" school and, realizing the truth, immediately put off all thought of sending her children to Washington. That was the last that Elinor, Blanche, or Bernard heard of the family of Franklin Benjamin Kemp.

In an interview in 1978, Frank's daughter (the son had died in 1945) revealed that she knew nothing whatever of the contact with Blanche, knew nothing of any Negro connection, and had always been curious about her father's background, since she had never seen a single relative on the paternal side.

Chapter Nineteen

Although the 1930s were a time of severe economic depression, Washington, DC, as the seat of government, suffered less acutely than many other places. Teachers and government workers took a pay cut, but few lost their jobs. Elinor continued to teach. In the summer of 1930 she visited her relatives in Morgan Park, in Chicago. Jayne recalled, "Elinor played jacks with me. She would get down on the floor. She was good at it. My mother had a good friend, Gertrude Swader, whose brother-in-law was Neal Swader. Elinor was introduced to him and he fell in love with Elinor. We saw a lot of him from then on. He wined and dined her. After she got back to Washington, he asked her to marry him, but she turned him down to our disappointment. We wanted her to stay in Chicago."[294]

Blanche continued to travel with Mrs. Thom. The only letter surviving from Blanche's pen was written August 6, 1930 from the Battle Creek Sanitarium in Michigan, where Mrs. Thom was staying. Blanche wrote: "Dearest Elinor—I was so glad to get your letter when I got here in Battle Creek today. We were to get here yesterday, but this old fool of a woman desided [sic] to stay in Toledo, Ohio another day. I only wish I were coming back home instead of just getting here. This old fool started moving furniture just as soon as she struck this place. I know these people here are sorry to see her come her. She is a dam nuciance [sic].

"Well, Elinor, I am real heart sick since reading your letter. You say you were sorry for our little difference on Sunday. It made me sad also, and my heart was nearly broken, not from anything you said, but because you don't seem to understand me. I just haven't scence [sic] enough to make my meaning plain. When I say, 'I got to work,' it is not because I mean it like you take it. I do not mean it in the way I must help you, not because I think you would not take care of me if I could not work. God knows I believe from the depths of my heart you would do the last thing on earth for me, it hurts me so when you speak like you do. I did not get anything from [Moser?] because I did not need anything, but you misunderstand me when I say you are stingy. I always tell you you are stingy with yourself, because you won't buy what I would like you to have. I could not say you were stingy when you have never refused me any thing in your life. You have not disappointed me in any way, for I think you are one of the best daughters [the] Lord ever gave to a woman and if I never see you again I want you to know I speak the truth from the depths of my soul. As for Jennings —I would not raise one hand to keep you two apart. I want you to have just whom you love, and I would do all in my power to help you be happy.

"It was cold in Ohio, but here in Battle Creek it is very pleasant tonight. I miss you all so much and hope everything will be all right. Don't you work too hard. Get all the rest you can before school opens. Tell Bernard to be good. I'll write him tomorrow. Will send the money for groceries & everything else. I have not been so well. You see we have been on a go since Tuesday morning and I have got to unpack 2 trunks tonight and tomorrow press all day. I started menustrating [sic] again yesterday. It was quite a bit but is better tonight. Give my love to all the folks, but keep the best for your self...

Love Always,

Ma

In the mid 1930s Blanche was back permanently in Washington, working as a seamstress at the Hotel Ambassador at 14th and K Streets, N.W. In 1933 she joined the Fifteenth Street Presbyterian Church, transferring her membership from Norfolk. There she served on the Ladies Aid Committee and helped to raise the money to build a brick retaining wall around the raised lawn around the church. A surviving member later said that the wall "ought to be Mrs. Ruffin's memorial." Unfortunately the wall, along with the church, was destroyed in the 1970s. Josephine Todd Walker remembered "Mrs. Ruffin" as an olive-skinned woman who was always elegantly dressed.[295] Alice Bamfield Hall, who also served on the committee, remembered Blanche was "sweet", "gentle", and "timid" and given to regaling her friends with funny stories about the eccentricities of her estranged husband.[296] Blanche was always in style. Around the age of 50, she took up smoking, and from then on, a lighted cigarette was always in her hand or lips. Helen Atkins recalled, "Beppie was a very good-looking woman. She looked just like a gypsy. She had beautiful black hair and she had that rich coloring of gypsies— ruddy, not really fair—and she was a nice size and she dressed nice and she had beautiful black eyes. But Beppie was spoiled. Elinor and Sissie spoiled her. Sissie had a lot of debts when she died. Beppie would go, 'I saw some shoes in Richards' window but they were' some impossible price, 'so I know I couldn't have them.' and Sissie would buy them for her. And when Elinor got to working, between the two of them, Beppie was always wanting something and she was an inquisitor and inquisitive. She was *spoiled.* They spoiled her."[297]

Sister Nonie, after living briefly with her daughter Florence in Bryn Mawr, Pennsylvania, returned to Norfolk to live with daughter Louise and son-in-law George Elliott, Jr. George Elliott, Sr. had recently lost his wife and visited his son's house with increasing frequency. Soon it was noticed by George, Jr. and Louise and their two teenaged children that George, Sr. and "Granny" were spending quite a bit of time on the front porch together. Then the two stunned their relatives and friends by announcing their plans to marry. Granddaughter Audrey remembered, "Everybody was in an uproar!" Neighbors said that her grandmother was "going to become her own mother-in-law." And so Elenora Virginia Kemp Jackson Manners Wilson Elliott moved into the Lexington Street home of her new husband, a retired postman. There were two adult Elliott daughters living at home, and relations between them and their stepmother became tense. Marian Elliott Bess was one of the few people who did not like Nonie. But soon, George, Sr.'s health began to wane and, on September 30, 1937, barely a year after the wedding, he died of bladder cancer and Nonie found herself for the fourth time without a husband.

At 63, Nonie Elliott was now single for life. She returned to the home of her daughter. She worked as a conference Bible worker and a literature evangelist for the Bethel Seventh Day Adventist Church of Norfolk, and was famous for the programs and plays that she organized. She continued to sing in sacred concerts, even though her soprano voice was growing frayed.

Elinor, who was described as "an excellent teacher, eminently superior"[298] seems to have been transferred every few years. In the early '30s she taught at Mott School, at 4th and W Sts, N.W. and then at the Morgan Demonstration School, then at Payne. A man friend once wrote, exhorting her, "Don't let the little thugs in that school run away with you or put you on the spot."[299] At one time she taught night high school, for $3.50 a day, at Garnett-Patterson.

Elinor, in the early 1930s, was planning to marry Jennings Newsom. Her friend Sara Davis Taylor dissuaded her. Taylor felt it necessary to reveal some damaging information about Newsome's private life. Elinor, horrified, broke off relations.[300] According to Atkins, "Some people said he turned gay. He died and I heard a lot of talk. I don't know what he died of. He died kind of young. Elinor was a nice girl and when Newsome died I went to see the body and I told Elinor, 'I went to see

Newsom.' She was then married and I thought she'd like to hear that. So she said, 'How did he look?' and I said, 'He looked very nice.'"[301]

For a time Elinor dated a man from a prominent old Washington family, but, according to Taylor, the man's mother strictly forbade her son to marry Elinor because she was not socially acceptable, being the daughter of a common domestic! Sometime during the summer of 1932 Elinor began to date Arthur Owen Waller, a native of Baltimore and a graduate of Springfield College in Massachusetts, an intelligent and cultured man, a lover, like her of the theatre, who had traveled extensively in Europe (apparently with the YMCA) and who was working as an instructor of physical education at Howard. (It was his uncle, the Rev. Owen Waller who had married Cousin Gertie Sparrow to William Glass Williams!) "I know that you have been unhappy for a long time," Art wrote Elinor, "and I want to undertake the pleasant job of trying to make you happy. I will dedicate the rest of my life to that job."[302] On November 30, 1934, Elinor and Art were married at the home of Dr. Taylor, the Presbyterian pastor.

Robert W. Wilson, one of Bernard's friends at the time, recalled, "We were in high school together... He was an all-around guy. We had a sort of a gang and we played baseball and had a team and it was the Columbia Cubs. We didn't have any backing...We did our own organizing. We had meetings...We didn't have uniforms or anything, but we had a team. We played mostly pickup teams. Bernard played a number of positions. He played second base sometimes. He was a pretty good athlete[303]."

Bernard was graduated from Dunbar in 1932, where he was a member of the Dramatic Guild and the swimming team and served as the art editor for the yearbook.[304] According to classmate Elaine Gates Magruder, "[Bernard] was a good student and he had a lot of friends. He was a nice-looking fellow, a *very* nice-looking fellow, a *very* nice-looking fellow, well-dressed and very good manners—*everything*! He was the type of fellow you wouldn't hesitate to bring to meet your parents. And your parent's wouldn't hesitate to allow you to go out with him. That's the type of person he was[305]." Another former classmate, Maxine Reynolds Baker, recalled, "He was nice-looking, very friendly, and so many of the young girls had a crush on him, including me. I just had a crush, that's all. He never paid me any mind[306]."

Bernard would preserved vivid memories of his teachers, such as

Ulysses Bassett, a science teacher who called his students "Wool-Gatherers" and upon entering the room, threw open the windows, roaring in stentorian tones, "Some one here is in need of H_2O and sopolio!" Another teacher, a grandson of Frederick Douglass, frequently told his classes, "The Negro isn't ready. He *just isn't ready.*" Bernard loved art and music and acted in the school plays. His favorite teachers seems to have been Miss Mary Burrill, who taught drama. A light-skinned lady who spoke in a stilted and excessively proper fashion, she subjected her students to vocal drills, to ensure distinct speaking, in which there was a repetition of the phrases, "Bah! Bee! Bye! Bo! Boo! A-wooh!" Every Christmas Eve, Miss Burrill held audiences spellbound at the Howard University Chapel where she would recite Henry Van Dyke's story *The Other Wise Man.*

Even when he was 18, Elinor was still extremely solicitous of her younger brother. In a letter to Art in September, 1932, with their mother away, she expressed misgivings about leaving him alone while she visited friends at the beach, prompting Art to write, "Don't be too hard on your kid brother. I'm sure he can at least be safe."[307]

After Dunbar, Bernard went to Howard. According to brother-in-law Art Waller, his father paid for his education and gave him enough spending change that he was one of the few students on campus who owned their own car. Most of his life-long associates were graduates of Dunbar who went on to Howard and then continued to live in the Washington area. He became a member of the fraternity Kappa Alpha Psi and majored in art. Benjamin Spaulding, a college classmate, recalled many years later, "Bernard liked the girls! They were not dark, I can say that! I've never seen Bernard with a black girl!"

Bernard said, in later years, that he wanted to be a veterinarian. Just before his graduation, he was dropped for poor scholarship, and, although he lacked but a few hours of credit for graduation, was too proud to go back. Apparently there had been a conflict with a Professor Herring in the Art department. According to one of Bernard's future sisters-in-law, his father, dissatisfied with his grades, refused to pay for further schooling. Elinor insisted that Bernard sacrificed his education to help put a future sister-in-law through school. This, however, the future sister-in-law vehemently denied.

Since 1931 Blanche and her family had lived in an apartment at 1905 15th Street. Some time after Elinor's marriage to Art, the Wallers, Blanche, and Bernard moved around 1937 to 124 Randolph Place, N.W.

in Washington. In November, 1936, Arthur Owen Waller, Jr., or "Little Art" was born. Bernard went to work as a messenger for the Department of Treasury. Atkins remembered, "Bernard was there and he was working and [Blanche and Elinor] wouldn't take any money from him. They told him to save his money...but I don't think he saved anything."[308] Art, who lost his job when Howard laid off younger faculty, became a probation officer with the Juvenile Court. Elinor, after a year's maternity leave, went back to Payne School, where she taught fifth grade for an annual salary of $2200.[309]

Atkins reminisced, "I think there was a little trouble between Art and Mrs. Ruffin. I think he was kind of jealous of Elinor. Mrs. Ruffin used to complain about that. They were *both* there and they *both* wanted Elinor and that was hard on her." In 1939 Elinor confined to her home with pneumonia and Art and Blanche almost fought over the right to take care of her. "You could feel that they were almost fighting over who was to take care of her," Atkins recounted, "till I think the doctor said something about it."[310]

According to Bernard, it was at a fraternity party that he met Lillian Jones of Chambersburg, Pennsylvania, who was then a freshman at Howard. It must have been in late 1934 or early 1935. She came to the party with a medical student from Connecticut and left with him. Lillian, remembered from those years by fellow clubwoman Ethel Browne O'Mealley, as "very pretty, very neat, very quiet, sedate, *very sedate*, and very friendly[311]"was a graduate of the then 99% white Chambersburg High School. She was one of the 14 children (including three sets of twins) of Lewis and Sarah (Cato) Jones. Lewis Jones, a man of negligible African roots, was a concrete contractor. Sarah, a light-brown- skinned woman of aristocratic bearing, seldom left their house. Lillian's second oldest sister, Mary, had come to Washington in 1920 to work as a stenographer in the Forest Service. She took night classes at Howard and was graduated in 1929 and, a few years later, became a teacher of business at Dunbar. The next oldest sister, Amy, came to Washington in 1926 and worked as assistant registrar and studied part-time at Howard. The youngest sister, Louise and her twin brother Jack, would come to Howard a few years later. All the Jones sisters were members of the Delta Sigma Theta fraternity and unusually close.

Lillian attended Howard full-time for a year, then, for financial reasons, worked full-time as secretary to the Dean of the Medical School and went to college part-time, earning a degree in Education in 1941.

When Bernard courted Lillian she was living with Amy and her husband Allan Atkinson at 2201 2nd Street, N.W., in the Claremont Courts apartment complex and most of their dates occurred in the Atkinson living room, with the older sister in the adjoining room, listening, to make sure that nothing improper occurred. This was not unique. Benjamin Spaulding, a long-time friend of Bernard, recalled, "You go home and hold hands in the living room. You were in the living room in those days. The parents were right there in the dining room. They would never let you alone! They were never too far away. When I courted [my wife] her mother was right there in the dining room.[312]" Around 1937, Lillian took an apartment across the hallway with her sister Mary Nightengale, but, evidently, she continued to be closely supervised by her older sisters.

In the spring of 1939, Lillian's widowed father, in failing health, came down from Chambersburg to stay at the Atkinson apartment, and, lovingly attended by his five daughters and granddaughter in his closing days, on May 23, he died. Shortly after that (as he later told his son) Bernard said to Lillian, "Why don't be get married some weekend?" She agreed and on August 10, they were married by the Rev. James Robert White, a family friend, at his home in Shippensburg, Pennsylvania. Lillian's sisters were there and so was Blanche, but Caulbert was not. According to Bernard, his father told him, "Lillian is an awfully nice girl for you to be marrying." When Lillian and Bernard married, Mary moved out of her apartment to another around the corner in the same complex and let the newlyweds take over her old place.

In April, 1940 Bernard obtained an appointment to the Metropolitan Police Force. According to Ben Spaulding, "There was terrible discrimination in the Government. Most of the people [who worked there] were messengers or laborers. You couldn't eat in the government cafeterias. You had to bring your own lunch...In those days in DC the highest paying jobs [for Negroes] were the police and fire department and post office and the school system. They were the top jobs...The lawyers largely starved to death. Just a few [were prosperous] and the rest of them were working in the Government and doing anything else. A lot of your physicians...were school teachers, dependent on their school-teacher's salaries until they began to get patients[313]."

Bernard was assigned to the Thirteenth Precinct at 9½ St, N.W. and U. According to Spaulding, "The Thirteenth Precinct on U Street was where the black people were. A few of them were in the precinct up on Park Road. But Bernard was on U Street. Smith's Storage Company was there. Well, the fellows used to hang out there and drink whiskey, which is illegal, and make a lot of noise. They were colored fellows. They worked for Smith's Storage. [Bernard] wanted to arrest two of them because they were doing things they shouldn't do. The owners of Smith's Storage didn't like that. They thought it was normal for colored men to drink whiskey and make a lot of noise. So Bernard arrested them. The owners went down to the Chief of Police—they were friends—and they transferred [Bernard] way out in Northeast, on night detail walking the streets out there. That's what happened. The captain warned Bernard, but it didn't do any good. 'We know it's illegal, but don't pay any attention.' He didn't do it. He kept on after them. So then [he] understood that you can't beat the system. It's heck to buck the system. Eventually the captain on U Street brought him back. Then he was in charge of the Boys' Clubs[314]."

From 1940 until 1947 Bernard was assigned to the eleventh precinct in Anacostia. It was during those days that World War II broke out, and Bernard's work as a policeman enabled him to escape the draft. Art Waller also escaped the military service by obtaining a position with the USO, which necessitated a temporary move to Seattle, Washington, but not to the battlefields of Europe or the Pacific. Elinor was then teaching the third grade at Phillips-Wormley School for $2200 a year. She applied for a leave of absence, with "part pay", which was granted in September, 1944, and set off for Seattle with Art, Jr.

Despite her European appearance and the fact that she was probably about one-sixteenth black, Elinor never considered herself anything other than a Negro and did not try to "pass." Mary Jones Nightengale Carter knew of fair-skinned ladies who would ignore their darker friends if they encountered them when shopping downtown—convinced that store clerks would recognize them as "colored" and subject them to inferior service. Helen Atkins affirmed, "You couldn't say that Elinor was a light girl that looked like white that put on airs with you, because if you were downtown at Hecht's and see saw you way across the aisle, she'd call you."[315] She later said that there was only once instance when she consciously "passed". This was during the long train trip to Washington State during the summer of 1944.

She and Art, Jr. had a roomette and were thus able to avoid "Jim Crow" accommodations south of Washington. Throughout the trip everyone was courteous and kind except a Pullman porter, who treated her with great rudeness and insolence. Everything was tolerable until she had to change trains in New Orleans, and found herself escorted with Art, Jr. into a hideous "colored" waiting room which looked like a prison. She found it so grim and dirty that she took seven year old Little Art by the hand and walked out and took a seat in the much nicer "white" waiting room. Nobody said anything and the trip proceeded without incident.

In Seattle Elinor, who had already earned a B.A. at Howard, worked studied full-time at the University of Washington and earned her master's degree. Atkins remembered, "When Elinor went out [to Seattle] Beppie had a fit....I don't think [Elinor] got a whole lot of money but she sent it to Beppie every month. Elinor thought Beppie lost the money, carrying it in her bosom. Beppie had a job and was renting out rooms[316]. Beppie didn't tell Elinor that. Beppie came over here and said, 'Helen, you got a whole lot of sheets. Give me some of those sheets because I need them for the rooms.' So I gave her some. Beppie was always nice and kind to me, but Beppie was *spoiled*."[317]

When he returned to Washington Art opened a clothing store, "The Fashion Mart", but, after a few years, was able to obtain a position as a physical education teacher in Shaw Junior High. Elinor returned to Phillips-Wormley School and her $2200 per annum salary. When the public schools of Washington were integrated in 1954, she was assigned to Petworth School at 8th and Shepherd Streets, N.W., where she taught fifth grade and served as assistant principal until 1957, when she became principal of Van Ness School in Southeast. In 1962 she was transferred to Langdon in Northeast, from which she retired six years later. In 1947 Bernard was made the director of the Police Boys' Club at 12th and U Streets, N.W. When the Boys' Clubs opened "Camp Number Two" for colored boys near Point Lookout, Maryland in 1950, Bernard was appointed director of that as well.

After seven years of marriage, Bernard and Lillian had their first child, a girl named Blanche Linda, after her grandmother and her maternal aunt, Blanche Louise. Bernard wanted her to be called Blanche *Lydia*, but Lillian objected (Bernard thought she must have known and disliked a girl by that name) so strenuously that they settled for "Linda." Linda Ruffin, as she was called, was a large, fair-skinned baby with black hair that formed a "widow's peak." She lived only long enough to break her parents' heart. As early as July there were rumors of an epidemic of diarrhea at Freedmen's. The obstetrician, Dr. Roland Scott, assured Bernard that there was no danger. (Freedmen's Hospital was not, at the time, the only hospital in Washington that delivered colored children, although the others, such as Garfield Memorial, which was a few blocks away from Freedmen's, had segregated wards.) The child was born on August 16 and immediately she contracted diarrhea. After a few days the doctors pronounced her healthy and the parents took her home. A few days later they had to rush her back to Freedmen's where she died of "circulatory collapse" on the 30th.

There was some disagreement as to how many babies died. Of the 200 babies delivered at Freedmen's during August, a group called the National Negro Congress insisted that 30 had died. Hospital officials put the number at 15. The chief pediatrician of the hospital insisted that although there were "several sporadic cases" of diarrhea among the newborn earlier the summer, such an experience was not unusual, and that it was not until late August that he realized that the diarrhea was "attaining mild epidemic proportions when the number of isolated babies with diarrhea reached a total of seven."[318] On August 28 (two days before Linda died) seven of the 60 babies in the nurseries had diarrhea.[319] An investigation blamed the epidemic on 1) overcrowding with lack of facilities for segregating well newborn infants into small units; 2) lack of sufficient and proper isolation facilities; 3) insufficient personnel to carry out aseptic nursing techniques; 4) improper handling of infants and preparation of formulae; 5) lack of adequate supplies, such as linens, etc. necessary to carry out aseptic nursing techniques, and 6) obsolete, insufficient, and poorly maintained equipment.[320] A newspaper reporter who visited the maternity ward at Freedmen's in September was appalled to find "(1) streams of water flowing from antiquated and leaky plumbing with cigarette butts floating in the water, making a ghastly sight near the entrance of one of the maternity wards; (2) walls of virtually all wards in dire need of paint, and in some instances, plaster; (3) the milk ward [of unsanitary appearance] with old and outmoded equipment...poor ventilated [and accessed through] rows of garbage cans; (4) the same elevator which was used to carry garbage to and from the wards was used to carry milk and food to the infants and...for transportation of the babies from one ward to another."[321] Although the executive secretary of the Washington Urban League blamed the epidemic at Freedmen's, which was dependent on federal funds, on "discrimination and segregation in the areas of health and medicine in the District"[322], the *Washington Afro-American*, while conceding this fact, insisted, "The hospital officials cannot escape responsibility for keeping the facilities on hand in the best of condition and by all means, clean."[323]

Though Lillian and Bernard were devastated, they did not sue. Lillian's sister, Mary Nightengale, later said that she wrote a letter to one of the local papers denouncing the staff at Freedmen's but that Bernard had written later, expressing his satisfaction with the hospital authorities! Another sister-in-law, Amy Atkinson, blamed Bernard for listening to his old crony, Dr. Scott, who assured him that there was no danger. A few months later Lillian conceived again, and the following November Caulbert Bernard Ruffin III was born. This time Lillian insisted on being returned home from Freedmen's immediately—by ambulance—and the child survived—to write this narrative.

In April, 1952 Bernard Ruffin, Jr. , became only the first Negro corporal in the history of the Metropolitan Police Department. The rank of corporal was fairly new in the department, and the only other policeman of color (in a department of 160) to attain a rank above private had a decade before been promoted from private to sergeant. The *Washington Afro-American* reported, "The new corporal, sporting two blue chevrons on his sleeve, the first of his race to attain such a rank, was sworn in to his elevated post Wednesday [April 16] at 10 p.m."[324] When Bernard came home wearing his new gold badge, his four year old son was quite distressed because he preferred the *color* silver and only with great difficulty was made to understand that the gold badge was a great honor.

The appointment was not without controversy. There were some complaints, within the African American community, that the police boys clubs, which served over 6000 children, had been split into two segregated divisions in order to justify the promotion. Indeed, there were now five clubs for white boys under a Corporal Marshall Cook in Division I and four clubs for Negro boys in Division II, under Corporal Ruffin. Major Robert Murray, chief of police, defended his decision by saying, "A group of colored citizens asked me to organize the boys clubs along these lines. The group had a chart outlining the then proposed organization that would make Ruffin coordinator for the color clubs and camps. I told the group that I would pass their recommendations on to a board that controls the boys clubs. I did so. And the board approved the recommendation. I thought I was doing something that would please a lot of people." Responding to the accusation that segregating the boys clubs was the only way to bring about Ruffin's promotion, Murray affirmed, "Officer Ruffin stood at the top of the civil service list and would have been promoted anyway. He would have received the same assignment as any other man. I have promised I would be fair in my promotional policy and I intend to fulfill that promise."[325]

Bernard also taught part-time at the Letcher School of Art on Logan Circle in Washington. Dr. Paul Phillips Cooke, a friend and fraternity brother, recalled in 1997 than in the late '40s or early '50s, Bernard developed a new, extremely vivid type of paint, which Cooke used for the sets of the plays at the college where he taught.

After his retirement from the police force, with the rank of sergeant, in 1964, Bernard served as director of safety and security at Howard University for three years before being appointed Associate Director for Training for the Office of Economic Opportunity's Pilot District Project, set up "to develop and implement training and educational programs adaptive to the changing environment in which police must work," specifically to develop programs "to prepare the law enforcement officer to be more effective in utilizing new methods of achieving the traditional law enforcement goals of preventing crime, apprehending criminals, and maintaining the peace."[326] After the Pilot District Project came to an end in 1971 Bernard was named to the newly created administrative position of Director of Security and Safety at the Rockville, Maryland campus of Montgomery College.

In the meantime Caulbert Bernard Ruffin, Sr. had continued his nomadic life after his separation from Blanche. For several years he rented an apartment at 1112 W Street, N.W. with his friend, Alphaeus Hunton, a professor at Howard. On June 11, 1941 he received a letter from the Post Office Department which read, "Under the provisions of the Retirement Act, as amended, you are hereby notified that the records of this office show that you will have attained the age of 62 years on August 20, 1941. Therefore, your service as a Railway Postal Clerk at $2450.00 per annum will, under the previsions of this law, terminate at the close of business August 31, 1941, when you will be automatically separated from the service." He was commended for his 29 year service and told, "You will be greatly missed by those with whom you have been associated on the road and by all members of the office, and on behalf of all I am taking the liberty of expressing the hope that you may enjoy many years of good health and happiness in your retirement."[327] It is interesting that the letter, which Caulbert preserved, was burnt through with a cigarette.

After his retirement, Caulbert moved from room to room. He worked for a time, in an unknown capacity, for one Dr. E.C. Wiggins, on 704 Q Street in Washington.[328] He worked part-time for the post office as a mail sorter for a time. In 1946 he moved to New York, where he worked for the Twentieth Century Fox Film Company[329], in an unrecorded capacity, perhaps in the mail room. Then he returned to Washington, where he worked as a watchman at Raleigh Haberdashers, a clothing store.[330] His personal papers reveal that there was some trouble with the Internal Revenue Service, for on December 22, 1947, just a month after the birth of his grandson, he was issue "a warrant of distraint" for the collection of his 1946 income tax.[331]

He appeared at the christening of his only grandchild Easter Sunday, 1948, at Fifteenth Street Presbyterian Church. He sat in the back of the nave and refused to enter the main part of the sanctuary with his family. This action, according to Bernard, Jr. was because of his hatred of organized religion. Yet his tax records show that he contributed (albeit less than $25 per annum) to Shiloh Baptist Church on 9th Street, N.W. Was his failure to sit with the rest of the family the result of his hatred of religion or, more likely, his hatred of Blanche?

In 1950 Caulbert, who, according to his son, had enjoyed fine health, suffered a heart attack and developed diabetes.[332] At that point Bernard, Jr. said that he went to live with his sister Adela. Adela had for more than 20 years been living in Asheville, North Carolina but, although she died there late in 1952, she disappears from the city directories during the year 1952 (which means that she was not there in 1951). So it is possible that she and Caulbert lived together somewhere. According to Bernard, Jr., the two could not get along. In 1951 Caulbert was living at 2406 Celia Avenue in Charlotte with a Perry family. Leroy Perry, Jr., who was seven at the time, remembered, in a telephone interview in the early 1990s, "a tall, light-skinned fellow who always wore a hat and sunglasses, even indoors," but who was kind and loved children. He was treated like a relative. Young Perry and his sister would tag along each day when the old man went to the bus stop. Just where he went, Perry had no idea.

Sometime in 1952 Caulbert was back in Washington, living on 13th Street, N.W., on the top floor of a small apartment building near

Logan Circle. His grandson has a vivid picture of him from this time: a tall, gaunt, rather irritable old man, wearing suspenders, tottering painfully about in a drab, sparsely furnished kitchen. He also recalls that during that summer, there were no apples in the local supermarkets and that his mother Lillian called "Granddaddy", who "always knew where to find everything". "Granddaddy" promised to get the apples and on a given day aunt Mary Jones Nightengale Carter drove "Peetie" to the apartment building on 13th Street, where "Granddaddy" stood in the doorway with the sack of apples. There was, it seems, no more than perfunctorily conversation with the boy, no invitation to come in.

By this time Caulbert was failing. He told his friend Dudley Tucker that he was suffering "bitterly" from pains in the legs and back. He entered Freedmen's Hospital around the time of his seventy-third birthday because of trouble with his heart and prostate. One day Lillian came home from the hospital and told her son, "Your granddaddy knows he can never get well, so he said he would just as soon die now." So Caulbert proceeded to starve himself to death, and, on October 14, he died of "inanition."[333]

While grandson Bernard, III remembered Caulbert as a rather cold, severe, even terrifying old man, Blanche, or "Granny" he recalled as approachable, warm, and loving. He frequently spent the day with her at the large, well-kept house at 124 Randolph Place where she lived with Elinor and Art, who were working during the day, and Art, Jr., who was at school. The rear bedroom, which had a porch that overlooked a small yard filled with flowers, was hers, with a rocking chair, four-poster bed, antique wash stand, and painted china figurines. She had a special cubby-hole in her pantry where she kept fig newtons and other goodies and no visit to her house was without a trip to the corner store for "nabiscoes." She taught "Peetie" to recite little rhymes such as one which began: "Come, little leaves, said the wind one day" and "Rain, rain, go away, come again some other day." Although Granny never drove a car, she would warn about the perils of crossing the railroad tracks and taught "Peetie" the phrase to remember when crossing: "Stop, look, and listen." By this time Granny's eyes were too "dim" to permit reading, but she would go through picture books. "Peetie" showed her his dinosaur books and she told funny stories, in a soft, mellifluous, aristocratic southern accent (which his Pennsylvania-born mother told him not to imitate) about what would happen if the creatures depicted were let loose on the streets of Washington. "If one of those came at me

I wouldn't *stop* running!" she said.

Granny would sit on the red painted steps in front of the house and reminisce about a magical place, a fairyland called "Norfolk" about a childhood in a never-never land long, long ago. She talked about the voyage by water from Washington to Norfolk, and how a boatman would warn non-passengers off by booming, "All ashore that's going ashore." He would call out the names of the ports where the boat stopped and she would imitate his voice, calling out the names of the places, like "Newport News! Old Point Comfort!"

It was in September, 1952[334] that "Peetie", along with his parents and Elinor, "Big Art", and "Little Art" saw Granny off to Norfolk to see her sister Nonie and niece Louise on *The District of Columbia*. That was her last journey to the place of her birth. Although only 68, she had begun to lose her memory fall and break bones and had to give up her job. Her condition would most certainly be described in late century as "Alzheimer's dementia", but at the time her doctors said she had "arteriosclerosis." Her personality changed. She became angry and irritable. She did things that did not make sense. In the summer of 1955, "to give Aunt Elinor a rest", "Granny", after a bad fall, came to live with her son and family at 303 Taylor Street. She stayed in the same room with her sister-in-law Louise Hubbard (not to be confused with Louise Elliott), who, with difficulty was able to restrain her from making and re-making her bed all night long. She insisted on washing dishes, but ordered her grandson to put them in the dining room instead of the cupboard where they belonged, and frightened him with her unaccustomed anger. Some nights family members would turn on the lights of the bathroom only to find "Granny" there, completely undressed, now almost a skeleton, cowering in fear and bewilderment. At he end of summer Blanche went back to Elinor's, where she would frequently escape the lady hired to watch her and wander the streets.

Helen Atkins recalled, "Elinor told me one tale. Mrs. Ruffin was a perfect housekeeper and so she would go out in the kitchen and help the maid. So the maid went to Safeway one time and took Mrs. Ruffin with her. Mrs. Ruffin got away from her and went on out and the woman couldn't find her. Mrs. Ruffin went the opposite way from where she was supposed to go. The girl went home and called the police. The police called Elinor. They told her, 'We have your mother here. She's a *delightful* old lady. You don't have to come. We'll take her home." She had told them, "My son is Corporal Bernard Ruffin and she told them [correctly] where he was stationed." She also named Elinor and accurately named the school where she was. [335]

In 1956 Blanche was placed in a private nursing home run by a Miss Wainwright. She was then only 72, and the other ladies, who were in their 80s and 90s, referred to her as "The Little Girl." Blanche continued to deteriorate, ceased to speak coherently, and then at all, sitting with her elbows on knees, staring dazedly, sometimes muttering incoherencies. By the fall of 1958 she was curled into a fetal position when daughter-in-law Lillian took her 11 year old son to see his grandmother on her 74th birthday. He hated the nickname "Peetie," but his mother explained that if Granny were to understand anything, it would pertain to the distant past, and so she called out, "Granny, Peetie is here." As if from the depths of the grave itself echoed the feeble response: "Peetie."

Two weeks later Blanche died. The funeral was conducted by Robert Pierre Johnson, pastor of the Fifteenth Street Church at the McGuire Funeral Home. An aged soloist, in a quavering voice, sang her favorite hymn "I Come to the Garden Alone." A carload of mourners came north from Norfolk: Nonie, her daughter Louise and Louise's son Allan, and cousin Janice. Peetie had seen or heard of none of them. His parents showed the greatest deference to a stiff little figure of alabaster white who sat in a big upholstered chair with carved arm rests that had been left to Blanche by her late employer Mrs. Thom. This was "Aunt Nonie," who, in a feeble, husky voice, called Peetie and asked for a glass of water. She spoke very little, except to explain that she had broken her spine by falling down the steps of her triangular back yard (she had neither broken her spine nor had a triangular backyard). Everyone fussed over her: "She's *the only one left!*" In her last years, according to her daughter-in-law, she would take to the streets, handing out old newspapers, thinking they were Bibles. Less than a year after Blanche died, on July 9, 1959, the oldest and the last of the "six beautiful girls" thanked daughter Louise for everything she had done for her, asked her, "Crack me some ice," and, clutching her Bible, died at 85.

Chapter Twenty

The descendants of Frank and Dodie were not blessed with longevity. Although Nonie lived to 85 and Blanche to 74, Carrie died at around 30, Frank at 41, Emma at 43, and Mattie at 45. Bernard, Jr., who died at 58 in 1972, was the longest-lived of the male grandchildren: Allan Jackson died at 40, William James at 54, and Frank's son Frank at 28. Florence (Nonie's younger daughter) lived to be 72, Janice 65, Viola 29, and Elinor 64. Only Frank's daughter Virginia, who lived to be 81 and Louise, the oldest of the cousins, who lived to be, at least according to her baptismal record, 90, attained a great age.

There are many descendants of William Greenwood and Martha Sparrow living today, but nearly all of them are through Billy Sparrow's daughter Gertrude Sparrow Williams White, the fourth of his eleven children, who died in Chicago in 1945 at the age of 74. On the other hand, there seem to be very few descendants of Sarah Kemp. Sarah Kemp had three children, four grandchildren, seven great-grandchildren, 13 second great-grandchildren, ten third great grandchildren, nine fourth great grandchildren, and, as of the 1990s, six fifth great grandchildren. Of the offspring of Sarah's grandson Frank Kemp, Blanche Kemp Robinson Ruffin is represented by one childless grandson, Bernard Ruffin III (Elinor's son Art Waller, Jr., died childless in 1973). Mattie's daughter Janice and Carrie's son William were childless, as were both children of young Frank. Russell Thomas Kemp, Sarah's great-grandson and the apparent child of the elder Frank, had two children, Russell Julian and Jayne. Russell was childless, as are both of Jayne's daughters, Karyn and Shelley. Elenora, or Nonie Kemp is represented, however, by Audrey Elliott Vagner, daughter of Louise, who, in turn has four children and two grandchildren (her brother Allan died childless in 1977), and three children of Florence, who in turn, have between them several grandchildren and, in the mid-90s, four great-grandchildren. Franklin Kemp's "white" family was, if anything, even less prolific. Of the five children of George Alexander Smith who lived to adulthood, two were childless (Thomas and George, Jr.) William, aside from Frank, had two sons who lived to adulthood, but neither of whom married. Ellen had two daughters, neither of whom produced offsrping. Murray had five children, but only two grandchildren—through one daughter—and just a handful of latter-day descendants.

Some might question the purpose of this life-long ancestor hunt.

It has produced no celebrities (except, perhaps, for the distantly related Alva Smith and her daughter Consuelo Vanderbilt, who were known primarily not for themselves but for the men they married), some solid substantial persons moderately successful in the world's eyes, and some failures. Why should these dead be raised from the dust where they slumber? While most are in agreement that succeeding generations should study the achievements of presidents, generals, politicians, and other "leaders", why should posterity concern itself with "little people just passing through"—especially "little people" who had few descendants?

The fact is, "little people" were just as much a part of history as the politicians and millionaires, and through public documents and oral history a fairly substantial account of the lives and fortunes of Sarah Kemp, Martha Sparrow, and William Greenwood can be put together, which provides insights, even to those not related, as to how people of their time, place, and circumstances met the challenges of life.

Would-be genealogists are always warned that their researches "might turn up a horse-thief." There seem to be no horse-thieves on the Kemp-Greenwood-Sparrow family trees, but not a few "bums", drunks, and ladies of questionable reputation. It is sad and silly to pursue the study of family history only in hopes of aggrandizing oneself through proof of descent from the powerful and prominent, an attitude that led Bernard Ruffin, Jr. to hold the hobby of "Genealogy" in contempt and prompted him to the frequent assertion that at death "the Almighty will not ask thy name or thy birth, but rather, 'What hast thou done on earth.'" What is fascinating is that in the objective study of family history one enters the past by little-known doors to see how ordinary people lived their lives. Many "skeletons" come tumbling forth from the "closet" but these are only a part of the entire picture of life, which at all times is checquered with times both fair and foul and individuals both bad and good. The story of the Kemp-Greenwood-Sparrow family may be the history of a "typical" "mixed" or "Eufrafrindian" family, or it may not be. Most likely the individuals in this relationship were "typical" only of themselves. But the history is of importance because, despite all the "Skeletons in the Closet", it is the story of human beings—unique, as all people are— and their struggle with the tempests and turmoils of life.

Table One: The Patrilinear Ancestors of Martin Greenwood

(By generations)

1. Oswald Grünewald
born circa 1540
married Elsa [surname unrecorded]
died Babenhausen October 1, 1614

2. Nicolaus Grünewald
born Babenhausen, Hessen-Darmstadt, circa 1569
married (1) Babenhausen, November 1, 1602 to Jacobë Hochsträsser
(c. 1578-February 22, 1628)
      (2) Babenhausen, November 28, 1632 to Barbara Kilian (1597-1673)
occupation: master butcher
died Babenhausen, October 21, 1635, of plague
children: Elsa (b. 1604), Anna (b. 1606), Helfrich (1608-1667), Anna Margaretha (1611-1683), Andreas (1616-1622), Petronella Amalia (1620-1620), Amalia (1623-1685), Anna (1633-1637)

3. Helfrich Grünewald
born Babenhausen, June, 1608
married Babenhausen, November 27, 1632 to Frau Anna May Kern
occupation: master butcher
children: Anna (1634-1635), Paulus (1636-1702), Anna Magdalena (b.1638), Margareth (b. 1640), Johann Helfrich (1643-1727), Barbara (1645-1645), Johann Nicolaus (1646-1647), Anna Susanna (b. 1648), Maria Elisabeth (1651-1652), Adelburgis (female) (1651-1656)

4. Paulus Grünewald
born Babenhausen, February 22, 1636
married Babenhausen April 22, 1661 to Luise Anna Zollman (1639-?)
occupation: master butcher, proprietor of the Black Lion Inn, and city councilman
died Babenahusen, May 5, 1702
children: Friedrich Philipp (1663-1736),), Hans Jacob (1666-d. early) Johann Ludwig (1664-1698), Hans Jacob (II) (b.1668), Johann Helfrich (1679-1767)

5. Johann Ludwig Grünewald
born Babenhausen December 4, 1664
married March 4, 1690 to Maria Eleonora Lottich (1665-1697)
occupation: surgeon-barber
died Babenhausen, March 18, 1698
children: Johann Georg (1690-1766), Georg Jacob Ludwig (b.1691),
Margaretha (b. 1694), Johann Christian (b.1696), JohannLudwig (1697-1697)

6. Johann Georg Grünewald
born Schaafheim, Hessen-Darmstadt, June 23, 1690
married Altheim, Hessen-Darmstadt, November 1, 1712 to Anna Klein (1691-1767)
occupation: hospital administrator (for 44 years) and teacher in the German school
died Babenhausen, September 20, 1766
children: Anna Elisabetha (md. Krapp) (1713-1781), Helena Johann (1714-1717), Maria Luise (b.1717), Johann Martin (1720-1781), Anthon Christian (1722-1723), Justus Adolph (1724-1761), Friedrich Phillip (1727-1772), Maria Catharina (1730-1732), Johann Michael (b.1732)

7. Friedrich Philipp Grünewald
born Babenhausen, January 19, 1727
married (1) Babenhausen, April 28, 1750 to Dorothea Francisca Müller (1729-1759)
        (2) around 1759 to Eleonora Elisabetha Schwind (1727-1761)
        (3) Babenhausen, November 12, 1761 to Maria Catharina Lemcke (1735-1808)
occupation: merchant, innkeeper, and lieutenant in town militia
died Babenhausen, December 19, 1772
children (by Dorothea) Johanna Catharina Francisca (b.1751), Maria Augusta Elisabeth (1752-1754), Johann Caspar Friedrich (b.1754), Wilhelmina Christiana (b.1756), Elisabath Dorothea Salome (b.1759) (by Eleonora) Ludwig Christian (1760-1761), (by Maria Catharina) Johann Martin Carl (1763-1825), Johann Georg Ernst (b.1765), August Daniel (b. 1767), Catharina Sybilla (1769-1776)

8. Johann Martin Carl Grünewald
born Babenhausen July 1, 1763
married (1) Babenhausen, September 14, 1795 to Anna Catharina Dickhaut (1757-1813)
  (2) Katharina Heinrietta Kopp Sauerwein (d.1825)
occupation: silkweaver and manufacturer of silk stockings; later a soap manufacturer
died Babenhausen June 11, 1825
children: Ernst Friedrich (Frederick) (1796-1855), Johann Martin (1799-1869)

Table Two, the Patrilinear Descendants of Hen Lotz (to Maria Eleonora Lottich Grünewald)

1. Hen Lotz the Elder
born Niederzell near Schlüchtern, before 1470
wife's name not known
occupation: peasant farmer
died Niederzel, after 1501

2. Jörg Lotz
born Niederzell about 1495
occupation: peasant farmer
wife's name not known
died after 1522

3. Wilhelm Lotichius
born Niederzell, about 1520
wife's name not known
graduate of Wittenberg University
occupation: Lutheran pastor
died Ulfa, Öberhessen, July 4, 1571

4. Zacharias Lotichius
born Ulfa, Öberhessen, about 1558
married Wolfskehlen, 1598, to Anna Angelus (b.1575), daughter of
Johannes Angelus (1542-1608), superintendent of the churches in the
city of Darmstadt
graduate of Marburg University
occupation: Pastor of the city church of Wolfskehlen and professor of
literature at the municipal grammar school there
died Wolfskehlen, Hessen-Darmstadt March 2, 1604

5. Johannes Lotichius
born Wolfskehlen, Hessen-Darmstadt, about 1600
married (1) Darmstadt, 1624 to Kunigunde Snyder
        (2) about 1634 to Anna Eleonora Voltz (1615-1670)
graduate of University of Giesen
occupation: Lutheran pastor in Crumstadt, Hofheim, and Zwingenberg

and definitor of the Synod from 1635 to 1649
died Zwingenberg, Hessen-Darmstadt, September 9, 1649

6. Johann Tobias Lotichius
born Zwingenberg, Hessen-Nassau, about 1635
married Frankfurt-am-Main, July 19, 1664 to Anna Maria Hellwig
occupation: tutor and imperial notary at court of the Holy Roman
Emperor
died Frankfurt-am-Main, November 26, 1666
children: Maria Eleonora Lottich (1665-1697), Johann Lottigius (1666-
c.1728)

The Children and Grandchildren of Martin and Margaret Greenwood

Martin Greenwood (born Johann Martin Grünewald)
born Babenhausen, March 26, 1799
married Babenhausen, January 2, 1825 to Margreth Koch
occupation: soap manufacturer
died Norfolk, VA December 26, 1869

Margaret Greenwood (born Margreth Koch)
born Babenhausen, April 5, 1825
parents: Johann Heinrich Koch (1752-1811), farm laborer and Anna
Catharina Lang Koch (1760-1826)
died Norfolk, VA June 6, 1866

1) William Greenwood (born Wilhelm Grünewald)
born Babenhausen, March 31, 1821
common-law marriage to Martha Sparrow (1824-1867) around 1840
occupation: soap manufacturer
died Norfolk, VA August 20, 1855
children: Josephine Sparrow (b.1841/2) William H. Sparrow (1844-
1908/9)→ Elenora Virginia Sparrow Wright Johnson (1849-1873),
Martha Missouri Sparrow Brock (1852-1910), Mary Louisa Sparrow
Kemp Bass→ (1854-1929)

2) Katharina Heinriette Maria Grünewald
born Babenhausen, March 11, 1824
died Babenhausen, March 21, 1824

3) Charles Frederick Greenwood (born Carl Friedrich Grünewald)
born Babenhausen, April 28, 1825
married (1) Norfolk, VA May 17,1848 to Mary Elizabeth Griffin (1832-
1889)
        (2) Norfolk, VA September, 1890 to Ann Robinson Todd (1837-
1921)
occupation: jeweller
died Norfolk, VA July 10, 1904
children: Margaret Elizabeth Greenwood Norsworthy→ (1849-1948),

Laura Virginia Greenwood Vesey→ (1851-1914), Elenora Grace Greenwood Catlin→ (1853-1923), Pauline Augusta Greenwood Peterson→ (1855-1939), Grace Edwards Greenwood Lee (1860-1884), Kate Lee Greenwood Stevens→ (1862-1938), Charles Frederick Greenwood, Jr. (1870-1904)

4) Margaret Elizabeth Greenwood (born Margaretha Elisabetha Grünewald)
born Babenhausen, April 26, 1827
married Norfolk, October 19, 1843 to Joaquin Martinez Bayto (born Baito) (1819-1868)
died Norfolk, January 18, 1852
children Josephine Bayto (1845/6-1850), Margaret Amelia Bayto Curdts (1848-1915), Mary Virginia Bayto (1849-1943), Joaquin Martinez Bayto, Jr. (1851-1852)

5) Friedrich Adam Grünewald
born Babenhausen, July 13, 1829
died Babenhausen, September 20, 1829

6) Martin Greenwood, Jr. (born Johann Martin Grünewald)
born Babenhausen, March 18, 1831
occupation: soap manufacturer
died Norfolk, September 20, 1852

7) Ellen Greenwood (born Magdalena Grünewald)
born Babenhausen, August 30, 1833
married Norfolk May 15, 1851 to George Louis Curdts (born Georg Ludwig Theodor Curdts) (1825-1906)
died Norfolk, May 22, 1915
children: Margaret Curdts (1852-1852), Edward William Curdts (1855-1945)→, Emma Louise Curdts (1857-1876), Columbia Virginia Curdts (1859-1863), Louis Martin Curdts (1861-1939), Charles Frederick Curdts (1863-1885), William Theodore Curdts, Sr. (1865-1930), Minnie Amelia Curdts (1869-1958), Robert Foster Curdts (1873-1876)

8) Frederick Greenwood
born Reisterstown, Maryland July 15, 1837
married (1) Portsmouth, VA October 10, 1860 to Columbia Parson

Minter (1840-1909)
    (2) Washington, DC September 28, 1910 to Rena Lee Fitchett
Crowell (1867-1945)
occupation: jeweller
died Norfolk, VA January 23, 1920
children: Charles Minter Greenwood (1861-1944), Martin Lee
Greenwood→ (1864-1925)

The Family of George Alexnder and Adeline M.McGehee Smith

George Alexander Smith
born Dumfries, VA November 10, 18073
married, place unknown, December 11, 1832 to Adeline M. McGehee
died Milton, NC April 7, 1860
occupation: tobacco planter and merchant
father: George Smith (b. Scotland, July 12, 1775—died Dumfries, VA August 29, 1822)
mother: Delia Stirling Forbes   (b. Dumfries, VA   July 12, 1780   d. April 8, 1841)4

Adeline Mildred McGehee
born Person County, NC December 16, 1813
died Milton, NC May 22, 1858
father: Thomas Mumford McGehee (c. 1784-1867)
mother: Elizabeth Jeffreys McGehee (1795-1825), daughter of Thomas and Mildred Mitchell Jeffreys

1. Thomas McGehee Smith
born Milton, NC March 12, 1834
married March 30, 1858 to Julia Alexander
died during battle of Cold Harbor, near Richmond, VA June 3, 18645
no children

---

3 His birthdate has been given also as December, 1807 and November 10, 1808
4 According to the *Sterling Genealogy*, written by Albert Sterling in 1908, Delia Forbes was the daughter of David Forbes (1752-1789), a native of Pitstigo, Scotland and a surgeon in the Continental Army and son of Sir William Forbes and Margaret Stirling (1754-1806), a native of Herbertshire, Scotland and daughter of George Stirling, Laird of Herbertshire (d. 1760)
5 His date has been also given as May 30, 1864. The Battle of Cold Harbor raged from late May to early June.

2. William Forbes Smith
born Milton, NC September 21, 1837
married Mary Ellen Huntington (1838-1918)
died Winston, NC   March 27, 1900
children: Benjamin Franklin Kemp, Sr.→ (1854-1897), Sterling Smith
(c.1860-1918), Henry Huntington Smith (1862-1890), Julia A. Smith
(1865-1877)

3. Delia Sterling Smith
born Milton, NC May 2, 1840
died Milton, NC June 16, 1853

4. Mumford Augustus Smith
born Milton, NC May 23, 1842
died Milton, NC February 24, 1845

5. Ellen Elizabeth Smith
born Milton, NC   August 1, 1844
married Preston Roan, M.D. (1840-1882)
died Winston, NC, October 25, 1909
children: Julia Roan Smoak (1864-1940) Ada McGehee Roan (1869-
1952)

6. George Alexander Smith, Jr.
born Milton, NC September 30, 1847
died Vicksburg, MS around 1900
Never married

7. Murray Forbes Smith
born Milton, NC   January 17, 1850
married 1874 to Kate Wilson (1855-1912)
died Vicksburg, MS September 27, 1909
children: Victor Conway Smith (1875-1953), Adeline McGehee Smith
Johnson→(1882-1969), Murray Forbes Smith, Jr. (1879-1949),
Clarence Carroll Smith (1883-1961), Lomie Lee Smith Johnson (1892-
1986)

8. Rosa Smith
born Milton, NC Jan 6, 1852
died Milton, NC February 5, 1855

The Children and Grandchildren of William and Lydia (I) Kemp

William Kemp
born Virginia
died probably before 1860

Lydia_____
born Virginia circa 1788
died, probably Norfolk, VA, 1860-1865

1) Sarah Kemp
born Norfolk, VA 1809/1810
perhaps married to Russell Kemp
died Norfolk, VA May 4, 1897
children: Lydia Kemp II (1837-1917), John Kemp (1839-1904), Samuel
Russell Kemp (1844-1896)

2) Joseph C. Kemp, Sr.
born Norfolk, VA circa 1819/20
married Minerva Tynes (b. Isle of Wight Co., Va. 1820/21, daughter of
Patsey Godwin d. Norfolk, 1860-1865)
died Norfolk, VA March 14, 1875
children: William Franklin Kemp (c.1847-?), Joseph C. Camp, Jr. (c.
1849-1882), John Kemp (c.1850-?), Timothy Kemp (1852-1874),
Alexander Kemp (c.1854-?), Raymond Kemp (1856-1914), Harriet
Kemp (b. 1860 d. 1860-1865)

The children of Lydia Kemp:
    1) Benjamin Franklin Kemp, Sr. (1854-1897)
The surviving children of Samuel R. Kemp
    1) William Kemp (1870-?)
    2) Sarah Jane Kemp (1873-1913)→
    3) Minnie Kemp (1877-?)

The children of Joseph Jr. and Martha (Gray) Kemp
    1) Christopher Kemp (c.1870-?)
    2) Frances M. Kemp (c.1872-?)
    3) Joseph C. Kemp, III (c.1878-?)
The children of John and Camilla (King) Kemp
    1) Anthony Kemp (c.1874-?)
The children of Raymond and Mary (Johnson) Kemp
    1) Frank Kemp (1880-1897)
    2) Raymond Kemp, Jr. (1881-1882)

The Children and Grandchildren of Franklin and Mary (Sparrow) Kemp

Benjamin Franklin Kemp
born Milton, NC 1854/55
married Norfolk, VA July 8, 1875 to Mary Louisa Sparrow
occupation: assistant jailer
died Norfolk, VA September 13, 1897
father: William Forbes Smith (1837-1900)
mother: Lydia Kemp (1837-1917)

Mary Louisa Sparrow
born Norfolk, VA November 25, 1854
married (2) Norfolk, VA July 10, 1896 to Armour W.D. Bass (1863-1896)
died Washington, DC May 14, 1929
father: William Greenwood (1821-1855)
mother: Martha Sparrow (1824-1867)

1. Elenora[6] Virginia Kemp (Nonie)
born Norfolk, VA March 6, 1874
married (1) New York City, September 19, 1893 to Samuel Joseph Jackson, Jr. (1871-1914)
  (2) ? George H. Manners (1873-1926)
  (3) Brooklyn, NY, January 10, 1928 to James Frederic Renshaw Wilson (1873-?) (Divorced)
  (4) Norfolk, VA July 28, 1936 to George Elliott, Sr. (1864-1937)
died Norfolk, VA July 9, 1959
children: Mary Louise Jackson Elliott→ (1892 or 1894-1983), Allan Joseph Jackson (1894 or 1896-1934), Florence Winifred Jackson Goude Johnson→ (1897 or 1900-1971)

2. Caledonia Kemp (Callie or Carrie)
born Norfolk, VA March 17, 1876

---

[6] As a young adult, she signed her name "Eleanor"; from 1928 on, she was "Elnora."

married (1) New York City, March 13, 1896 to Benjamin James, Jr.
      (2) ?   to James (?) Jones
died (place unknown) between 1906 and 1910
children: Harold James (?-?), William George James (1896-1950), Benjamin James III (b.1899 probably died young)   James D. Jones (b.1906/7)

3. Martha R. Kemp (Mattie)
born Norfolk, VA June 22, 1878
married (?) Joseph Walton Brock (b.c.1884)
      Norfolk, VA March 21, 1918 to John Anderson (b.c.1884)
died Norfolk, VA February 18, 1924
children: Janice Meredith Kemp Ogburn (1903-1968)

4. Benjamin Franklin Kemp, Jr.
born Norfolk, VA April, 1880
died Norfolk, VA July 21, 1881

5. Emma Maud Kemp
born Norfolk, VA , April 17, 1882
married Norfolk, VA April 17, 1900 to George William Gatling (1871-1950)
died Norfolk, VA October 2, 1925
No children

6. Blanche Franklin Kemp
born Norfolk, VA October 11, 1884
common law wife of Walter S. Robinson (1876-?)
married Washington, D.C. October 23, 1912 to Caulbert Bernard Ruffin, Sr. (1879-1952)
children: Viola Herbert Robinson Burgess (1899-1928) Elinor Virginia Robinson Waller→ (1907-1971) Caulbert Bernard Ruffin, Jr. →(1914-1972)

7. Franklin Benjamin Kemp
born Norfolk, VA November 19, 1888 (or 1887)
married New York City, April 12, 1915 to Maud Cornell (1893-1976)
died Bronx, New York, February 18, 1930

children: Eleanor Virginia Kemp Hall (1915-1996) Franklin Joseph Kemp (1917-1945)

1. e.g. Nancy Moler Poeter, *The Comegys Family.* Baltimore: Gateway Press, 1981

2. Norfolk City Corporation Court, Register of Marriages, Book 1, p. 171

3. *Ibid.* Book 1, p. 75, p. 108, p. 140, Book 2, p. 30

4. *Ibid.*, Book 1, p. 75

5. *Norfolk and Portsmouth Daily Advertiser,* January 9, 1840

6. *Ibid.* January 19, 1840

7. *Ibid.* January 14, 1840

8. *Ibid.* July 5, 1840

9. *Ibid.* November 2, 1840

10. *Ibid.* November 26, 1840

11. *Ibid.* February 1, 1840

12. *Ibid.* January 1, 1840

13. *Ibid.* November 2, 1840

14. *Ibid.* November 26, 1840

15. Register of Deaths, Corporation Court, Norfolk, VA, Volume I (1853-1871)

16. Tommy L. Bogger, *The Slave and Free Black Community in Norfolk, 1775-1865.* Charlottesville, VA, 1976, p. 200

17. *Norfolk Beacon,* January 1, 1849

18. *Norfolk and Portsmouth Daily Advertiser,* January 29, 1840

19. *Norfolk Beacon,* December 5, 1848

---

20. Wills, Person County, NC, Book 6, pp. 82-84

21. *Norfolk and Portsmouth Daily Advertiser*, January 16, 1840

22. *Ibid.*   September 3, 1840

23. *Ibid.*   January 16, 1840

24. The U.S. Supreme Court, in the notorious *[Dred] Scott v. Sandford* decision, would, among other things, rule in 1857 that people of colored were not United States citizens.

25. Louise Jackson Elliott, oral history

26. Elinor Robinson Waller, oral history

27. Conversation with Dr. Tommy L. Bogger, Norfolk State University, Norfolk, VA, July, 1992

28. From the signature cards of depositors in the Freedmen's Savings Bank of Norfolk, VA (1871-1874), on microfilm at the National Archives, Washington, DC

29. Photocopy of a document in the possession of Alfred L. Melenbacker of Camden, ME.

30. Norfolk Corporation Court, Marriage Register I, 1853-1879

31. This is an assumption. The families of Sarah and Joseph were clearly related, but there are no documents that state the exact relationship between the two. The fact that Sarah's mother Lydia was living with Joseph's wife and family in 1860 would seem to indicate that Joseph and Lydia were brother and sister. It is also possible that Joseph, who was ten years younger, was a nephew.

32. Norfolk Corporation Court, Law Causes, Registration, Minerva Tynes, November 1, 1842

33. U.S. Census, Virginia, City of Norfolk, County of Norfolk, August 9, 1860

34. Charles L. Perdue, ed., *Weevils in the Wheat: Interviews with Virginia Ex-Slaves.* (Charlottresville, VA, 1976), p. 282 (I have "translated" some of the dialect in this and subsequent slave interviews into English comprehensible for most readers).

35. *Norfolk Beacon,* July 19, 1848

36. George P. Rawick, ed., *The American Slave, A Composite Autobiography.* Vol. 14, Part One. (Westport, CT, 1972), p.139

37. *Ibid.* p. 140

38. Rawick, *op. cit.* P. 290

39. *Ibid.* p. 286-288

40. Perdue, *op.cit.* pp. 315-318

41. *Ibid.* p. 319-320

42. Rawick, *op.cit.* p. 312

43. *Ibid.* pp. 44-50

44. Ethel C. Woodall Grider, *McGehee Descendents.* Vol. I. (Baltimore, 1987), pp. 1-34

45. Records of the Daughters of the American Revolution, file for Mumford McGehee

46. Person County, North Carolina, Will Book G, pp. 82-84

47. Jane N. And Ethel C. Woodall Grider, *McGehee Descendants,* Vol. III. (Baltimore, 1991),
pp. 299-301

48. *Roxboro [NC] Courier.* August 5, 1941

49. Caswell County Deed Book [???   ]

50. Elinor Robinson Wallers, interviews between 1963 and 1970

51. Albert M. Sterling, *The Sterling Genealogy.* (New York. 1909), Vol. II., p. 1201

52.   *Ibid.* ***

53. U.S. Slave Census, Caswell County, NC, 1850

54. Caswell County Court, Inventory Book S, pp. 312-320

55. Minutes of the Milton Presbyterian Church, Vol. I. (On microfilm, courtesy of Presbyterian Historical Society, Montreat, NC)

56.   *Ibid.*

57. The historian of the Milton Presbyterian Church told the author the following anecdote when he visited Milton in 1991: Tom Day offered to make the pews for the church on condition that he and his family were allowed to sit on the first floor of the church, in the front, with the white members. It was agreed. The pews were still in place at the time of the author's visit.

58. U.S. Census, 1850; U.S. Slave Census, 1850, both for Caswell County, NC

59. Elinor Robinson Waller, conversations, 1963-1971

60. Christian Feest, *The Powhatan Tribes.* (New York: Chelsea House, 1990), p. 68

61.   *Ibid.*

62. Norfolk County Court, *Register for Free Negros & Mulattos, December 25, 1809—May 19, 1852,* no. 390

63.   *Ibid.* No. 487

64. Norfolk County Court, Minute Book 23, p. 6

65. This can be deduced simply by the fact that Martha's oldest daughter, Josephine, is listed as 8 years old in the census of 1850 and nineteen in the census of 1860.

66. National Archives, microfilm M255, *Passenger List of Vessels Arriving at Baltimore 1820-1891, Roll 1, September 2, 1820—March 30, 1837.*

67. Babenhausen Parish Register, Volume I, Deaths, p. 670

68. Babenhausen Parish Register, microfilm 1340325, Church of Jesus Christ of Latter-Day Saints.

69.   *Ibid.*

70.   *Ibid.*

71.   *Ibid.*

72.   *Ibid.*

73. Keerner, Bernhard, *Genealogisches Handbuch: Bürglicher Familien.* (Berlin, 1903),
pp. 391-394

74. Burial Register, Frankfurt-am-Main, Vol. 7., p. 416, 1666

75. Keerner, *op.cit.* p. 394

76. Parish Register, Babenhausen, Deaths, 1697, p. 858

77. Parish Register, Babenhausen, microfilm 134 0 328, LDS (the page numbers are not evident on the microfilm

78. Parish Register, Altheim, microfilm 134 0 323, LDS

79. Parish Register, Babenhausen, Marriages, 1750, p. 51, no. 6, 1761, p. 76, no. 9

80. Parish Register, Wollbach, Germany, as research by Friedrich Wollmershausen, Ostelsheim, Germany, 1982

81. Parish Register, Kandern, researched by Friedrich Wollmershausen, 1982

214

82. London City Postal Directories, 1808-1861, LDS Library, Salt Lake City

83. London Census, 1861

84. Parish register, Babenhausen, Register of Baptisms, 1796, p. 70 and 1799, p. 179, no. 104

85. Obituary in vertical file, Kirn Memorial Library, Norfolk, VA

86. Parish registers, Babenhausen, microfilm 134 0 326, LDS

87. This is a result of my own informal research, based on Babenhausen's death registers.

88. Law Cause file 1851, Circuit Court, Norfolk, VA

89. Norfolk City Corporation Court, Deed Book 25, 143

90.   *Ibid.* Deed Book 29, p. 384

91.   *Ibid.* Deed Book 30, p. 195

92. Elizabeth B. Wingo and W. Bruce Wingo, eds., *Naturalizations and Declarations of Intention, Norfolk Borough/City, Norfolk County (Now Chesapeake), Princess Anne County (now Virginia Beach), Portsmouth, Eastern District Court, VA.* (Norfolk, 1987), p. 47

93.   *Ibid.* pp. 2-64

94. Vertical File, Kirn Memorial Library, Norfolk, VA

95. A similar story was related by another descendant of Louis Theodore Curdts, Bayto's son-in-law.

96. Document in the possession of Alfred L. Melenbacker, Camden, Maine

97. Personal Property Tax Records, Norfolk City, 1851, Virginia State Library, Richmond, VA

98.   *Ibid.*

99. Letter, The Rev. Ira Austin, First Methodist Church, Norfolk, VA, to C. Bernard Ruffin, ca. 1967

100. Newspaper obituary in possession of Virginia Burger Sessoms, Richmond

101. Telephone interview, Margaret Seville Bacchus Lambert, circa 1975

102. Thomas J. Wertenbaker, *Norfolk, Historical Southern Port.* (Durham, NC: Duke University Press, 1962), p. 189

103. *Ibid.*

104. Clipping in the possession of Virginia Burger Sessoms, Richmond, VA

104.. Wertenbaker, *op.cit.* p. 191

105. Roderick E. McGrew, *Encyclopedia of Medical History.* (London: Macmillan, 1985), p. 361

106.. William S. Forrest, *The Great Pestilence in Virginia, Being an Historical Account of the Origins, Character, and Ravages of Yellow Fever in Norfolk and Portsmouth in 1855.* (New York: Derby & Jackson, 1856), p. 29

107.. McGrew, *op.cit.* p. 357

109. Forrest, *op.cit.* pp. 101-104

110. Perdue, *op.cit.* p. 258

111. Forrest, *op.cit.* pp. 94-97

111. Caswell County Superior Court, Will Book S, p. 307

113. Mortality Census, 1860, Caswell County, NC, p. 6, line 16

114. Caswell County Superior Court, Will Book S, p. 356

115. *Milton Chronicle*, April 12, 1861 (North Carolina State Archives, Raleigh, NC)

116. William S. Powell, *When the Past Refused to Die: A History of Caswell County, North Carolina, 1777-1977.* (Durham, NC, 1977), p. 204

117. Rawick, *op.cit.* p. 397

118.   *Ibid.* p. 312

119.   *Ibid.* p. 185

120. Rawick, Vol. 14, Part Two, p. 28

121.   *Ibid.* p. 35

122. *Durham Morning Herald,* April 15, 1956 (Personal County Historical Society, Roxboro, NC)

123. Cassandra Newby, *The World Was All Before Them.* (Williamsburg, VA, 1992), pp. 31-32

124.   *Ibid.* p. 32-33

125.   *Ibid.* p. 104

126. Michael Edward Hucles, *Postbellum Urban Black Economic Development: The Case of Norfolk, Virginia, 1860-1890.* (Ann Arbor, MI, 1990), p. 50

127.   *Ibid.* p.55

128.   *Ibid.*

129.   *Ibid.*

130. Perdue, *op.cit.* p. 18

131.   *Ibid.* p. 241

132.   *Ibid.* p. 262

133. Powell, *op.cit.* p. 227

134. *Ibid.* p. 228

135. *Ibid.*

136. *Milton Chronicle,* May 24, 1861

137. Ms. by John G. Lee in the North Carolina State Archives, Raleigh, NC

138. *Ibid.*

139. *Ibid.*

140. *Ibid.*

141. Stuart McIver, "The Murder of a Scalawag," *American History Illustrated.* April, 1973, p. 16

142. Lea, *op.cit.*

143. *Ibid.*

144. McIver, *op.cit.*, p. 16

145. Newby, *op.cit.* p. 104

146. *Ibid.*

147. *Ibid.* p. 112

148. *Ibid.* p. 113

149. *Ibid.* p.138

150. *Ibid.*

151. Hucles, *op.cit.* pp. 82-83

152. *Ibid.* p. 83

153. *Ibid.*

154. Newby, *op.cit.* p. 184

155. She appears in the 1860 census of free inhabitants.

156. Microfilm of signature cards for Freedmen's Bank, Norfolk, National Archives, Washington

157. Elinor Robinson Waller

158. Norfolk Corporation Court, Will Book 9, p. 15

159. Newby, *op.cit.* p. 276

160. Obituary

161. Arthur T. Vanderbilt, *Fortune's Children: The Fall of the House of Vanderbilt.* (New York, 1989), p. 88

162. *Ibid.* p. 89

163. *Ibid.* p. 121

164. Obituary, Norfolk *Virginian-Pilot*, January 24, 1920

165. *Ibid.*

166. Interview, Dudley Tucker, March 27, 1969

167. Norfolk Corporation Court, Death Registers (as of August 12, 1999, these could not longer be located in the Courthouse!)

168. Norfolk City Directory 1888

169. Norfolk City Directory 1889

170. U.S. Census of 1880, Norfolk, VA, June 5, 1880, dwelling #136, family #238

171. Norfolk Corproation Court, Marriage Register, Book 1, p. 137

172. Dudley Tucker is the sole source of the name of Frank Kemp's boss.

173. Norfolk city directories, 1880s

174. Dudley Tucker

175. *Ibid.*

176. Catalogue of Norfolk Mission College, circa 1899, in archives of Norfolk State University

177. Hucles, *op.cit.* p. 241

178. Vanderbilt, *op.cit.* p. 149-150

179.Curiously, when he filled out his application for a social security card (710-03-6356) on June 30, 1937, Russell Thomas Kemp gave his parents' names as Samuel Kemp and Sadie Lee Bullitt. Sadie, as far as can be determined, was never married until she was wed to James Lovett many years later. If *Samuel* Kemp was Russell's father, this would mean that Samuel *had a child by his own daughter!* Russell also gave his birthplace as "Norfolk, Princess Ann, Va". Norfolk City, Norfolk County, and Princess Anne County were three separate entities. He could have been born in Norfolk City or County, or in Princess Anne County, but *not* in "Norfolk, Princess Ann, Va." It is hard to know what to make of this curious document. Since Sadie (whose second name was, by tradition, Jane, not Lee) was unmarried and living at home, perhaps her father Samuel became the child's legal guardian.

180. Marriage license, Corporation Court, Norfolk County

181. Death register, Norfolk County, on microfilm, Virginia State Archives, Richmond

182. Will of Armour Bass, Corporation Court of Chesapeake, VA, Book 8, p. 294

183. Elinor Robinson Waller, interview, spring 1969

184. Norfolk Corporation Court, Death Register No. 4 (1892-1897)

185. Winston-Salem *Republican,* February 13, 1890

186. Winston-Salem *Union-Republican*, March 29, 1900

187. Forsyth County Superior Court, Case X3929

188. *Winston-Salem Journal*, August 21, 1918

189. Scrapbook in the possession of Virginia Burger Sessoms, Richmond, Virginia

190. Mary Griffin Greenwood died in 1889. C.F. remarried the next year to Anne Robinson Todd.

191. Will, C.F. Greenwood, Norfolk Corporation Court_____

192. Norfolk Corporation Court, Inventory Book 6, pp. 315-317

193. Norfolk Circuit Court, Will Book 2, p. 11

194. Telephone interviews with Mildred Curdts Fitzpatrick, 1975-1984

195. Death certificate, Norfolk Department of Health

196. Louise Jackson Elliott, interview, September, 1966

197. This was Ruth Harris (1905-1950), who married Joseph C. Barnes. She left no children.

198. Interview, Miss Ora Churchill, Portsmouth, VA, circa 1980. Lillian and Henry Ballentine had three children: Goldie (1906-1933), a teacher who married Jordan Sayles and died suddenly after becoming ill at a Christmas party; Evans (1908-1968), who went to New York, married twice, and seems to have been unsuccessful in life; and Oswald (1910-1930), who died in a car crash while studying at St. Paul's College, in Virginia. The Ballentines had no grandchildren.

199. George Elliott, Jr., September, 1966

200. C. Bernard Ruffin, Jr., circa 1970

201.Norfolk *County*did not keep consistent death records. The approximately date of W.H. Sparrow's death is deduced from his disappearance from the Norfolk city directories. West Point Cemetery, which has records dating to the 1880s, has no record of William Sparrow and

Calvary Cemetery has no burial records dating to the time of Sparrow's death.

202. There is some question about the birth years of the children of Elenora Kemp Jackson. Louise was the oldest and she always maintained that she was born in 1894 and that Allan was two years younger and Florence three years Allan's junior. The record of Louise's baptism, in the early 1900s, gives her birth year as 1892. According to her confirmation record, she was born in 1893. According to Allan's military records, he was born in 1894. Florence always insisted that she was born in 1900. Unfortunately, the three Jackson children seem to have been missed by the 1900 census, since they appear neither with their parents in New York nor with their grandmother in Norfolk County.

203. Recollections of Louise Jackson Elliott, 1966-1968

204.   *Ibid.*

205. Caledonia Kemp seems to have had three sons by her marriage to Benjamin James. Louise Elliott recalled that the children of "Aunt Carrie" were William, Harold, and Bennie. The U.S. Census of 1900 states that "Carrie" James, enumerated at her mother's home, had given birth to three children, of whom two were alive: William, born in 1896, and Benjamin, born in 1899. William alone seems to have lived to maturity. When asked about Harold and Bennie, Louise Elliott replaced, "They've been dead so long I don't remember when they died." Obviously, Harold must have died before 1900, and it seems as that by the time of the 1910 census Bennie was also dead.

206. According to the U.S. Census of 1910, Mary Bass (Dodie) was the mother of seven children, of whom only five were alive. Enumerated in her household is a grandchild, James D. Jones, age three, born in New York. This is evidently a child of Caledonia. Since Elinor Robinson (later Waller), who was the very same age and who was living in the same household had no recollection of this cousin, one would assume that this child died shortly afterwards.

207. It should be pointed out that one cannot be certain that the "Mrs. W.H. Anderson" arrested for running a bordello in 1921 was indeed Mattie, but the imprisonment is in accord with the memory of Bernard Ruffin, Jr. who insisted that when "a little boy" his mother took him to see his Aunt Mattie, who was in jail. There is also no *proof* that Mattie Smith the Richmond

boarding-house keeper was in fact Mattie Kemp or that her boarders were all prostitutes. The fact that her boarder, Emma Kemp, is almost certainly her sister and that no Mattie Kemp, Mattie Brock, or Mattie Young of the appropriate age or description appears in the census provides a likely association.

208. Letter, O.L. Murden, Captain, Central Files and Communcations, City of Norfolk, Division of Police, August 30, 1968

209. Norfolk Corporation Court, Common Law Book 34, p. 281, 299, 319

210. *Ibid.* Book 48, p. 174

211. Marian Elliott Bess, interview, April 13, 1978

212. *Ibid.*

213. Louise Jackson Elliott, interview, summer 1970

214. Interview, Helen Ogle Atkins, circa 1990

215. Interview, Sarah Davis Taylor, circa 1991

216. Interview, Elinor Robinson Waller, spring, 1969

217. Interview, George Elliott, Jr., September, 1966

218. Interview, Richard W. Bright, August, 1973

219. Norfolk Corporation Court, Will Book 8, p. 123

220. Registration of free negroes, Norfolk Corporation Court, Law Causes, 1858

221. Interview, Dr. John R. Custis, Jr., 1980

222. *Ibid.*

223. *Ibid.*

224. Statement by C. Bernard Ruffin, Jr., made in the 1960s

225. Interview, Margaret Saunders Manning (first cousin of Caulbert B.

Ruffin, Sr.), August, 1987

226.   *Ibid.*

227.   *Ibid.*

228. Letter, James O. Sorrell, Registrar, North Carolina State Archives, June 21, 1999

229. Statement by George Elliott, Jr., circa 1968

230. Washington, D.C. city directories

231. U.S. Census, Town of Stonington, New London, Connecticut, 1850, 1860, 1870, 1880

232. U.S. Census of 1900, City of Philadelphia; Philadelphia city drectories; marrige license for William G. Williams and Gertrude Lillian Sparrow (no. 59268, Office of Clerk of Orphan's Court, Dvision of the Court of Common Pleas, Philadelphia). Fortunately, the couple did not change the names of their sons, otherwise they would have proved untraceable!

233. Interviews with Dorothy Douglas Williams and Marie Madden Williams Ford.

234. Records of First United Presbyterian Church, Norfolk

235. Elinor Robinson Waller and Louise Jackson Elliott

236. Tuition, according to Ethel Browne O'Mealley, was $6 a semester when she attended in the 1930s.

237. Helen Irene Ogle Atkins, telephone interview, July 6, 1999

238. Constance McLaughlin Green, *The Secret City: A History of Race Relations in the Nation's Capital.*
Princeton, NJ, 1967, pp. 171-175

239. Joseph L. Drew, interview, January 3, 1987

240.   *Ibid.*

241. Peter Perl, "Nation's Capital Held at Mercy of Mob," *The Washington Post Magazine,* July 16, 1989, p. 21

242. Rosina Corrothers-Tucker, interviews, 1974-1976

243. Joseph L. Drew, *op.cit.*

244. Willard B. Gatewood, *Aristocrats of Color: The Black Elite, 1880-1920.* Bloomington, IN, 1990, p. 39

245. *Ibid.* p. 44

246. Helen Irene Ogle Atkins, interview, January 16, 1993

247. *Ibid.* p. 64

248. Helen Irene Ogle Atkins, interview, January 16, 1993

249. Dudley Tucker

250. Marie Taylor Primas, interview, June 7, 1995

251. Gatewood, *op.cit.* p. 287

252. *Ibid.*

253. *Ibid.*

254. Marie Taylor Primas, *op.cit.*

255. *Ibid.*

256. Helen Irene Ogle Atkins, interview, January 16, 1993

257. *Ibid.*

258. *Ibid.*

259. *Washington Tribune,* January 4, 1929

260. Maxine Reynolds Baker, telephone interview, June 24, 1999

261. Joseph L. Drew, interview, January 3, 1987

262. Mary Jones Nightengale Carter, taped memoir, circa 1987

263. Joseph L. Drew, *op.cit.*

264. Mary Jones Nightengale Carter, *op.cit.*

265. *Ibid.*

266. *Ibid.*

267. Grace Ridgeley Drew, interview, January 3, 1987

268. Mary Jones Nightengale Carter, *op.cit*

269. Joseph L. Drew, *op.cit.*

270. Grace Ridgeley Drew, *op.cit.*

271. Helen Ogle Atkins, interview, January 16, 1993

272. Helen Ogle Atkinson, telephone interview, July 6, 1999

273. *Ibid.*

274. Liber Anni 1925, Dunbar High School

275. Helen Ogle Atkins, interviews January 16, 1993 and July 6, 1999

276. Marie Taylor Primas, interview, June 7, 1995

277. *Washington Tribune,* January 4, 1929

278. Helen Ogle Atkins, telephone interview, July 6, 1999

279. Helen Ogle Atkins, interview, January 16, 1993

280. *Ibid.*

281. Marie Taylor Primas, *op.cit.*

282. Norfolk City Corporation Court, Deed Book RB41, p. 374

283. This story was recounted by C. Bernard Ruffin, Jr. during the 1960s.

284. Interview with George and Louise Elliott, September, 1966

285. This is the version told by Elinor Robinson Waller. Bernard Ruffin, Jr. said only that his parents separated when he was 13. Dudley Tucker said that Caulbert left his wife because she insisted on working and "whenever a woman goes to work, that's the end of the marriage."

286. Dorothy Goude Bryant

287. According to their marriage license, at least, James F.R. Wilson was only a year older than Nonie.

288. Helen Ogle Atkins, interview, January 16, 1993

289. Interview, Kathryn Payne Carr, January, 1985

290.   *Ibid.*

291. Helen Ogle Atkins, interview, January 16, 1993

292. Helen Ogle Atkins, interview in the mid 1970s and January 16, 1993

293. Jayne Kemp Taylor, interview, July 20, 1999

294.   *Ibid.*

295. Josephine Todd Walker, telephone interview, July 22, 1999

296. Alice Bamfield Hall, interview, circa 1973

297. Helen Ogle Atkins, interview, January 16, 1993

298. Helen Ogle Atkins, telephone interview, July 6, 1999

299. Letter, Arthur O. Waller to Elinor R. Robinson, September 22, 1932

300. Sara Davis Taylor, interview, early 1990s

301. Helen Ogle Atkinson, telephone interview, July 6, 1999

302. Letter, Arthur O. Waller to Elinor R. Robinson, undated, circa 1934

303. Robert W. Wilson, telephone interview, August 29, 1999

304. *Liber Anni* (Dunbar Yearbook) 1932

305. Elaine Gates Magruder, telephone interview, June 24, 1999

306. Maxine Reynolds Baker, telephone interview, June 24, 1999

307. Letter, Arthur O. Waller to Elinor R. Robinson, September 5, 1932

308. Helen Ogle Atkins, telephone interview, July 6, 1999

309. Papers of Elinor Robinson Waller

310. Helen Ogle Atkins, interviews, January 16, 1993 and July 6, 1999

311. Ethel Browne O'Mealley, telephone interview, June 22, 1999

312. Benjamin L. Spaudling, interview, January 9, 1999

313. *Ibid.*

314. *Ibid.*

315. Helen Ogle Atkins, telephone interview, July 6, 1999

316. According to Wilhelmina Allen Garner, in an interview on August 18, 1999, the tenants were her husband, William Garner, a medical student, and her brother, Hayes Allen, a dental student.

317. Helen Ogle Atkins, interview, January 16, 1993

318. *Washington Afro-American,* November 2, 1946

319. *Ibid.* October 19, 1946

320. *Ibid.*

321. *Ibid.* September 28, 1946

322. *Ibid.*, September 21, 1946

323. *Ibid,* September 28, 1946

324. *Washington Afro-American,* April 19, 1952

325. *Ibid.*

326. Memorandum, Ross Morgan, Director of Pilot District Project to Mayor Walter E. Washington, "Recommendation for Cash Award to C. Bernard Ruffin, Sustained Superior Performance."

327.Notice of Retirement, Civil Service Retirement Standard Form 37, signed by J.W. Johnson, Superintendent, and letter, D.D. Brower to C.B. Ruffin, RPC, August 21, 1941

328. U.S. Individual Income Tax Return, 1944

329. U.S. Individual Income Tax Return, 1946

330. U.S. Individual Income Tax Return, 1947

331. Letter, D. Sullivan, Deputy Collector, District of Maryland, to Caulbert Ruffin, December 22, 1947

332. Personal effects of Caulbert Bernard Ruffin, Sr., including a urine test strip.

333. Death certificate of Caulbert Bernard Ruffin, Sr, District of Columbia, Vital Statistics

334. The narrator was less than five and had no knowledge of the date until it was specified by George Elliott, Jr. in 1966 as that of "Blanche's last trip to Norfolk."

335. Helen Ogle Atkins, telephone interview, July 6, 1999

* 9 7 8 0 7 8 8 4 1 4 6 6 4 *